W9-BJR-848

DISCOVER

QUICKEN WS®

DISCOVER QUICKEN 6 FOR WINDOWS

Icon Bar Buttons

 Registr — Move to current account register

 Accts — Go to the Account List

 Recon — Balance your account

 Reports — Go to Reports

 Home & Car — Go to Online Banking

 Calendar — Display the Financial Calendar

 AddrBk — Open the Address Book

 Index — Open the Help index

 Investr — Access Investor Insight

 Inventry — Start Home Inventory

 MutualF — Go to the Mutual Fund Finder

 Help — Go to Quicken Help

Activity Bar Buttons

 My Accounts — Create, view, and reconcile accounts

 Bills — Write checks, make online payments, record paid bills

 Planning — Create budgets, plan for taxes, reduce debt

 Investments — Track and work with investments

 Home & Car — Track assets and home inventory

 Online — Do all your banking online

 Reports — Create reports to quickly view status of finances

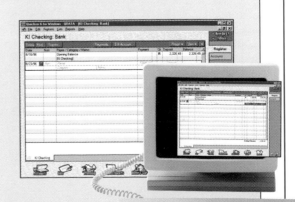

Other Main Window Buttons

▼ How Do I? **Find answers to common questions**

▼ Advice **Get expert financial advice**

Register / Accounts **Quickly switch between open windows (actual tab names vary by window)**

◀) **Turn the QCards features on and off**

To Do! **Bring up the Quicken Reminders windows**

Keyboard Shortcuts

Shortcut	*Go to...*
CTRL+A	**Account List**
CTRL+C	**Category List**
CTRL+H	**Loans List**
CTRL+T	**Memorized Transaction List**
CTRL+J	**Scheduled Transaction List**
CTRL+R	**Register**
CTRL+U	**Portfolio List**
CTRL+W	**Write Checks**

Shortcuts for Entering Dates

Keystroke	*Date Change*
+	**Increases the date by one day**
-	**Decreases the date by one day**
T	**Today's date**
M	**First day of this month**
M,M	**First day of previous month (M,M,M for the month before that, etc.)**
H	**Last day of the month**
H,H	**Last day of the next month (H,H,H for the month after that, etc.)**
R	**Last day of the year**
R,R	**Last day of the next year (R,R,R the year after that, etc.)**

DISCOVERY CENTRAL

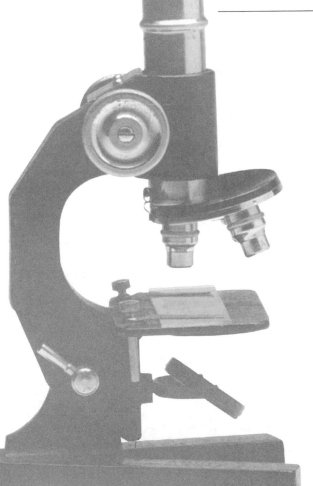

DISCOVER
QUICKEN 6®
FOR WINDOWS®

BY KATHY IVENS
WITH TAX TIPS FROM
STEPHEN I. BUSH, CPA

IDG BOOKS

IDG BOOKS WORLDWIDE, INC.

AN INTERNATIONAL
DATA GROUP COMPANY

FOSTER CITY, CA • CHICAGO, IL •
INDIANAPOLIS, IN • SOUTHLAKE, TX

Discover Quicken 6® for Windows®

Published by
IDG Books Worldwide, Inc.
An International Data Group Company
919 E. Hillsdale Blvd., Suite 400
Foster City, CA 94404

http://www.idgbooks.com (IDG Books Worldwide Web site)

Library of Congress Catalog Card No.: 96-79753

ISBN: 0-7645-3048-8

Printed in the United States of America

10 9 8 7 6 5 4 3 2 1

1IPC/RU/QT/ZX/FC

Distributed in the United States by IDG Books Worldwide, Inc.

Distributed by Macmillan Canada for Canada; by Contemporanea de Ediciones for Venezuela; by Distribuidora Cuspide for Argentina; by CITEC for Brazil; by Ediciones ZETA S.C.R. Ltda. for Peru; by Editorial Limusa SA for Mexico; by Transworld Publishers Limited in the United Kingdom and Europe; by Academic Bookshop for Egypt; by Levant Distributors S.A.R.L. for Lebanon; by Al Jassim for Saudi Arabia; by Simron Pty. Ltd. for South Africa; by Pustak Mahal for India; by The Computer Bookshop for India; by Toppan Company Ltd. for Japan; by Addison Wesley Publishing Company for Korea; by Longman Singapore Publishers Ltd. for Singapore, Malaysia, Thailand, and Indonesia; by Unalis Corporation for Taiwan; by WS Computer Publishing Company, Inc. for the Philippines; by WoodsLane Pty. Ltd. for Australia; by WoodsLane Enterprises Ltd. for New Zealand. Authorized Sales Agent: Anthony Rudkin Associates for the Middle East and North Africa.

For general information on IDG Books Worldwide's books in the U.S., please call our Consumer Customer Service department at 800-762-2974. For reseller information, including discounts and premium sales, please call our Reseller Customer Service department at 800-434-3422.

For information on where to purchase IDG Books Worldwide's books outside the U.S., please contact our International Sales department at 415-655-3172 or fax 415-655-3295.

For information on foreign language translations, please contact our Foreign & Subsidiary Rights department at 415-655-3021 or fax 415-655-3281.

For sales inquiries and special prices for bulk quantities, please contact our Sales department at 415-655-3200 or write to the address above.

For information on using IDG Books Worldwide's books in the classroom or for ordering examination copies, please contact our Educational Sales department at 800-434-2086 or fax 817-251-8174.

For press review copies, author interviews, or other publicity information, please contact our Public Relations department at 415-655-3000 or fax 415-655-3299.

For authorization to photocopy items for corporate, personal, or educational use, please contact Copyright Clearance Center, 222 Rosewood Drive, Danvers, MA 01923, or fax 508-750-4470.

 is a trademark under exclusive license to IDG Books Worldwide, Inc., from International Data Group, Inc.

ABOUT IDG BOOKS WORLDWIDE

Welcome to the world of IDG Books Worldwide.

IDG Books Worldwide, Inc., is a subsidiary of International Data Group, the world's largest publisher of computer-related information and the leading global provider of information services on information technology. IDG was founded more than 25 years ago and now employs more than 8,500 people worldwide. IDG publishes more than 275 computer publications in over 75 countries (see listing below). More than 60 million people read one or more IDG publications each month.

Launched in 1990, IDG Books Worldwide is today the #1 publisher of best-selling computer books in the United States. We are proud to have received eight awards from the Computer Press Association in recognition of editorial excellence and three from *Computer Currents'* First Annual Readers' Choice Awards. Our best-selling *...For Dummies®* series has more than 30 million copies in print with translations in 30 languages. IDG Books Worldwide, through a joint venture with IDG's Hi Tech Beijing, became the first U.S. publisher to publish a computer book in the People's Republic of China. In record time, IDG Books Worldwide has become the first choice for millions of readers around the world who want to learn how to better manage their businesses.

Our mission is simple: Every one of our books is designed to bring extra value and skill-building instructions to the reader. Our books are written by experts who understand and care about our readers. The knowledge base of our editorial staff comes from years of experience in publishing, education, and journalism — experience we use to produce books for the '90s. In short, we care about books, so we attract the best people. We devote special attention to details such as audience, interior design, use of icons, and illustrations. And because we use an efficient process of authoring, editing, and desktop publishing our books electronically, we can spend more time ensuring superior content and spend less time on the technicalities of making books.

You can count on our commitment to deliver high-quality books at competitive prices on topics you want to read about. At IDG Books Worldwide, we continue in the IDG tradition of delivering quality for more than 25 years. You'll find no better book on a subject than one from IDG Books Worldwide.

John Kilcullen
CEO
IDG Books Worldwide, Inc.

**Eighth Annual
Computer Press
Awards ≥1992**

**Ninth Annual
Computer Press
Awards ≥1993**

**Tenth Annual
Computer Press
Awards ≥1994**

**Eleventh Annual
Computer Press
Awards ≥1995**

IDG Books Worldwide, Inc., is a subsidiary of International Data Group, the world's largest publisher of computer-related information and the leading global provider of information services on information technology. International Data Group publishes over 275 computer publications in over 75 countries. Sixty million people read one or more International Data Group publications each month. International Data Group's publications include: **ARGENTINA:** Buyer's Guide, Computerworld Argentina, PC World Argentina; **AUSTRALIA:** Australian Macworld, Australian PC World, Australian Reseller News, Computerworld, IT Casebook, Network World, Publish, Webmaster; **AUSTRIA:** Computerwelt Österreich, Networks Austria, PC Tip Austria; **BANGLADESH:** PC World Bangladesh; **BELARUS:** PC World Belarus; **BELGIUM:** Data News; **BRAZIL:** Annuário de Informática, Computerworld, Connections, Macworld, PC Player, PC World, Publish, Reseller News, Supergamepower; **BULGARIA:** Computerworld Bulgaria, Network World Bulgaria, PC & MacWorld Bulgaria; **CANADA:** CIO Canada, Client/Server World, ComputerWorld Canada, InfoWorld Canada, NetworkWorld Canada, WebWorld; **CHILE:** Computerworld Chile, PC World Chile; **COLOMBIA:** Computerworld Colombia, PC World Colombia; **COSTA RICA:** PC World Centro America; **THE CZECH AND SLOVAK REPUBLICS:** Computerworld Czechoslovakia, Macworld Czech Republic, PC World Czechoslovakia; **DENMARK:** Communications World Danmark, Computerworld Danmark, Macworld Danmark, PC World Danmark, Techworld Denmark; **DOMINICAN REPUBLIC:** PC World Republica Dominicana; **ECUADOR:** PC World Ecuador; **EGYPT:** Computerworld Middle East, PC World Middle East; **EL SALVADOR:** PC World Centro America; **FINLAND:** MikroPC, Tietoverkko, Tietoviikko; **FRANCE:** Distributique, Hebdo, Info PC, Le Monde Informatique, Macworld, Reseaux & Telecoms, WebMaster France; **GERMANY:** Computer Partner, Computerwoche, Computerwoche Extra, Computerwoche FOCUS, Global Online, Macwelt, PC Welt; **GREECE:** Amiga Computing, GamePro Greece, Multimedia World; **GUATEMALA:** PC World Centro America; **HONDURAS:** PC World Centro America; **HONG KONG:** Computerworld Hong Kong, PC World Hong Kong, Publish in Asia; **HUNGARY:** ABCD CD-ROM, Computerworld Szamitastechnika, Internetto online Magazine, PC World Hungary, PC-X Magazin Hungary; **ICELAND:** Tolvuheimur PC World Island; **INDIA:** Information Communications World, Information Systems Computerworld, PC World India, Publish in Asia; **INDONESIA:** InfoKomputer PC World, Komputek Computerworld, Publish in Asia; **IRELAND:** ComputerScope, PC Live!; **ISRAEL:** Macworld Israel, People & Computers/Computerworld; **ITALY:** Computerworld Italia, Macworld Italia, Networking Italia, PC World Italia; **JAPAN:** DTP World, Macworld Japan, Nikkei Personal Computing, OS/2 World Japan, SunWorld Japan, Windows NT World, Windows World Japan; **KENYA:** PC World East African; **KOREA:** Hi-Tech Information, Macworld Korea, PC World Korea; **MACEDONIA:** PC World Macedonia; **MALAYSIA:** Computerworld Malaysia, PC World Malaysia, Publish in Asia; **MALTA:** PC World Malta; **MEXICO:** Computerworld Mexico, PC World Mexico; **MYANMAR:** PC World Myanmar; **NETHERLANDS:** Computer! Totaal, LAN Internetworking Magazine, LAN World Buyers Guide, Macworld Netherlands, Net, WebWereld; **NEW ZEALAND:** Absolute Beginners Guide and Plain & Simple Series, Computer Buyer, Computer Industry Directory, Computerworld New Zealand, MTB, Network World, PC World New Zealand; **NICARAGUA:** PC World Centro America; **NORWAY:** Computerworld Norge, CW Rapport, Datamagasinet, Financial Rapport, Kursguide Norge, Macworld Norge, Multimediaworld Norge, PC World Ekspress Norge, PC World Nettverk, PC World Norge, PC World ProduktGuide Norge; **PAKISTAN:** Computerworld Pakistan; **PANAMA:** PC World Panama; **PEOPLE'S REPUBLIC OF CHINA:** China Computer Users, China Computerworld, China InfoWorld, China Telecom World Weekly, Computer & Communication, Electronic Design China, Electronics Today, Electronics Weekly, Game Software, PC World China, Popular Computer Week, Software Weekly, Software World, Telecom World; **PERU:** Computerworld Peru, PC World Profesional Peru, PC World SoHo Peru; **PHILIPPINES:** Click!, Computerworld Philippines, PC World Philippines, Publish in Asia; **POLAND:** Computerworld Poland, Computerworld Special Report Poland, Cyber, Macworld Poland, Networld Poland, PC World Komputer; **PORTUGAL:** Cerebro/PC World, Computerworld/Correio Informático, Dealer World Portugal, Mac*In/PC*In Portugal, Multimedia World; **PUERTO RICO:** PC World Puerto Rico; **ROMANIA:** Computerworld Romania, PC World Romania, Telecom Romania; **RUSSIA:** Computerworld Russia, Mir PK, Publish, Seti; **SINGAPORE:** Computerworld Singapore, PC World Singapore, Publish in Asia; **SLOVENIA:** Monitor; **SOUTH AFRICA:** Computing SA, Network World SA, Software World SA; **SPAIN:** Communicaciones World España, Computerworld España, Dealer World España, Macworld España, PC World España; **SRI LANKA:** Infolink PC World; **SWEDEN:** CAP&Design, Computer Sweden, Corporate Computing Sweden, Internetworld Sweden, it.branschen, Macworld Sweden, MaxiData Sweden, MikroDatorn, Natverk & Kommunikation, PC World Sweden, PCaktiv, Windows World Sweden; **SWITZERLAND:** Computerworld Schweiz, Macworld Schweiz, PCtip; **TAIWAN:** Computerworld Taiwan, Macworld Taiwan, NEW ViSiON/Publish, PC World Taiwan, Windows World Taiwan; **THAILAND:** Publish in Asia, Thai Computerworld; **TURKEY:** Computerworld Turkiye, Macworld Turkiye, Network World Turkiye, PC World Turkiye; **UKRAINE:** Computerworld Kiev, Multimedia World Ukraine, PC World Ukraine; **UNITED KINGDOM:** Acorn User UK, Amiga Action UK, Amiga Computing UK, Apple Talk UK, Computing, Macworld, Parents and Computers UK, PC Advisor, PC Home, PSX Pro, The WEB; **UNITED STATES:** Cable in the Classroom, CIO Magazine, Computerworld, DOS World, Federal Computer Week, GamePro Magazine, InfoWorld, I-Way, Macworld, Network World, PC Games, PC World, Publish, Video Event, THE WEB Magazine, and WebMaster; online webzines: JavaWorld, NetscapeWorld, and SunWorld Online; **URUGUAY:** InfoWorld Uruguay; **VENEZUELA:** Computerworld Venezuela, PC World Venezuela; and **VIETNAM:** PC World Vietnam. 2/14/97

Welcome to the Discover Series

Do you want to discover the best and most efficient ways to use your computer and learn about technology? Books in the Discover series teach you the essentials of technology with a friendly, confident approach. You'll find a Discover book on almost any subject — from the Internet to intranets, from Web design and programming to the business programs that make your life easier.

We've provided valuable, real-world examples that help you relate to topics faster. Discover books begin by introducing you to the main features of programs, so you start by doing something *immediately*. The focus is to teach you how to perform tasks that are useful and meaningful in your day-to-day work. You might create a document or graphic, explore your computer, surf the Web, or write a program. Whatever the task, you learn the most commonly used features, and focus on the best tips and techniques for doing your work. You'll get results quickly, and discover the best ways to use software and technology in your everyday life.

You may find the following elements and features in this book:

Discovery Central: This tearout card is a handy quick reference to important tasks or ideas covered in the book.

Quick Tour: The Quick Tour gets you started working with the book right away.

Real-Life Vignettes: Throughout the book you'll see one-page scenarios illustrating a real-life application of a topic covered.

Goals: Each chapter opens with a list of goals you can achieve by reading the chapter.

Side Trips: These asides include additional information about alternative or advanced ways to approach the topic covered.

Bonuses: Timesaving tips and more advanced techniques are covered in each chapter.

Discovery Center: This guide illustrates key procedures covered throughout the book.

Visual Index: You'll find real-world documents in the Visual Index, with page numbers pointing you to where you should turn to achieve the effects shown.

Throughout the book, you'll also notice some special icons and formatting:

 A Feature Focus icon highlights new features in the software's latest release, and points out significant differences between it and the previous version.

 Web Paths refer you to Web sites that provide additional information about the topic.

TIP Tips offer timesaving shortcuts, expert advice, quick techniques, or brief reminders.

 The X-Ref icon refers you to other chapters or sections for more information.

Pull Quotes emphasize important ideas that are covered in the chapter.

NOTE Notes provide additional information or highlight special points of interest about a topic.

 The Caution icon alerts you to potential problems you should watch out for.

The Discover series delivers interesting, insightful, and inspiring information about technology to help you learn faster and retain more. So the next time you want to find answers to your technology questions, reach for a Discover book. We hope the entertaining, easy-to-read style puts you at ease and makes learning fun.

Credits

ACQUISITIONS EDITOR
Ellen Camm

DEVELOPMENT EDITOR
Susan Pines

TECHNICAL EDITOR
Tom Barich, Frameworx Consulting

COPY EDITOR
Kerrie Klein

PROJECT COORDINATOR
Ben Schroeter

GRAPHICS AND PRODUCTION SPECIALIST
Renée Dunn

QUALITY CONTROL SPECIALIST
Mick Arellano

PROOFREADERS
Desne Border
Andrew Davis
Stacey Lynn
Candace Ward
Anne Weinberger

INDEXER
Lori Lathrop

BOOK DESIGN
Seventeenth Street Studios
Phyllis Beaty
Kurt Krames

About the Author

Kathy Ivens has been a computer consultant since 1985 and has authored and co-authored many books on computer subjects. She is a frequent contributor to national magazines, writing articles and reviewing software. Before becoming an expert in computing, she spent many years as a television producer, where she had fun producing sports and was mildly amused producing news and entertainment programs. Preceding that career, she spent some time as a community organizer and also as a political consultant. She still doesn't know what she wants to be when she grows up (although she's a grandmother now and it's about time she decided and settled down).

The tax tips for this book were provided by **Stephen I. Bush**, CPA, a senior partner at Bush, Levin, & Tecosky, with offices in Pennsylvania and New Jersey. He's been practicing his profession for many years and has a wide range of clients for whom he performs services that include tax matters, business planning, management consulting, and other important business ministrations.

THIS BOOK IS DEDICATED TO E.T., THE MOST CONGENIAL GUY I KNOW, WHO HAS BEEN SUCH A GOOD INFLUENCE ON ME. HE WROTE THAT OUT FOR ME TO SAY ABOUT HIM, BUT I'LL ADD SOME STUFF OF MY OWN: THANKS, e.t., FOR YOUR HELP AND ENCOURAGEMENT, FOR BRINGING THE SUNSHINE OF LAUGHTER INTO MY LIFE EVERY DAY, AND FOR BEING A SPECIAL PERSON AND A SPECIAL FRIEND.

PREFACE

This book is written to get you up and running as quickly as possible in Quicken. Instructions for all the important basic steps are here, and they're presented in a simple, easy-to-follow manner. And I've explained many of the more advanced tasks Quicken can handle for you. As you gain confidence in your knowledge of the software, try some of the operations that may seem complicated when you first look at them — you'll find that they're not all that complex, and they can help you get the most out of Quicken.

I've written this book for people who run Quicken on Windows 95 or Windows 3.*x*. Where there are real differences, I've approached the elements separately (the Help system is a bit different, as is the process of starting up the software). But the instructions, the figures, and even the hints and tips work for everybody. Although most figures in this book are from my Windows 95 version of Quicken, you'll find that they pretty much match the way Quicken looks in Windows 3.*x*.

Each chapter in this book is aimed at a task or a set of related tasks. There's an overview before the meat of the chapter begins, so as you get comfortable with Quicken, you can try the procedures in the overview and shorten your learning time a bit. At the end of each chapter is a Bonus section. Sometimes that section explains how to move beyond the basic procedures and try some of the more complicated stuff; sometimes it discusses related topics such as the tax ramifications of the different ways you can choose to use Quicken.

Throughout the book, you'll find hints and information from a CPA, which should help you make some of the decisions needed to have a smooth tax preparation period.

You don't have to read this book in order; it's not a mystery novel. But you do have to read the Chapters 1 and 2 first so that you can install and set up the software and learn how to enter information in Quicken. After that, you can use the Index, the Table of Contents, or just flip through the pages to find the chapter that has information on what you want to do now.

Enjoy the learning, enjoy the power you'll gain from the information in this book, enjoy Quicken.

Acknowledgments

Thanks to Michele F. Lapera of Chestnut Hill National Bank and Ira Feldman of Bush, Levin, & Tecosky for providing great answers to all my questions.

At IDG Books Worldwide, a great many talented people put time, effort, and skills into this book. Ellen Camm, the Acquisitions Editor, has been supportive and helpful well beyond anything I had a right to expect, and I'm glad we finally found a chance to work together. Kudos to Sue Pines, a Development Editor extraordinaire, for being an excellent resource and a funny, bright person who is a pleasure to work with. Thomas Barich provided the technical editing that makes me look accurate and efficient, for which I thank him.

IDG Books Worldwide gathered a whole bunch of really professional people who put their skills into this project to make it work. So, my sincere appreciation to Copy Editor Kerrie Klein, Project Coordinator Ben Schroeter, and all the folks in Production and Manufacturing.

— *Kathy Ivens*

CONTENTS AT A GLANCE

CONTENTS

QUICKEN 6® FOR WINDOWS® QUICK TOUR

HERE YOU LEARN THESE KEY SKILLS:

ANSWERING THE STARTUP QUESTIONS   PAGE 2

SETTING UP YOUR BANK ACCOUNT   PAGE 3

Before you can do anything in Quicken, you have to set up and configure your Quicken system. Once you've done that, you can start keeping your financial records using Quicken's easy-to-use features.

The first time you use Quicken, the New User Setup process begins. The Quicken Welcome screen (Figure 1) is the first thing you see.

Figure 1   Welcome to Quicken, but there's work to do before you start using the software.

You have these options:

- ✳ Click Cancel to leave the setup program.
- ✳ Use the Help button to get more information about this dialog box.
- ✳ Click Next to move to the next step.

Answering the Startup Questions

The next setup dialog box (Figure 2) contains a number of questions designed to help you set up Quicken especially for your needs.

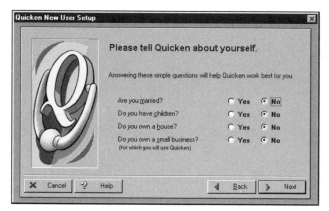

Figure 2 Answer these questions to set up your Quicken categories.

The answers you select let Quicken set up the software so it can track the information you need to keep financial records and get ready for tax time. The categories Quicken uses to track your spending change depending on the information you enter here. All the answers are preset to No:

1. Click Yes as necessary to match your circumstances.

2. Click Next when you have finished.

The answers you select affect the number of categories Quicken sets up for your bookkeeping. A *category* is way to explain and summarize expenses and income. For example, your heating, electric, and water bill payments are grouped in a category named utilities.

Don't worry, however, about whether or not you're establishing the absolutely perfect configuration. As you work in Quicken, you can add and change categories, decide which items you need to track for tax purposes, and decide what expenses you want to track and how you want to track them.

Setting Up Your Bank Account

You can't begin to use Quicken until you've set up at least one bank account. During the New User Setup process, the bank account you set up should be your main checking account — the one you use to write the checks that pay your bills. You can add more accounts later.

Naming the bank account

The first thing you have to do is give this account a name, as shown in Figure 3.

Figure 3 Name your bank account during the setup process.

The name you select doesn't appear on the checks you print, so you don't have to worry about whether the name makes sense to anyone but you. No one else will know about it. Whatever you do is just fine — as long as you recognize the name as belonging to this bank account when you see it on your screen while you work in Quicken.

You can use any letter or number in this name and can even use spaces and other keyboard characters. The only characters you can't use are the following:

[ ] / : | ^

Deciding on a starting point

Quicken asks if you have your last statement for this checking account (Figure 4).

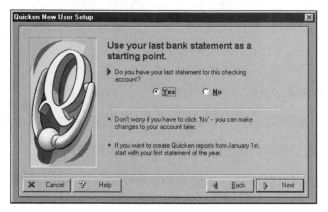

Figure 4 Do you have your last statement for this account?

Here's what you need to know about answering this question:

* If you answer Yes, the next dialog box asks you about the statement date. Quicken uses that date as a starting point for tracking this account and asks you to enter the bank balance for that statement date.

* If you say No, Quicken uses today's date as the starting point for tracking the account and places a zero balance in the account.

* No matter what you say, you can make adjustments later.

* You don't have to use the latest statement; use an earlier statement. You may want to use the last statement that actually balanced and reconciled (which may be several months old).

* Another acceptable option is to use the last date and amount in your manual checkbook stub (if it's accurate).

* You can use the first statement you received in January (or the last statement you received last December) as the statement date and use that statement's balance figure to begin your bookkeeping for the year.

If you use real statement dates instead of the last date and amount in your manual checkbook, you have to enter all the uncleared transactions. If you use January 1, you have to enter all the transactions since then (if you're reading this in February or March, that's not quite as daunting as it is if you're reading this in August). That's not as much work as it seems, however, so don't panic. You don't have to do it all at once and you can enter a few transactions every time you have a spare moment.

Once you've selected Yes or No, click Next.

Entering the starting date and balance

If you chose Yes in the previous dialog box, the next dialog box is where you enter the starting date and the balance (Figure 5):

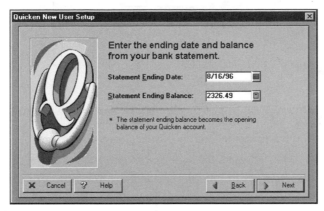

Figure 5 Enter information to establish your Quicken starting date and balance.

1. Enter a starting date by entering the numbers (you don't have to type the slashes). The format is MM/DD/YY.

2. Enter the amount. Don't use any commas. Use a decimal point to separate the dollars from the cents.

3. Click Next.

Remember that although the dialog box fields say Statement Date and Ending Balance, you can invent your own definitions for both terms.

If you change your mind about whether you want to enter a starting date and balance, click Back in the dialog box to change your answer in the previous section. (If you chose No in the previous dialog box, a message displays telling you that the account is being opened with a zero balance, and you can just click Next to move on).

Checking the information

The last setup screen displays all the information you've just entered about your first Quicken bank account (Figure 6).

You can change anything you want. Once this summary window has everything the way you want it, click Next.

Figure 6 Confirm that the information you entered is accurate.

If you want to make changes to any item, you can move through the summary window as follows:

1. The Account Name field is highlighted, indicating it's in "ready to edit" mode. If you want to change the account name, just start typing and the new name you enter replaces the current name.

2. Press Tab to move to the Statement Date field.

3. To change the statement date, enter a new date or click the button to the right of the text box to bring up a calendar. Then click a new date, which is entered automatically as the statement date in the Statement Date field.

4. Use Tab to move to the Ending Balance field.

5. To change the balance, enter a new figure or click the button to the right of the text box to launch the Quicken calculator. Click the calculator buttons to do your figuring and then click the calculator's Enter button to transfer your total to the Ending Balance text box.

6. Click Next once you're happy with the information in the dialog box.

The New User Setup process is complete, and your data files are established, so you can now begin to use Quicken. By default, Quicken names your file QDATA — if you establish additional files (for business or for other members of the family), you give those files a different name.

One of the disadvantages that comes with living in a fast-paced, overachieving society is that the demands we place on ourselves are often accompanied by unfounded neuroses. In our constant quest to attain new goals, we often take a self-deprecating position and focus on what we haven't achieved and ignore what we have. Groucho Marx said that he would never belong to a club that would have him as a member. Likewise, we often shy away from software that's easy for us to use. If it's easy for me, how could it be any good?

Attitudes like Groucho's have been a challenge for Quicken. When a software package like Quicken revolutionizes the home and small office market, professionals in the field — accountants and financial advisors, for example — sometimes scoff at the tiny program with universal appeal. And sometimes they go back to see what the fuss is about.

Jim Vasecky has worked for a large public accounting firm for 16 years. Jim's firm has, in the past, purchased several, expensive, heavy-duty accounting software programs. These programs have "bells and whistles" that make for great packaging and ads, but in actual, everyday use, Jim and many of his coworkers have no need for these features. The result is a large, slow-to-load program that is difficult to learn — yet workers use it mostly for its basic features.

Jim and many of his colleagues figured that there had to be a better way. There was — Quicken. In the world of billable hours, Jim says, "Time is money. I don't want to sit there spending this week and next week learning some program when with Quicken, I can pick it up and I'm off and running." You can sit and learn a program for a week, or you can be working for a client and making money. It doesn't take an accountant to pick the better choice there.

Another reason that Jim likes Quicken is that when a client calls him needing information about a profit and loss statement, Jim can find the information quickly on his computer, answering the client's questions right over the phone. Previously, to answer these types of questions, Jim had to request this information from the Data Processing department. He then had a minimum three-day wait until he received the information. And finally, he would have to recontact the client to convey the information.

In its small, intuitive package, Quicken has made it easy for Jim and his coworkers to be more productive, flexible, and responsive to their customers' needs. And if that makes his customers happy and keeps them coming back, Jim is happy to be a member of that club.

GETTING STARTED

B efore you can use Quicken to enter transactions, write checks, and keep track of what you're spending, you have to perform a few setup chores. This chapter covers all the steps in the New User Setup procedure that Quicken automatically presents the first time you use it.

TIP **Have your checkbook and last bank statement available because you can use that information to set up Quicken.**

Once the setup is complete, you see Quicken's main software window whenever you use Quicken. This window is filled with shortcuts, help, and other easy-to-use features.

TIP **Before you can enter your setup data, Quicken must be installed on your computer. To install the software, follow the directions that came with your Quicken CD-ROM or disks. You install Quicken just as you install any other Windows program. After the installation process is complete, you're ready to use Quicken.**

Starting Quicken for the First Time

To start Quicken from Windows 95, select Start → Programs, move your mouse pointer to highlight Quicken, and choose Quicken 6 for Windows from the submenu.

To start Quicken from Window 3.*x*, open the Quicken program group and double-click the Quicken 6 for Windows icon.

The first time you use Quicken, the New User Setup process begins. The Quicken Welcome screen is the first thing you see (Figure 1-1). Click Next to continue.

Get more information about this dialog box

Leave the setup program

Move to the next step

Figure 1-1 The Welcome dialog box explains the setup procedure.

TIP If you're already a Quicken user, you won't see opening setup dialog boxes. During the software installation, Quicken finds your existing files and converts them for this new version of Quicken. When you use Quicken for the first time, you go right back to work in the Quicken window you last used.

The next setup dialog box lists questions designed to obtain information about you (Figure 1-2). The answers to these questions help Quicken set up the software so that it can track the information you need to keep financial records and get ready for tax time. The categories that Quicken uses to track your spending change depending on the information you enter here. The answers are preset to No.

To help Quicken set up categories, follow these steps:

1. Click Yes as necessary to match your circumstances.

2. Click Next after you finish.

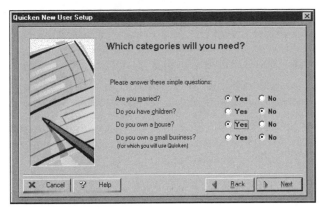

Figure 1-2 Click Yes to change the answer to any question that doesn't match your profile.

The answers to some startup questions affect the categories that Quicken sets up for your bookkeeping data. A *category* is way to explain and summarize expenses and income. For example, your heating, electric, and water bill payments are grouped in a category named *utilities*.

X-REF **For more information about adding and using categories, see Chapter 8.**

If you own a home, you need categories for tracking tax-deductible expenses, such as mortgage interest and real estate tax. Being married and having children affect your taxes, and Quicken establishes categories you can use for tax reports. If you indicate that you will use Quicken to track business expenses, it sets up business categories in your system.

X-REF **You learn more about using Quicken for business expenses in Chapter 9.**

Don't worry about establishing the perfect configuration. Nothing is etched in cement, and as you work in Quicken, you can add and change categories, decide which items you need to track for tax purposes, and decide which expenses you want to track and how to track them.

Setting Up Your Checking Account

You can't begin using Quicken until you've set up at least one bank account. During the setup process, the bank account you set up should be your main checking account — the one you will use to write the checks that pay your bills.

TIP If you have multiple checking accounts and don't pay all your bills from just one, don't worry about deciding on a main account now. Just pick one account (toss a coin or throw darts at a dartboard to decide) and tell Quicken about it at this point in the setup procedure. Later you can add as many accounts as you need.

Naming the bank account

The first thing you have to do is give this account a name (Figure 1-3). If you only have one checking account, you can call it My Account, Bank, Checks, or even X. The name you give the account in Quicken doesn't appear on the checks you print or in the transactions you perform online, so don't worry about whether the name makes sense to anyone else. No one else will know about it. Whatever you choose is fine — as long as you recognize the name as belonging to the bank account when you see it on-screen while you work in Quicken. After you've entered the name, click Next to move on to the next window.

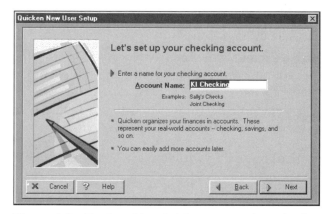

Figure 1-3 The first thing Quicken wants to know is what you want to call this bank account.

You can use any letter or number in this name, including spaces and most other keyboard characters. The only characters you can't use are these:

[ ] / : | ^

Deciding on a starting point

Quicken next asks if you have your last statement for this checking account (Figure 1-4). This question isn't a quick survey about how efficiently you keep records or a test to see if you have a good filing system; rather, it's part of the decision-making process.

Here's what you need to know about answering this question:

* If you answer Yes, the next dialog box asks you about the statement date. Quicken uses that date as a starting point for tracking this account and asks you to enter the bank balance for that statement date.

* If you answer No, Quicken uses today's date as the starting point for tracking this account and places a zero balance in this account.

* No matter how you answer, you can make adjustments later.

Once you've selected Yes or No, click Next.

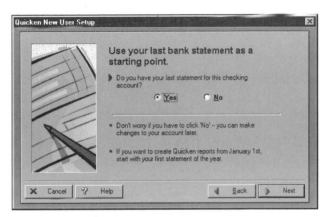

Figure 1-4 Decide whether you're ready to set up a starting point for tracking this bank account.

TIP If you answer Yes, you have to enter data in the next dialog box. You may want to think about some options you have for starting points, other than information from your last statement:

* You can "lie." Don't use the latest statement; use an earlier statement. You may want to use the last statement that actually balanced and reconciled (which may be several months old).

* Another acceptable "lie" is to use the last date and amount in your manual checkbook stub (if it's accurate).

* Use the first statement you received in January (or the final statement you received last December) as the statement date. Use that statement's balance to begin your bookkeeping at the start of the year.

If you use real statement dates instead of the last date and amount in your manual checkbook, you have to enter all the uncleared transactions. If you use January 1, you have to enter all the transactions since then (if you're reading this in February or March, the task is not quite as daunting as if you're reading this in August). That's not as much work as it seems, however, so don't panic.

You don't have to do it all at once, and you can enter a few transactions every time you have a spare moment.

X-REF See Chapter 2 to learn how to enter transactions.

Entering the starting date and balance

If you chose Yes in the preceding dialog box, you enter the starting date and balance in the next dialog box (Figure 1-5):

1. Enter a starting date by typing the numbers (you don't have to type the slashes). The format is MM/DD/YY.

2. Enter the amount. Don't use commas. Use a decimal point to separate the dollars from the cents.

3. Click Next.

Back up to the preceding question

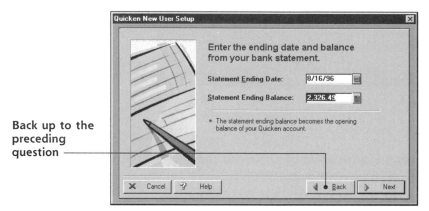

Figure 1-5 Enter a statement date and a starting balance for this account.

Remember that although the dialog box requests statement ending date and ending balance, you can invent your own definitions for both terms. If you change your mind about whether to enter a starting date and balance, click Back to switch your answer in the preceding dialog box.

If you chose No in the preceding dialog box, a message displays, telling you that the account is being opened with a zero balance. Simply click Next to move on.

Checking the information

The last setup screen displays all the information you've entered about your first Quicken bank account (Figure 1-6). You can change anything you want.

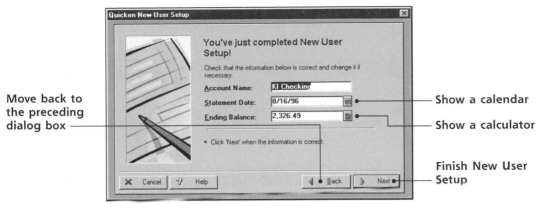

Move back to the preceding dialog box ⎯⎯⎯

Show a calendar

Show a calculator

Finish New User Setup

Figure 1-6 The summary window displays all your information so you can approve it or change it.

If the summary window has everything the way you want it, click Next. If you want to change any item, you can move through the summary window as follows:

1. The Account Name field is highlighted, indicating that it's in ready-to-edit mode. If you want to change the account name, start typing. The new name you enter replaces the current name.

2. Press Tab to move to the Statement Date text box.

3. To change the statement date, enter a new date or click the button to the right of the text box to bring up a calendar (Figure 1-7). Then click a new date, which is entered automatically as the statement date.

4. Use Tab to move to the Ending Balance text box.

5. To change the balance, enter a new figure or click the button to the right of the text box to launch the Quicken calculator (Figure 1-8). Click the calculator buttons to do your figuring and then click the calculator's Enter button to transfer your total to the Ending Balance text box.

6. Click Next when you are happy with the information in the dialog box.

Move back to previous months ⎯⎯⎯

Move ahead to subsequent months

Figure 1-7 Clicking the calendar is a quick way to enter a date.

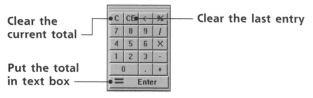

Clear the current total

Clear the last entry

Put the total in text box

Figure 1-8 Use the calculator if you have to tally numbers.

TIP The calendar and calculator are available everywhere in Quicken, not just in the New User Setup process. Whenever you have to enter a date, you see the Calendar icon next to the text box that accepts the date. The Calculator icon appears next to all entry fields for entering amounts.

The New User Setup process is over, and your data files are established. You can now begin to use Quicken. By default, Quicken names your file QDATA. If you establish additional files (for business or for other family members), you will give those files different names.

Exploring the Startup Window

Immediately upon opening, Quicken offers helpful advice in the form of a *Quicken Tip*. Quicken Tips provide information on using and customizing features as well as navigating around the program.

Once you familiarize yourself with Quicken, you can turn off the automatic tips by clearing the Show Tips at Startup option box (click the box to clear it; click again to select it — it's a toggle switch).

The dialog box also offers you the capability to view upcoming tips and previous tips by using Next Tip and Prev Tip. If you find the suspense unbearable, you can use the Contents button to view the entire collection of Quicken Tips at once. Finally, the More Info button takes you to more detailed help information on the specific topic covered in the current tip (if there isn't any additional information, the More Info button is greyed out). When you're through with the tips and want to move on, click Done.

Once you finish examining the Tip of the Day, Quicken presents you with the main window. The Quicken window is precisely that: a window into your financial world. Properly set up and maintained, Quicken presents you with an organized and accurate view of your finances. This is something that most of us long for but rarely achieve — akin to wishing the kids would stop turning into aliens every time you take them to a fancy restaurant.

To get the most out of Quicken, you must be able to navigate through the program with ease and confidence. A good understanding of the Quicken window puts you in complete command of your finances.

See all Quicken Tips

Disable automatic startup tips

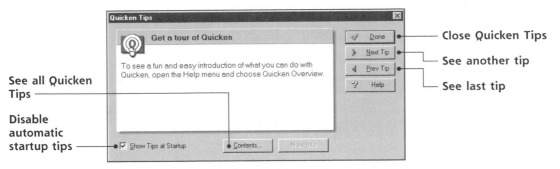

Close Quicken Tips

See another tip

See last tip

Figure 1-9   Take a tip from Quicken. In fact, take as
many as you need.

The Quicken window is made up of various components, and you learn about all of them in more detail in this chapter. The window includes the following:

* At center stage is your *account register*, which holds all your transaction entries and is where you record your transactions.

* To the right of the register, you find *QuickTabs*, which help you move easily through the Quicken windows.

* At the base of the QuickTabs column is a *To Do! icon* for the Quicken Reminder feature and a *Speaker icon* that turns QCards off and on (QCards provide additional help on a task).

* Also on the right are two help-related buttons. The *How Do I? icon* provides answers to common questions. The *Advice icon* offers expert financial guidance.

* The *Activity Bar* and its icons are located on the bottom of the screen. These items provide easy access to many of Quicken's most frequently used features.

* At the top of the window are the *title and menu bars*. The title bar displays the name of the current Quicken window. The menu bar gives you access to Quicken commands. The register has a button bar that contains shortcut buttons for using the register.

As you can see in Figure 1-10, everything you need to put Quicken to work for you is at your fingertips.

The register

By default, Quicken opens with the main window as you last left it. If you're working in Quicken for the first time, the register of the account you established during setup appears.

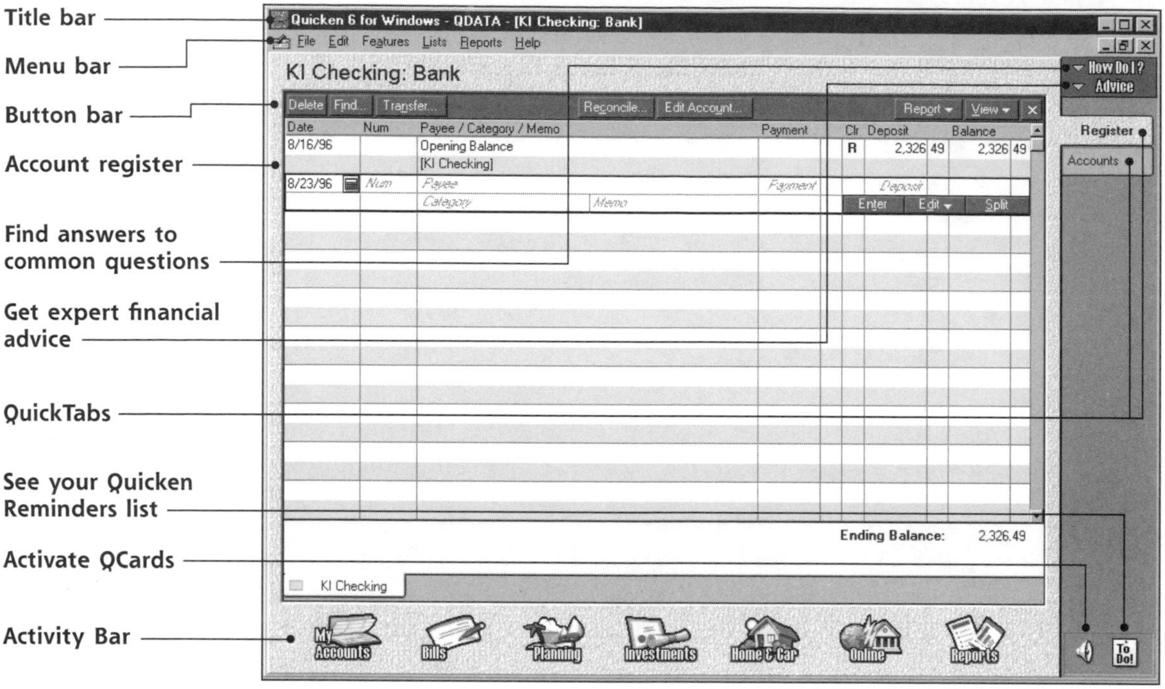
Title bar
Menu bar
Button bar
Account register
Find answers to common questions
Get expert financial advice
QuickTabs
See your Quicken Reminders list
Activate QCards
Activity Bar
Quicken 6 for Windows - QDATA - [KI Checking: Bank]
File Edit Features Lists Reports Help
KI Checking: Bank
Delete Find... Transfer... Reconcile... Edit Account... Report View
How Do I?
Advice
Register
Accounts
Date Num Payee / Category / Memo Payment Clr Deposit Balance
8/16/96 Opening Balance [KI Checking] R 2,326 49 2,326 49
Enter Edit Split
Ending Balance: 2,326.49
KI Checking
My Accounts
Bills
Planning
Investments
Home & Car
Online
Reports
To Do!

Figure 1-10 Quicken's main window provides access to all the program's features.

The register is the heart of your record keeping. Almost identical to its paper counterpart in your checkbook, the register is where you keep track of all your transactions. Here you record your checks, deposits, transfers, ATM withdrawals, and other items affecting your bank account. If you add more bank accounts to your Quicken system, you'll have a register for each account. You spend almost all of your Quicken working time in the registers.

X-REF **Chapter 2 contains information about using the register to enter transactions.**

At the top of the register is the button bar, which provides buttons that enable you to perform the most common banking functions quickly — Delete, Find, Transfer, Reconcile, Edit, Report, and View.

QuickTabs for quick work

QuickTabs are your ticket to fast and easy navigation through every open Quicken window. Each time you open a new window, a QuickTab appears in the QuickTabs column bearing the window's name. The QuickTabs (and the Quicken windows to which they're attached) that appear when you finish your work and exit Quicken are there when you return to Quicken. As you add accounts and use some of the more advanced Quicken features, such as creating classes and categories, a window will be available for each feature you use.

To Do! icon

The To Do! icon brings up the Quicken Reminders window (Figure 1-11). The Reminders window is where Quicken keeps track of all the transactions that you've scheduled for a future date.

X-REF Information about using the Reminders window appears in Chapter 6.

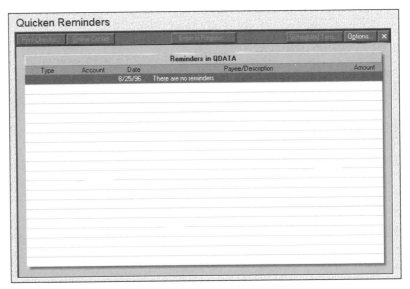

Figure 1-11   The Reminders window lists the transactions that you must complete.

Speaker icon

As mentioned earlier, the Speaker icon turns the QCards feature on and off (you can also do this task from the menu bar, but the Speaker icon is faster and easier). The icon changes when the QCard window is displayed — you see little, radiating lines coming from the speaker. QCards are part of Quicken's Help system and are discussed later in this chapter, in the "Using Quicken Help" section.

Activity Bar

If you're looking for a fast, intuitive way to navigate in Quicken, look no further than the Activity Bar. When you place your mouse pointer over one of the Activity Bar icons, a list of features appears above the icon. Just choose any item from that list to move to that activity. Information about using the features is found throughout this book.

The Activity Bar icons are as follows:

 My Accounts. The My Accounts icon covers account functions. This includes creating, viewing, and reconciling accounts, as well as entering transactions in the register and downloading online transactions.

 Bills. If you want to write checks, make a payment online, record a paid bill, or enter a future transaction, you want to move to this icon.

 Planning. This icon is the one you may try to pass over quickly. I recommend that you avoid the temptation and stop anyway. How many times did your mother tell you that a stitch in time saves nine? Well, she was right (as a mother myself, I learned that mothers are always right). Here's where a little planning can make your future much more pleasant. Budgeting, tax planning, and debt reduction are all part of this category.

 Investments. Once you've done a little planning and decided to forego that new, hot pink convertible you've been pining away for, check out the Investments icon. Take all the money you were going to spend on the new car and put it to work for you in investments. Eventually, you'll have enough for the car and your retirement.

 Home & Car. Okay, so you didn't take my advice, and now you're going to buy that hot little sports car. Quicken enables you to keep track of the bank loan, upkeep, and maintenance. You can also keep track of your assets and home inventory by using the Home & Car icon.

 Online. Quicken offers you the ability to do your banking right from your computer. You can check your account balances, transfer money, and pay bills, all with a few keystrokes and a modem.

 Reports. In reality, reports are one of the main reasons for taking the time and effort to input all your financial data into Quicken. Reports enable you to see the status of your finances, make intelligent money decisions, and plan for the future.

Quicken mouse power

Quicken has a few special mouse moves, including the capability to open short-cut menus with a click of the right mouse button. For Windows 95 users, the concept of a shortcut menu that appears when you click the right mouse button isn't anything new. But if you're using Quicken in Windows 3.x, you'll be delighted with the time you save by using a shortcut menu that appears with a click of the right button.

The content of these shortcut menus changes depending on where your mouse is when you click the right button, because the choices are directly connected to the current task. Shortcut menus are available in many Quicken windows, and as I cover these windows throughout the book, I also discuss their shortcut menu options.

To access the shortcut menus of the Activity Bar icons, do the following:

1. Move your mouse pointer over the icon.

2. Pause the mouse pointer — you don't have to click.

3. A menu appears, and you can click the choice you need.

Incidentally, if you have a sound card, the menu pop-up action is accompanied by an interesting sound effect — the whooshing wind.

Using Quicken Help

Quicken has a multitude of features. Fortunately, it also has an extensive Help system to assist you in harnessing the power of all those features. Not only does Quicken contain the standard Help system, it also offers advice, answers common questions, plays audio and video clips, gives hints on field entries, troubleshoots, and does the dishes. Okay, so it doesn't do dishes.

There is one caveat, however. If your computer does not contain a sound card and speakers, you will not benefit a great deal from the video or the audio help. The reason for the audio is obvious. The video requires a sound system because video clips are frequently unclear without the accompanying audio explanations.

Quicken's Help system is so extensive that at first glance you may think it requires its own Help system to ensure that you don't get lost. The truth is that although the Help system is extensive, it's also easy to navigate. You can find help a couple of ways. There is a standard Help system just as there is in all Windows programs, and there are QCards and Advice pages.

The quickest and most obvious approach is to select Help from the Quicken menu. This opens a submenu with seven help options:

* **Contents.** A table of contents for the entire Help system.

* **Index.** A searchable index of major topics covered in the Help system.

* **Help on This Window.** A help screen specific to the current window.

* **Troubleshooting This Window.** Common problems and their solutions related to the current window.
* **Quicken Overview.** A guided tour of Quicken's key features.
* **Quicken Tips.** Helpful hints on how to get the most out of Quicken.
* **Show QCards.** Audio or text-based assistance for your current task.

The basic Help system

Choose Contents or Index from the Help menu to bring up the basic Quicken Help system. The Help Topics dialog box has three tabs: Contents, Index, and Find. Each tab works in a different way, but no matter which tab you use, you end up with the same information from the help files. In this section, we start with the Contents tab and use it to get to a help page, where a topic is explained. Then we look at the other tabs, which you can use to get to the same help page.

HELP CONTENTS TAB

Use the Contents tab to get help on general topics. Topics are divided into books, and each book covers a help category. When you open a book, you see the topics for that category. Most of the Quicken Help books open to reveal additional books, and you can keep opening books to move through the Help system. Eventually, you will find the specific topic you need (Figure 1-12). To open a book, double-click it, or select it and click Open. To open a topic, double-click it, or select it and click Display.

The Display button in Figure 1-12 changes its title depending on the item you've selected (highlighted):

* When you select a closed book, the button says Open.
* When you select an opened book, the button says Close.
* When you select a topic, the button says Display.

TIP You can print the selected object by choosing Print from the dialog box. If you have selected a book, however, the entire book prints, and it could be a very long document. Wait until you have found a topic, display it, and then print it if you need a hard copy.

HELP TOPIC PAGE

When you find the topic you need, double-click it to open the topic's help page. Reading the text usually gives you the information you need to perform the task. The Windows 95 version of the help page looks like Figure 1-13.

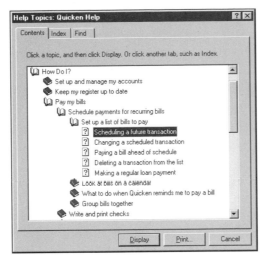

Figure 1-12 Open the book named How Do I?
to find out how to schedule a
bill for payment next week.

Get a general
explanation
of topic ———

See additional
information
about topic ———

See list of
related topics ———

Click underlined green text for help on
that text's subject

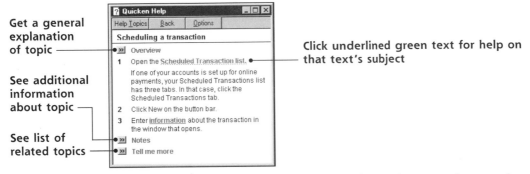

Figure 1-13 The help page gives you instructions on how to perform a task.

If you're running Quicken in Windows 3.*x*, you can click the underlined color text in the help page to achieve the same results as in the Windows 95 version.

HELP PAGE OPTIONS

You can do more than read the help text on a help page. Plenty of options make help pages even more useful. In this section, we look at the options that are the most useful (and interesting).

Note that a small difference exists in the appearance of the help page and in the available options between the Windows 95 version of Quicken and the version that runs on Windows 3.*x*:

* In Windows 95, you can right-click any blank spot inside the help page to see the options available (or click Options at the top of the page).

* In Windows 3.*x*, you use the Help menu bar to get the help page options.

ANNOTATING A HELP TOPIC

You can add your own notes to any help page. This capability can be useful if you went through more than one help page to learn how to perform a task and you don't want to repeat that process the next time you need assistance.

The following list tells you how to annotate a help page depending on which version of Windows you use:

* To annotate a help topic in Windows 95, choose Annotate from the shortcut menu you see when you right-click in the window.

* To annotate a help topic in Windows 3.*x*, choose Edit → Annotate from the menu bar.

When the Annotate dialog box displays, enter your note (Figure 1-14) and then select Save. A paper clip icon is placed on the help page. The next time you use this help page, click the paper clip to see your note.

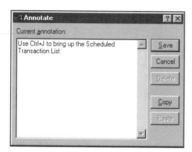

Figure 1-14 Put notes to yourself, for yourself, on the help pages.

PRINTING A HELP TOPIC

You can print the text of a help topic page so that you have hard copy in front of you while you work (*hard copy* is computer jargon for a printed copy of a document). To do so, follow these steps (depending on which version of Windows you use):

* To print from Windows 95, select Print Topic from the shortcut menu or click Options → Print Topic .

* To print from Windows 3.*x*, click the Print button or select File → Print Topic .

ADDING BOOKMARKS FOR HELP TOPICS

A *bookmark* is a place marker in the help files that you can create to make it easy to jump to that topic. Bookmarks are only available in the Windows 3.*x* version of Quicken.

When you're looking at the help topic window you want to mark, click Bookmark → Define. The Bookmark Define dialog box opens with the title of the help topic inserted as the name of the bookmark (Figure 1-15). You can change that name by entering your own text.

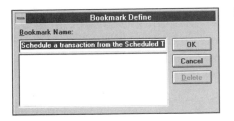

Figure 1-15 Enter a bookmark for this help topic page so you can jump to it whenever you need it.

Hereafter, whenever you're looking at any help topic page, select Bookmark to see a list of all the bookmarks you've created. Click the bookmark representing the help topic page you want and save the keystrokes needed to move through the Help system.

HELP INDEX TAB

A sometimes faster approach is to use the Index tab of the Help Topics dialog box to get to the help topic page you need. The Index is a list of topics (just like an index in a book). When you type characters in the top section of the Index tab, the Index entry section of the tab displays any index entry with matching characters (Figure 1-16). Click the entry you want and click Display to get to that help topic page.

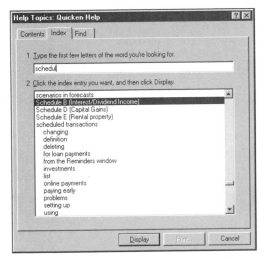

Figure 1-16 As you enter characters, the index list moves to entries that match those characters.

Most of the time, you don't have to enter all the characters in a word, because as soon as you get close to a match with an index entry, you see the listing for which you're looking.

HELP FIND TAB

The Index tab only lists those words contained in the Help system index. You can also search for words that are contained in the text of the help topic pages (that are not words in the Index) by using the Find tab. This is another feature that works differently in Windows 3.*x* than it does in Windows 95.

USING FIND IN WINDOWS 95

In Windows 95, the first time you use the Find tab, you have to build the database of words you'll use when you want to find a word (Figure 1-17).

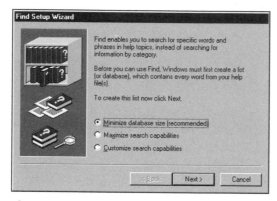

Figure 1-17 You have to build the database of all the words in the help topics before you can use the Find tab.

Three options for building this database are as follows:

✳ Minimized, which creates a database of all the important words in the help topics files.

✳ Maximized, which builds a larger database and adds some more powerful search features to the Find functions.

✳ Customized, which builds a larger database and lets you customize the way the Find functions work.

To build the database, follow these steps:

1. Select an option and click Next.

2. Click Finish in the next dialog box.

That's all it takes to create the database. Now you can use the Find tab to search for words in the help text files (Figure 1-18).

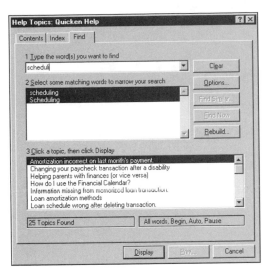

Figure 1-18 Enter characters in the Find tab to search for matching words in the help topic files.

To find words in the help files, follow these steps:

1. Begin typing in the top section of the Find window.

2. When matching words appear in the middle section, select one.

3. Select a topic from the bottom section (which lists the topics that contain the words in the middle section).

4. Click Display to see the help page for your selected topic.

TIP Choose a minimized database, because most of the time that option provides all the Find functions you need, and it's faster than the other choices. If you want to experiment with the other choices, however, click Rebuild from the Find tab to begin the database building process again and choose a different option.

Using Find in Windows 3.x

When you use the Help Find tab in Windows 3.x, you must enter the complete word you want to search for and then click Find. The text pages that contain that word display in the bottom section of the dialog box, and the Index entry for the topic appears in the middle section (Figure 1-19).

Look at the other topic pages that contain the word you're searching for by pressing Ctrl+N to move to the next topic.

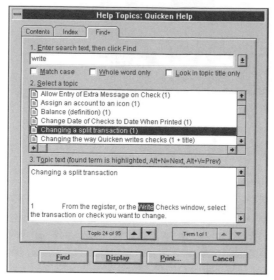

Figure 1-19 Enter the word you want to search for and then choose Find to locate all topics containing that word.

QCards

QCards are short, help paragraphs about the specific task in which you are engaged. You can use them as audio help or text help. For audio QCards, your Quicken CD-ROM must be inserted in your CD-ROM drive. Then when you're performing a task, a voice coaches you by telling you what each step of that task requires.

For example, if you're in the Date field of a blank transaction in the register, a pleasant voice tells you to enter the date and press Tab to move to the next field. As you fill in each field and move to the next, an appropriate audio QCard plays, giving you brief instructions on entering data.

Click the Speaker icon on the bottom right of your Quicken screen to turn the QCards off and on (you can also use the Help menu to select or deselect QCards). When QCards are turned on, the QCard window with its controls is on your Quicken screen (Figure 1-20).

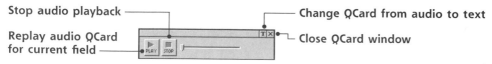

Figure 1-20 The QCard window looks like a control panel for tapes.

If your Quicken CD-ROM is not in the CD-ROM drive, you can change the QCard feature so that you see text, which is, in fact, the script for the audio feature. As you move from field to field, the text changes to match the instructions needed (Figure 1-21).

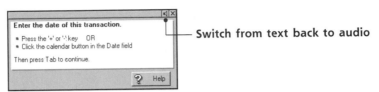

Switch from text back to audio

Figure 1-21   If your CD-ROM isn't inserted in the drive, you can still get help from the QCard window because you can see the text of the audio script.

Show Me

This version of Quicken provides animated video clips, called Show Me videos, that provide step-by-step, mini-tutorials for some of the program's more important features. Each Show Me video has accompanying audio and walks you through the steps for the task. The videos, which are found in select Help screens and in the Help contents under Show Me, last less than two minutes. To play a Show Me, use the VCR-like controls shown in Figure 1-22.

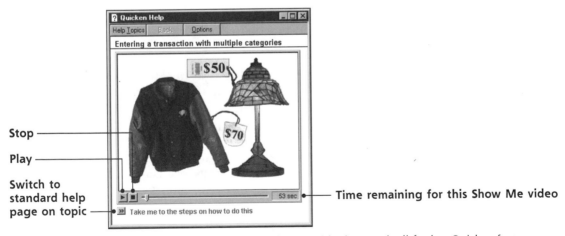

Stop

Play

Switch to standard help page on topic

Time remaining for this Show Me video

Figure 1-22   Show Me video clips provide show-and-tell for key Quicken features.

Most Show Me video clips offer a toggle switch so that you can move to a standard help file topic page if you find it easier to look at steps to complete a task. The same applies in reverse (Figure 1-23).

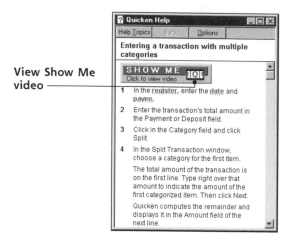

Figure 1-23 You can read the instructions and then switch to an animated video clip with a click of the mouse.

View Show Me video

To view a listing of all the available Show Me video clips, follow these steps:

1. From the Quicken menu, select Help → Index.

2. In the first text box, type **show me** (actually, you only have to type **show**, and the index listing moves to Show Me).

3. This brings up an index entry that says "Show Me. See Videos." Click Display to see topics with Show Me videos available.

4. Scroll through the list and choose any Show Me by double-clicking it.

How Do I?

Click How Do I? to see the help file topics listed as questions. The questions are directly related to the current Quicken window, so that when you're working in the register, the questions are about those tasks (Figure 1-24). Click any item in the list to see instructions on accomplishing that task.

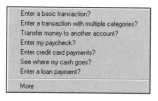

Figure 1-24 The common endings to the beginning of the question How Do I? are listed when you use this feature.

The last item in the list is More, and you can select it to see more questions that are grouped with a number of selected help topics (Figure 1-25). Click any topic to see detailed instructions on how to accomplish the task.

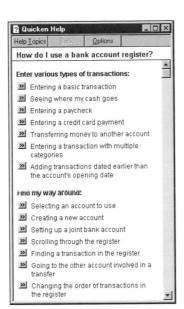

Figure 1-25 All the help topics for the current Quicken window are grouped to match the common questions about accomplishing tasks.

Many of the How Do I? answers have a Show Me button, so if you use this feature frequently, make sure that you keep your Quicken CD-ROM in the CD-ROM drive.

Advice

FEATURE FOCUS

New to Quicken 6 is the Advice button, which delivers recommendations and helpful hints on planning for the future and dealing with circumstances that can impact your financial situation. The advice is provided by three financial experts: Jayne Bryant Quinn, columnist and author; Marshall Loeb, former Managing Editor of *Fortune* and *Money* magazines; and Eric Tyson, MBA and author.

When you click Advice, you're offered several categories of counsel. These Advice topics are like mini-books that provide plenty of wisdom (Figure 1-26).

Planning & Prioritizing is filled with expert advice about how to plan ahead for everything from paying off debts, to buying a house, to having a comfortable retirement.

Life Events discusses ways to plan the financial aspects of the events that occur in most lives, including marriage, having children, divorce, and handling responsibility for aging parents.

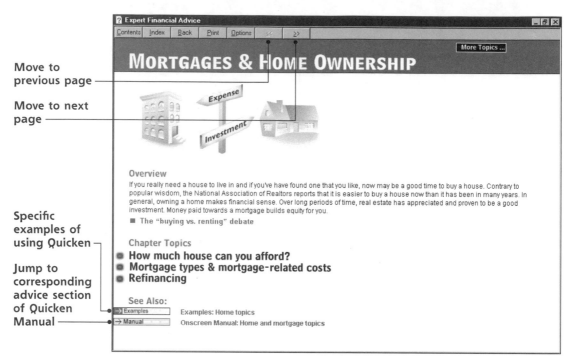

Move to previous page —

Move to next page —

Specific examples of using Quicken —

Jump to corresponding advice section of Quicken Manual —

Figure 1-26 Expert advice is available with plenty of guidance and specific examples.

Quicken Examples, the third option, lists all the Quicken features you can use to track or plan the finances for a host of situations. This advice window is from Quicken, not from the experts who contributed to the preceding two advice features.

Closing Quicken

I f you're using Quicken in Windows 95, close (exit) Quicken by clicking the Close button, which is the X in the upper-right corner of the Quicken software window. If you're using Quicken in Windows 3.*x*, go to the menu bar and select File → Exit.

Whenever you close Quicken, all the transactions you've entered are saved automatically. In addition, you are reminded to back up your files if you haven't used the backup feature recently.

X-REF Chapter 16 discusses Quicken's backup feature in more detail.

BONUS

The bank account you enter during startup may not be your only bank account.

Tracking multiple bank accounts

If you have a bunch of bank accounts, you may want to track them in Quicken, even if you don't use them to pay bills. In that case, give some thought to the naming procedure you use for this first account you're entering. If you have two accounts at the National Bank of East Overcoat, Iowa, don't name this account with that bank name, because you'll be stuck for a name when you add the other account from that bank (of course, you could name the second account "the other account," but then you'd have to remember which is which). Find some unique name for each account. One may be "Main Account" or "Account with Green Checks," and the other "Backup Account" or "Account with Yellow Checks." (See Chapter 7 for more on adding accounts.)

If you and your spouse each have individual accounts and also share a joint account, make the first Quicken account the one you use to pay most of the bills.

Try these shortcuts

Each task you perform in Quicken has its own window. You can move quickly to other windows and avoid the extra keystrokes of using the menu system by using these keyboard shortcuts:

Shortcut	Go to...
CTRL+A	Account List
CTRL+C	Category List
CTRL+H	Loans List
CTRL+T	Memorized Transaction List
CTRL+J	Scheduled Transaction List
CTRL+R	Register

(continued)

Shortcut	Go to...
CTRL+U	Portfolio List
CTRL+W	Write checks

Nifty trick for keeping help topics handy

You can copy the text in a help topic page by doing one of the following, depending on which version of Windows you use:

* To copy the text in the help topic window in Windows 95, select [Copy] from the shortcut menu that appears when you right-click.

* To copy the text in the help topic window in Windows 3.*x*, choose [Edit] → [Copy].

When you do this, the text is placed on the Windows Clipboard, and you can paste the text into another Windows program. In case you don't see the usefulness of this capability, let me tell you what I do with this feature.

When I'm working with certain features I don't use frequently, I don't always remember how to use those features when I need them. So, I open up the program's help files and go through the topics I need to accomplish my task. The next time I have to perform the same task, however, I don't want to bother going through that entire process again.

Therefore, when I'm using the help file, I open my word processor (isn't multitasking wonderful?), copy each help topic I need, and paste it into my word processor document. Eventually I have a handbook. I print my handbook and keep it on my desk. In fact, because I do this with so many software applications, my handbook consists of a three-ring binder with dividers for each software package. In addition to the copies of the help text, I have my own notes, so this handbook is a terrifically useful tool.

Summary

The New User Setup process is a one-time procedure that gets the Quicken software ready to track your finances properly. Now that it's over, you're ready to use Quicken for your bill paying and other financial transactions. This chapter also gives you a full tour of all the elements and features on the Quicken window, so it will be easy to jump right in and start entering transactions.

CHAPTER TWO

ENTERING CHECKBOOK TRANSACTIONS

2

IN THIS CHAPTER YOU LEARN THESE KEY SKILLS:

I f you've had a checkbook for any length of time and have been writing checks and making deposits, then you already have experience entering transactions. Now you must carry over that experience and apply it to the Quicken register. Maintaining a computerized checkbook may seem time-consuming at first, but it saves you effort, aggravation, and time in the long run. The ability to review the status of your individual accounts and locate specific transactions at the touch of a keystroke is invaluable.

Tracking income and expenses, printing reports, and compiling information for your taxes are tasks that cannot be accomplished by filling out your checkbook. Once you enter information in Quicken's register, however, you have the ability to sort it, manipulate it, graph it, and view it in a dozen different ways. The act of entering transactions into Quicken offers you control of your finances in a way that simple, paper bookkeeping cannot.

To ensure that you are getting the most out of Quicken, you must understand not only what you are doing but why you are doing it. Because transactions are the building blocks of your financial house, understanding the various parts of a transaction and the role each plays in the overall picture is essential. This chapter covers the steps you take when you enter a checkbook transaction.

Understanding Transactions

Simply put, a *transaction* is anything that affects your account's bottom line. If an item changes the balance negatively or positively, it is a transaction. Examples of transactions are checks, deposits, transfers of money between two accounts, interest earned, bank charges, ATM withdrawals, and online payments.

Transactions are recorded in the register, which is pretty much the same as the paper register in your checkbook. As with all record keeping, keeping specific information about each transaction is important. These pieces of information form the basis for the transaction entry fields. The accuracy of this information enables you to see when and where your money is going and to budget and forecast with confidence. The two-line transaction shown in Figure 2-1 is composed of the following entry fields:

Date	Num	Payee / Category / Memo	Payment	Clr	Deposit	Balance
8/16/96		Opening Balance		R	2,326 49	2,326 49
		[KI Checking]				

Figure 2-1   Quicken's two-line transaction closely resembles the one in your checkbook register.

* **Date.** The date the transaction occurred. Without the correct date, monthly, quarterly, and annual reports do not reflect a true picture of your spending habits.

* **Num.** The number of the check. Keeping track of the numbers alerts you when a check is missing or written out of sequence. Enter Deposit (choose it from the pop-up list that appears automatically) for any transaction that increases the balance of your account.

* **Payee.** The person or company to whom the check was written. If you enter **Deposit** in the Num field, the Payee field changes to Paid By. For a deposit, enter the source of the money.

* **Payment.** The amount of the check or transfer. Be sure to double-check this one. I hate it when my statement shows that I have less money than I thought because I entered the wrong amount of a check. If you're entering a deposit, leave this field blank.

* **Clr.** Cleared items. You use this field during statement reconciliation to confirm that you and the bank agree on the checks that have been cleared through the bank and on the deposits that have been received.

* **Deposit.** The amount of the deposit. As with the Payment amount, be sure to enter the correct number here.

* **Balance.** A running total of your account balance, including all transactions through the last one recorded. Quicken keeps track of this total for you by recalculating the balance every time you enter a transaction.

* **Category.** A means of tracking income and expenses by assigning similar transactions to the same income or expense group. This field is very important when it comes to producing meaningful reports that show you exactly where your money is going.

* **Memo.** A brief description of the transaction may not be necessary, but it sure helps when you wonder what the check you wrote to Sharkey's Pool Hall, Pizzeria, and All-Night Laundromat was really for. You know that the category Childcare doesn't seem appropriate, but that's what you put down. If you have a written memo that indicates you cashed a check to pay the baby-sitter, the entry may make a little more sense.

Entering Transactions

Regardless of the transaction type, the mechanics of entering transactions in the register are very similar. Every transaction should have an entry in the Date field, the Num field, the Payee field, either the Payment or the Deposit field (not both!), and the Category field. The Memo field can be helpful as a reminder of the reason for the transaction, but it is not critical.

As soon as you begin working, the check register presents you with the next available (blank) transaction record. The cursor is positioned in the Date field, which is today's date. You are now on your way to entering your first transaction. Actually, this is your second transaction if you filled in an opening balance during setup.

TIP You probably thought that if nothing else, the computer would at least do what you told it and not talk back. Well, you were only half right. If this is your first time using the program and you have the Quicken CD in your CD-ROM drive, Quicken's QCard feature gives you an unsolicited audio prompt to fill in the Date field. Each time you move to a new field, you receive brief audio instructions for that field. If you find it disconcerting to have your computer talk to you, turn it off by clicking the X in the corner of the QCard (if you need help later, you can turn this feature back on by clicking the Speaker icon in the lower-right portion of your Quicken screen). Audio QCards automatically play every time you start Quicken as long as they were turned on when you last closed Quicken.

Recording a check

Because most activity in a checking account takes the form of check writing (mine certainly does), this transaction makes an ideal starting point.

To record a check, follow these steps:

1. Quicken automatically fills in the Date field with today's date. If you wrote the check today, press Tab to move to the next field.

2. If the date is incorrect, type the correct date (you don't have to enter the slash marks) or click the calendar button to the right of the Date field and choose the correct date from the pop-up calendar (Figure 2-2). In addition, there are a number of shortcut keystrokes for entering dates, which are listed in Table 2-1.

Move through the previous months —————— Move through the next months

Figure 2-2 The pop-up calendar makes changing the date quick and easy.

TABLE 2-1 Shortcuts for Entering Dates

Keystroke	Date Change
+	Increases the date by one day
-	Decreases the date by one day
T	Today's date
M	First day of this month
M,M	First day of the previous month (M,M,M, the month before that, and so on)
H	Last day of the month
H,H	Last day of the next month (H,H,H, the month after that, and so on)
Y	First day of the year
Y,Y	First day of the previous year (Y,Y,Y, the year before that, and so on)
R	Last day of the year
R,R	Last day of the next year (R,R,R, the year after that, and so on)

TIP Sometimes I instinctively hit Enter when I'm ready to move on. I find it more intuitive than the Tab key that all Windows programs use in dialog boxes. Therefore, I appreciate the fact that Quicken offers the option of using either Tab or Enter to move from field to field. The first time you press Enter after making a transaction entry, a pop-up dialog box asks if you want to use Enter to move from field to field. Click Yes to enable Enter or No to stick with Tab. If you change your mind later, you can reverse your decision (see Chapter 15).

3. Enter the check number or choose Next Check Num (only if it is the next check number you're entering) from the drop-down list that appears when you move to the Num field (Figure 2-3).

Figure 2-3 Select Next Check Num from Quicken's drop-down list or enter the check number for this transaction.

4. Move to the Payee field.

5. Enter the name of the person or company to whom the check was written.

TIP After you've entered a name in the Payee field, Quicken remembers it and adds it to a Payee drop-down list. As each subsequent Payee is entered, Quicken searches the list for a match while you type. If it finds one, Quicken inserts it in the Payee field. If it is correct, you can move on; if it is incorrect, keep typing until Quicken finds the next match or until you've typed the full name of the new payee. Not only does this feature speed up the entry process, but it also ensures that misspelling a name does not result in multiple payee names for the same person.

6. Press Tab (or Enter) to move to the Payment field.

7. Record the amount of the check. If you need to do any calculations at this point, Quicken thoughtfully provides a pop-up calculator (Figure 2-4).

Figure 2-4 To make things add up, use Quicken's pop-up calculator.

8. Move to the Category field.

9. Choose a category from the drop-down list (Figure 2-5).

TIP **Using categories is such an important part of tracking your finances that Quicken reminds you to select one if you attempt to finalize a transaction that has not been assigned to a category. A dialog box pops up and asks if you would like to select one from the Category & Transfer List.**

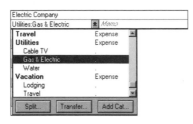

Figure 2-5 Assign a category to each check for accurate tracking.

10. Press Tab to move to the Memo field.

11. Enter a brief description of the reason for this check.

12. Check your entries to make sure that they're accurate.

13. Press Enter (*not* Tab) or click the Enter button on the right side of the transaction line to save the transaction and move to the next one.

Entering a deposit

Now on to the most important transaction of all: the deposit. Any transaction that increases the balance of your account is a deposit. Paychecks deposited, interest earned, and transfers from other accounts are all deposits.

Although the process for entering a deposit is very similar to the process for entering a check, a few significant differences exist. Starting with the next blank transaction record, follow these steps to enter a deposit:

1. Enter the Date as you would for a check.

2. Press Tab or Enter to move to the Num field.

3. In the Num field, choose Deposit from the drop-down list. Be sure not to enter a check number, or all subsequent checks will be misnumbered.

4. Press Tab to move to the next field.

TIP **Entering Deposit in the Num field causes the Payee field to become the Paid By field. In addition, the Payment field is automatically skipped, and you move directly from the Paid By field to the Deposit field.**

5. Use the Description field to record a name or description for the source of the deposit.

6. Press Tab and move to the Deposit field.

7. Enter the amount of the deposit.

8. Move to the Category field.

9. In the Category field, select an appropriate income category.

10. Press Tab to move to the Memo field.

11. Type an optional description or explanation of the transaction.

12. To finalize and save the deposit, press Enter or click the Enter button to the right of the Memo field.

With any luck, the sum of your deposits is larger than sum of the checks written. If this is not the case, your balance appears in red to indicate a negative balance.

Entering a transfer

A *transfer* is the movement of funds from one account to another. It can take the form of a check written on one account and deposited in another. The movement of money from your savings account to cover shortages in your checking account (overdraft protection) is an automatic transfer. Recording such activities as transfers eliminates the need to enter the transaction in both account registers. By entering it in one account as a transfer, Quicken automatically records it as a deposit in the other account.

Like checks and deposits, transfers are recorded in the account register. And like checks and deposits, the basic steps are similar.

Follow these steps to enter a transfer:

1. Enter the Date of the transfer.

2. Press Tab or Enter to move to the Num field.

3. Choose Transfer Funds from the drop-down list in the Num field. The descriptor TXFR is placed in the Num field to indicate a transfer.

TIP **Choosing Transfer Funds in the Num field automatically changes the Payee field to Description. It also converts the Category field into the Xfer Acct field and replaces the drop-down list of categories with a list of your existing accounts. If you have no other accounts, moving to the Xfer Acct field causes Quicken to offer you the opportunity to create a new account.**

4. Move to the Description field.

5. Enter a brief explanation of the transfer.

6. Press Tab or Enter to move to the Payment field.

7. Enter the amount of the transfer.

8. Press Tab to move to the Xfer Acct.

9. If you do not have any other accounts, Quicken asks if you want to add a new one. Say Yes and answer all the questions to create the account so that Quicken can enter the offsetting amount in this new account. (For detailed steps on setting up a new account, see Chapter 7.) If you already have other accounts, select the appropriate one from the Xfer Acct drop-down list (Figure 2-6).

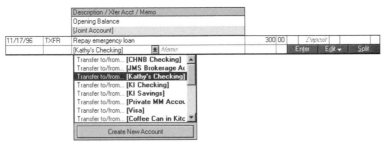

Figure 2-6   Select an account for this transfer from the Xfer Acct drop-down list.

10. Press Tab.

11. Move to the Memo field.

12. Enter a brief description of the transfer.

13. To finalize the transfer, press Enter or click the Enter button to the right of the Memo field.

Quicken offers an alternate means of entering a transfer by using a transfer form. You may find it a little more intuitive and easier to complete (Figure 2-7).

Figure 2-7   Making a transfer is as easy as filling in the blanks.

Filling out the form is as simple as following these steps:

1. Click the Transfer button just above the Num field heading in the account register.

2. In the Transfer Money From field, select the account from which to initiate the transfer (the default is the current account). Use the drop-down list to change the account.

3. Use the Tab key to move to the To Account field.

4. From the drop-down list, choose the existing account to receive the transfer or select Create New Account to add an account.

5. Move to the Date field.

6. Enter the date of the transfer.

7. Press Tab to move to the Description field.

8. Enter a short explanation of the transfer.

9. Use Tab to move to the Amount field.

10. Enter the amount of the transfer.

11. Click OK to save the transfer.

Because you're only moving money when you transfer, you cannot use income and expense categories to track transfers. You can, however, group transfers by assigning them to classes, which is a way to categorize them for reports.

Splitting a check

The reason you're taking the time to enter all this information into Quicken is so that you have a clear view of your financial picture. Unless you enter accurate information, you're defeating the purpose of computerizing your checkbook. One area that often gets overlooked is a single check written for multiple items, each of which belongs in a different category. The easy (and wrong!) way to handle such a check is to assign it to the category that corresponds to the largest amount. The right way to handle this check is to split it into all the various categories needed.

Say, for example, that on your next trip to the local discount store, you pick up a case of motor oil, some socks for the kids, and some cleaning supplies. You pay by check. Which category do you use? That's easy. All three: Auto, Clothing, and Household. Record the check as you would any other check until you reach the Category field. At this point, select the Split button from the drop-down list. In the Split Transaction window that appears, fill in the detailed information for the transaction (Figure 2-8):

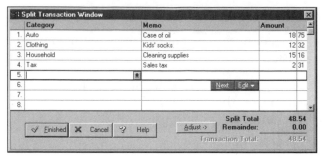

Figure 2-8 Splitting the check lets you know where your money goes.

1. For the kids' socks, select Clothing from the drop-down Category list.

2. Tab to the Memo field.

3. Enter a description (**Kids' socks**) in the Memo field.

4. Press Tab to move to the Amount field.

5. In the Amount field, enter the total you spent on the socks.

6. Use Tab to move to Line 2.

7. Repeat the preceding steps for the oil, cleaning supplies, and sales tax (if applicable).

TIP As you enter items in the Split Transaction window, Quicken calculates the total, deducting each entry from the amount you originally placed in the Payment field. If you're entering prices from your cash register receipt, you end up with a left-over amount that should equal the sales tax charged on the purchased items.

8. After you finish entering items, select Finished to close the Split Transaction window.

9. Use Tab to move to the Memo field.

TIP You can enter a brief description or leave the Description field blank because each item in the split has its own description.

10. To finalize the transaction, press Enter or click the Enter button.

The benefits gained by splitting checks as needed are well worth the minimal time and effort required to enter the data. You can have as many as 30 different entries per split, so there is no reason not to track your spending accurately.

Viewing Your Work

The reason for entering all this information is to get a clear picture of your financial situation. To that end, the Quicken Register offers several ways to view the transactions you enter. Although Quicken offers extensive reporting features, it also provides a handy Register Report and an expense graph that you access directly from the register. In addition, Quicken gives you several options for sorting the register to help you find and analyze your data.

The Report button

The Report button, located above the Deposit field heading in the account register, offers you a couple of quick ways to view your account without having to go to the report window and create a report. The information is limited, but it gives you a quick overview of the entire account or the expenditures made to one specific payee or category.

To view the Register Report, follow these steps:

1. Place the cursor in the first blank transaction and click Report button.

2. Select Register Report to view a transaction report with a running balance of your account, as in Figure 2-9.

3. To close the report and return to the register, click the X button.

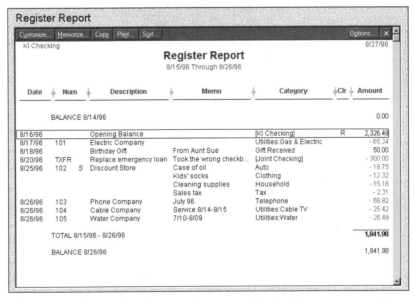

Figure 2-9 The Register Report gives you a clear look at your transactions and running balance.

You can also access two additional, quick reports that give you a breakdown of all transactions for a specific payee or category (Figure 2-10). Follow these steps to see those reports:

1. Place the cursor on the specific transaction for which you want a payee or category report.

2. Click the Report button.

3. Choose the desired report.

4. Click the X in the top right-hand corner of the Report button bar to close the report and return to the register.

Figure 2-10 Select a Category Report or a Payee Report.

A visual representation of data often gives me a clearer understanding of its importance than lists of numbers and figures. Therefore, I find the Expense Summary graph to be very useful in getting a snapshot of where I'm spending my money (Figure 2-11).

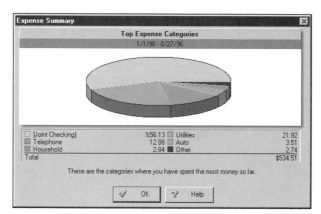

Figure 2-11 Seeing is believing! The Expense Summary graph shows where your money went.

To view the graph, follow these steps:

1. Click the Report button.

2. Select Expense Summary Graph.

3. Click OK to close the graph and return to the Register view.

The View button

Another way of viewing the register information is to switch from the two-line view of each transaction to a one-line view, as seen in Figure 2-12. This enables you to fit more transactions on the screen at one time while retaining all the transaction information except the Memo field. The Memo field information is not lost, simply hidden from view.

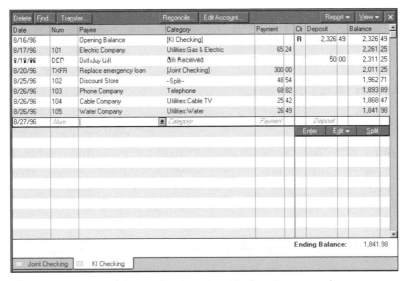

Figure 2-12 Switching to the One-Line Display gives you a less cluttered view of the register.

To change views, follow these steps:

1. Click the View button, which is located above the Balance field heading on the account register.

2. Select One-Line Display to convert the transactions to one liners (no joking).

FEATURE FOCUS The View button also offers a number of sorting options so that you can rearrange your transaction information in a manner suited to your specific needs. As Figure 2-13 shows, the options are self-explanatory.

Figure 2-13 Quicken's sort options let you have things your way.

TIP Items on the View menu can be toggled off and on by clicking them. A check mark to left of the item indicates that it is currently on.

Making Changes

As much as I hate to admit it, I occasionally make a mistake. It's at those times that I'm thankful I'm using a computer. Although the computer takes all my instructions literally, doing what I tell it to do, not what I want it to do, it is quite forgiving in allowing me to change my mind whenever I choose.

Editing a transaction

Editing entries is a necessity when you enter the wrong amount or the wrong date for a transaction and don't realize it until a later time. With the exception of the Balance field, you can edit any field in a transaction.

To edit a transaction, follow these steps:

1. To highlight the information to be changed, place the cursor in the transaction field you want to edit.

2. Begin typing the new information to overwrite the existing entry entirely.

3. To change part of the entry, move the cursor to the desired position and insert or replace individual characters.

4. To edit another field in the same transaction, Tab to the field and repeat Steps 2 and 3.

5. To save the changes, press Enter or click the Enter button.

If perchance you change your mind, click the Edit button, which is located between the Enter and Split buttons to the right of the Memo field. Among the numerous options available on the Edit menu is Restore Transaction. Selecting this option returns the transaction to its condition before you made any changes.

Deleting a transaction

There are times when the entire transaction is inaccurate and needs to be deleted. This action is irreversible, however, and should be done only if you are completely sure you want to delete the transaction and not merely edit it. One nice thing about the delete feature is that deleting one side of a transfer automatically removes the other:

1. Highlight the transaction you want to eliminate.

2. Click the Delete button found at the top, left-hand corner of the account register, above the Date field heading.

3. When Quicken prompts you to confirm the deletion, select Yes if you are sure; otherwise, select No.

Protecting Transactions with Passwords

Once you've set up Quicken and entered all your data, the last thing you want is for someone to come along and mess everything up. In fact, it's not a bad idea to protect your data from accidental changes or deletions that you might make.

To protect your transaction information from being unintentionally modified, follow these steps:

1. Select File → Passwords → Transaction from the Quicken menu to bring up the Password to Modify Existing Transactions dialog box (Figure 2-14).

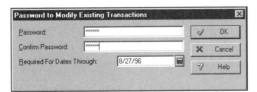

Figure 2-14 Password-protecting your transactions ensures that they will not be accidentally altered or deleted.

2. Enter your chosen password in the Password field.

3. Press Tab to move to the Confirm Password field.

TIP Notice that as you type your password into the Password field, none of the letters you typed actually shows up in the field. To eliminate the possibility of someone else inadvertently seeing your password, Quicken replaces the letters you type with asterisks. Because you can't really see what you're typing, be sure to choose a password that's easy to enter so you won't make a typo when you want to use it.

4. Type the password in the Confirm Password field again to verify that you typed the password correctly. If you do not type the same word here, Quicken balks and takes you back to the Password field to start over.

5. Once you have confirmed your password, press Tab to move to the Required For Dates Through field.

 It is very important that you write down your password and put it in a safe place. If you forget it, you will have to send your file to Intuit's data recovery department to have the password removed. Until the file is returned, you will not have access to the restricted transactions except to view them.

6. In the Required For Dates Through field, enter the effective date for password protection to begin. All transactions on or before that date become inaccessible without the password.

7. To accept password protection with your chosen password on the transactions you've indicated, click OK.

The next time you edit a transaction covered by password protection, Quicken asks you for the password when you attempt to save your changes. If you do not provide it, the changes are not accepted.

BONUS

S ome decisions about using Quicken can be put off for a while. If you're not used to bookkeeping software, it may be better to wait until you've been using Quicken for a time before you make it more complicated.

Start with the basics

It's not necessary to start off with the idea that you're going to know everything about your cash, investments, pension, and assets. You can operate Quicken perfectly well with only your checking account. Entering every deposit you make to your account and every check you write gives you plenty of information about your financial status.

All categories are not equal

The most important items to track are those that are tax deductible. These items are more important than how much you spent on clothing or even on utilities. Keep careful, detailed category entries on tax-deductible expenses; you can put everything else under Quicken's catch-all category, Misc.

If that's not clear enough for you, go ahead and add a category called *non-deductible expense*. Adding a category while you're entering transactions is easy:

1. When you get to the Category field during a transaction entry, start typing the new category name you want (ignore the pop-up category list).

2. Press Tab to move to the next field.

3. Quicken catches on to what you did and pops up a little message saying "Do you want to create a new category with the name...(the name you entered goes here)?"

4. Click Yes.

5. Fill out the Set Up Category dialog box that looks like Figure 2-15.

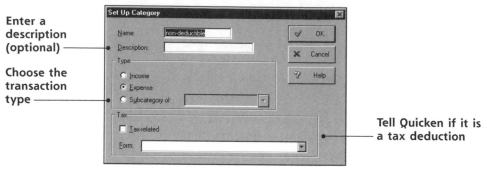

Enter a description (optional)

Choose the transaction type

Tell Quicken if it is a tax deduction

Figure 2-15 The Set Up Category dialog box.

Get the information you need from the payee

If you don't want to bother with multitudinous categories, here's a trick that works almost all the time — get a report on the payee. Why do you need to track the amount you're spending for electricity by tracking it by category? Just ask Quicken how much money you sent to the payee named The Electric Company (or whatever your power company is named). After all, it's not very likely that you wrote a check to them to pay for your new shoes.

To get payee information, follow these steps:

1. Click any transaction line that has the payee you need information about.

2. Click the Report button.

3. Select Payments made to (the name of the payee appears here).

Quicken displays a report that shows you every transaction for that payee along with a total.

Summary

In this chapter, you learned about the most important task you'll perform in Quicken: entering transactions. It's possible to use Quicken without ever using another feature beyond this one (except for running reports, of course). If you want to learn more about your spending habits, however, and you want to plan your spending intelligently, there are plenty of Quicken features discussed in this book to help you.

PRINTING CHECKS

IN THIS CHAPTER YOU LEARN THESE KEY SKILLS:

3

The preceding chapter covers entering manually written checks into the register. That's fine if you only write a handful of checks every month. If you have a large number of checks to write, however, or if most of your bills are due at the same time of the month, it makes sense to use Quicken's check-writing feature. With preprinted computer checks, you can have Quicken do everything but sign the check for you.

This Quicken feature eliminates the worry of illegible handwriting or the possibility of entering a written amount different from the numerical amount of the check. Used in conjunction with window envelopes, you can even include the payee's address on the check and forget about addressing the envelope.

In this chapter, you discover how to write checks that will be printed, set up your printer, select your print options, and then print the checks.

Writing Checks

Aside from the checks you write while out shopping, most checks are generally written at home to pay the bills. With proper planning, you probably can narrow it down to one or two check-writing sessions a month. That is when Quicken's check-writing feature comes in handy.

To access the Write Checks window, click the Bills icon in the Activity Bar and select Write a Check to Print. As you can see in Figure 3-1, the Write Checks window closely resembles a paper check from your checkbook.

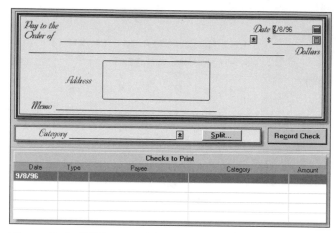

Figure 3-1 Writing an electronic check isn't much different than writing one from your checkbook.

 TIP   If you're using Quicken in Windows 3.*x*, the Write Checks window does not have the Checks to Print/Send register at the bottom. Instead, it has a scroll bar that takes you through the actual checks one at a time.

The account tabs

The first order of business is to be sure you're writing the checks from the correct account. Because the Write Checks window has the same appearance no matter which account you're using, it's easy to start writing checks in the wrong checkbook. To ensure that doesn't happen, the account tabs appear at the bottom of the Write Checks window so you can click the appropriate tab.

The check fields

The fields for the check are filled in following these guidelines:

* **Date.** The date of the transaction. Because you may be writing checks to be paid at a later date, you can "postdate" your check for printing at that time.

* **Pay to the Order of.** The payee, or person to whom the check is written.

* **$ (Amount).** The exact amount of the check.

* **Dollars.** The dollar amount spelled out to ensure that the correct amount is given to the payee.

* **Address.** The field used when a check is being mailed in the appropriate window envelope. The payee's name and address appear in the window.

* **Memo.** As in the register, the memo is an optional field for entering a brief description of the check. One thing to note here is that the Memo field may be visible if you are using window envelopes.

TIP If you're using window envelopes and your memo appears in the window, you may want to select the Extra Message option in the Check Options window (select Options on the Write Checks window). Selecting Allow Entry of Extra Message on Check creates a separate Message field to the right of the Address field on the check. The Message field, unlike the Memo field, is not visible from the envelope window. For more information, see Chapter 15.

* **Category.** If you're interested in keeping an eye on where your money is going, use categories. Assigning similar transactions to the same category makes it easy to see how much money is being spent in a particular area.

* **Online Payment.** This checkbox option, which enables you to write a check and send it as an online payment, appears only if the account in which you're working is set up for online payments. Notice in Figure 3-2 that selecting the Online Payment option changes the date to ASAP, causes the address box to disappear, and converts Checks to Print to Checks to Send. Because the payment will be made online, you do not need to fill in an address. If you want to send the payment at a later date, you can change ASAP to the appropriate date.

* **Split.** Split enables you to assign one check to multiple categories.

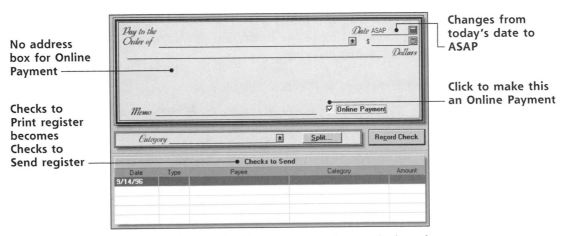

Figure 3-2 The Online Payment option changes the face of the check as well as its purpose.

Filling out the check

To write an electronic check, you must enter all the necessary information you would normally include on a paper check from your checkbook. Because Quicken automatically places you in the Date field when you enter the Write Checks window, you want to start there. The default date is today's date.

Follow these steps to fill out the check:

1. If the date is correct, go to Step 2. If the date is incorrect, type in the correct date (you do not have to type the /; it is entered automatically).

2. Press Tab to move to the Pay to the Order of field.

3. Enter the name of the person to whom the check is being written or click the down arrow at the end of the Pay to the Order of field to access a drop-down list of existing payees.

4. Press Tab to move to the $ (amount) field.

5. Type in *the exact numerical amount of the check.* Don't forget to use a decimal point to separate dollars and cents (no need to worry about a comma to separate thousands and hundreds because Quicken does it for you).

TIP **Quicken automatically converts the numerical amount in the $ field to text and places it in the Dollars field. The only way to change the text amount is to return to the $ field and change the numerical amount.**

6. Use Tab to move to the Address field.

7. If you plan use window envelopes to mail the check, fill out the payee's address.

TIP **Quicken does not automatically insert the payee's name, so be sure to include it as the first line of the address if you're going to mail the check using a window envelope.**

8. Press Tab to move to the Memo field.

9. Enter an account number or brief description of the check in the Memo field.

10. Move to the Category field by pressing Tab.

11. Enter the appropriate category for the check or choose one from the drop-down list. You can add a new category by typing it in and filling out the Set Up Category dialog box that appears (Figure 3-3).

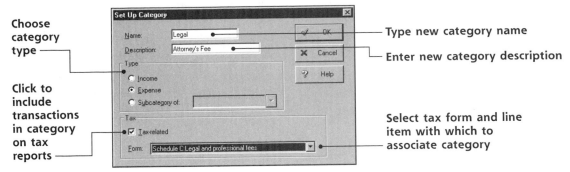

Choose category type ⎯

Click to include transactions in category on tax reports ⎯

Type new category name

Enter new category description

Select tax form and line item with which to associate category

Figure 3-3 If Quicken doesn't provide the right category, add your own.

12. Press Tab to move to the Record Check button.

TIP If you write a check to a single payee for multiple items of completely different types, you should split the check to track your expenses accurately. Click the Split button to assign each amount to the appropriate category. Enter the category, a brief description (memo), and the amount for each item.

13. To finalize the check and save it, press Enter or click Record Check. Once the check is saved, it appears in the Checks to Print register (Figure 3-4).

Checks to Print				
Date	Type	Payee	Category	Amount
9/14/96	Print	Berryl Coronet	Legal	200.00
9/14/96				

Figure 3-4 The Checks to Print (or Send, for online payments) register enables you to view and review checks that you write.

TIP In Quicken for Windows 3.*x*, there is no Checks To Print register — each specific check has a notation, and you can scroll through the window to see the final list.

One nice feature that Quicken provides is the capability to see not only your ending balance, but your current balance and the total of the checks to be printed (sent). The ending balance includes all the checks you've written, including those that are still to be printed. When postdating checks to be sent at a later time, however, the current balance gives your balance as of today. This balance comes in handy when you're trying to figure out just how much you need to cover upcoming payments. The To Print figure to the left of the current balance keeps track of the total of all checks to be printed (sent).

Changing Checks

Writing checks is no different than other activities that make up part of your everyday life. You will always have times when you make a mistake or just change your mind after the fact. Fortunately, changing your mind or correcting your mistakes in Quicken is a rather simple process.

Editing

Before printing a batch of checks, it is always a good idea to review them to make sure all the information is accurate. If you find something that is in error or you just have a change of heart, you can make the changes before printing. Editing a check in Quicken's Write Checks window is a relatively simple matter:

1. In the Checks to Print register, choose the check to be edited by clicking it. This immediately fills in the blank check form with the information from the selected transaction.

2. Move to the fields to be edited.

3. Make the necessary changes.

4. After you're finished editing the check, click Record Check to save the changes.

Deleting

Occasionally editing a check is just not enough. If you change your mind entirely or write a check that is a duplicate of another, you can delete the transaction completely, as long as you have not yet printed the check.

Deleting a check is as easy as following these steps:

1. Highlight the check in the Checks to Print register by clicking it.

2. Select Delete from the Write Checks button bar at the top of the Write Checks window.

3. If you're sure you want to eliminate this transaction, confirm your decision to delete the check by clicking OK.

Voiding

Deleting a check once it's printed is inadvisable, because doing so will wreak havoc on your check numbering system. To ensure that you don't lose your mind looking for a check that doesn't exist, a good idea is to void a check that's been printed but is no longer valid. Because a printed check no longer appears in the Write Checks window, however, the only way to void it is to return to the register for the account on which the check was written.

Do not void an online payment that has been already been sent. Doing so eliminates your ability to get a confirmation number, which is necessary to effect a stop payment on the check. Instead, go to the Online Banking Center and select the correct account and payment. Then select Cancel Payment to prevent the payment from being processed. If it is not too late to stop the payment, Quicken changes the payment status from Sent to Cancel. If the payment has been processed, Quicken alerts you to contact the bank and request a stop payment order.

To void a check, follow these steps:

1. From the Quicken Activity Bar, point to the My Accounts icon and click Use My Register.

2. If you're not in the right account, select the correct account tab from the bottom of the register window.

3. Highlight the check to be voided by clicking it.

4. Select $\boxed{\text{Edit}} \rightarrow \boxed{\text{Transaction}} \rightarrow \boxed{\text{Void}}$ from the menu bar.

TIP **Once you're in the correct account register, you can easily void a check by right-clicking it and selecting Void Transaction from the resulting pop-up menu.**

5. To save the voided check, click the Enter button located on the second line of the transaction below the Deposit field. Quicken adds the check amount back to your account.

Ordering Checks

Now comes the best part of letting Quicken write the checks for you: automatic printing. You don't have to lift a pen or write a stroke except to sign the checks. If you use double-window envelopes, you won't even have to address the envelope. Add the fact that no guesswork is involved regarding the amount of the checks or to whom they're written, and you may wonder why you ever hand-wrote a check. To make the printing process as easy as the rest of Quicken's check-writing procedure, you must attend to a few details before starting.

Types of checks

The first matter of business is to determine the type of check you are going to use. The two types of available computer checks are *continuous feed* and *single feed* checks. The types of checks from which you can choose is governed by the printer you use. A dot-matrix printer without a sheet feeder accepts only continuous form checks. Laser and ink-jet printers, which do not have tractor feeds, can use single sheet checks but not continuous form checks.

TIP **One of the drawbacks to printing checks is having to load and unload the checks from the printer every time you do a print run. Using an old, slow, dot-matrix printer as a dedicated check printer is an ideal way to get that old "doorstop" back into service and to eliminate the hassle of switching the checks every time. If you don't have one, you can probably pick one up for next to nothing at a used computer shop or through the classified ads.**

Once you've decided which type of check to use, the next decision involves the size. Generally, you have three sizes to choose from for both single sheet and continuous form checks:

* **Standard size.** This is the most basic check. It comes three checks to a page and has no stub or voucher. The approximate size of these checks in 8.5 inches × 3.5 inches.

* **Wallet size.** If you want a printed record of the transaction for your files, the wallet check offers a stub in addition to the check itself. The checks are approximately 6 inches × 2.8 inches and also come three to a page.

* **Voucher size.** These are typically used for accounts payable or payroll because they have a large stub at the bottom to accommodate all necessary transaction information. Voucher size checks come one 8.5-inch × 3.5-inch check to a sheet with the remainder of the page available as the stub.

TIP **If you're using a dot-matrix or ink-jet printer, you should consider reusable forms leaders that attach to the pages and reduce check waste. Some dot-matrix printers, because of the print head setup, cannot print the first check of a page. Attaching form leaders allows you to line up the checks so that every one can be used. Ink-jet printers do not allow you to print a three-check sheet with only one or two checks remaining. Attaching forms leaders enables you to print a single check at a time if necessary.**

The ordering process

Quicken has made ordering checks as simple and easy as the rest of the check-writing process. Once you've determined the type and size checks you want, you can place your order through the Intuit Marketplace (Figure 3-5). Of course, you need to go online to the Internet to do this.

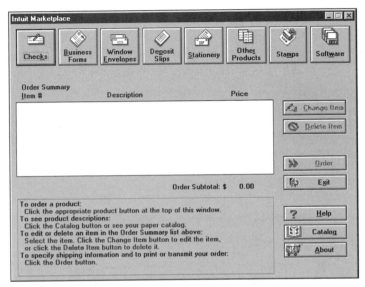

Figure 3-5 The Intuit Marketplace offers one-stop shopping for your check printing needs.

CHOOSING THE CHECK TYPE

To select a check type, follow these steps:

1. From the Quicken menu bar, select `Features` → `Online` → `Intuit Marketplace`.

2. Select Checks from the toolbar at the top of the Intuit Marketplace window.

3. Enter your Bank Account Number (Figure 3-6).

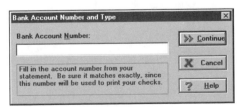

Figure 3-6 Make sure that you enter your correct account number.

TIP Because the numbers on the bottom of your check include routing information and the check number in addition to the account number, sometimes it is hard to tell which is the account number. The easiest way to get your account number and be sure that it is accurate is to take it directly from a recent bank statement.

4. Click Continue to proceed.

5. Because it is critical to have the correct account number, Quicken seeks verification by requiring you to enter the account number a second time.

6. After you re-enter your account number, click Continue to move forward.

7. From the Paper Type dialog box, select the type of paper checks you want to use (Figure 3-7).

8. Click Continue to proceed.

For use with dot-matrix or other tractor feed printer

For use with a laser or ink-jet printer

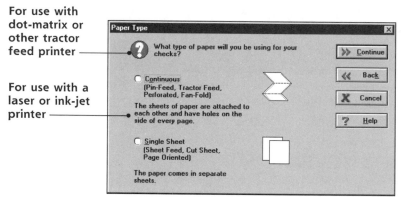

Figure 3-7 Your choice of check type depends on the printer you plan to use.

SELECTING SIZE, COLOR, AND QUANTITY

Whether you select Continuous or Single Sheet checks, the remaining information that you must provide is the same. The Size and Style window offers you the choice of size, color, and quantity (Figure 3-8).

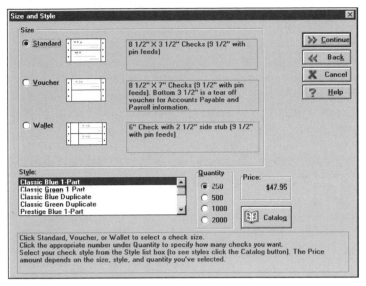

Figure 3-8   The Size and Style window gives you basic layout and design choices.

To specify which layout you want, the color of your checks, and how many you want to purchase, follow these steps:

1. Select Standard, Voucher, or Wallet by clicking the radio button to left of the desired size.

2. Press Tab to move to the Style box.

3. Use the scroll bar to select the color and style of your checks.

4. Press Tab to move to the Quantity options.

5. Click the radio button to the left of your desired Quantity.

T I P   When you select the different quantities, the price is shown in the Price box to the right. As is usually the case, the larger the quantity, the smaller the per unit cost. Before you succumb to the temptation to "save" money by ordering a large quantity, however, take your lifestyle into account. Do you write enough checks to warrant a large order? Is your situation stable enough to make using all the checks you order feasible? If you're considering a move or must relocate frequently, you may save money by buying a smaller quantity.

6. Press Tab to move to the Catalog button.

7. Click the Catalog button for information on additional sizes and styles.

8. Click Continue to proceed.

PROVIDING PERSONAL AND BANK INFORMATION

Computer checks are no different than any other check in that they must carry the same basic preprinted information. You will probably want each check to include your name, address, and phone number, the name and location of the bank, and possibly a logo or monogram. Once you've selected size and color, the next dialog box asks you to enter the personal information you want printed on your checks (Figure 3-9).

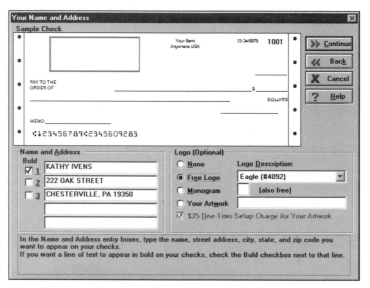

Figure 3-9   Enter your personal information exactly as you want it to appear on your checks.

1. Enter your name and address on the five lines provided in the Name and Address box.

2. Place a check mark in the Bold boxes of the lines you want to appear in bold.

3. Select your logo option from the following choices located in the Logo (Optional) section:

   ✱ **None.** Choose this option if you do not want a logo or monogram on your checks.

   ✱ **Free Logo.** To select free logo, check this option and choose a logo from the Logo Description drop-down list.

   ✱ **Monogram.** To include a monogram on your checks, select this option and type the letter of your choice in the box to the right.

* **Your Artwork.** If you're supplying your own camera-ready artwork, select this option and type a brief description of it in the box to the right.

* **$35 One-Time Setup Charge for Your Artwork.** This box is automatically checked if you select the Your Artwork option.

4. Click Continue to proceed to the Bank Name and Address window as seen in Figure 3-10.

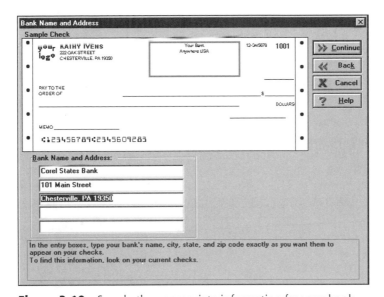

Figure 3-10 Supply the appropriate information for your bank.

5. Enter your bank's name and address using as many of the five lines as you need.

6. Click Continue to move to the Bank Fractional Number dialog box (Figure 3-11).

7. Enter the fractional number using Tab to move between entry boxes.

T I P   **Don't worry if your fractional numbers don't fit precisely in the entry boxes. The important thing is to include all the numbers. If your bank does not use fractional numbers, place an X in each entry box.**

8. Click Continue to move to the Starting Check Number window, as seen in Figure 3-12.

9. Enter the starting number for this order of checks.

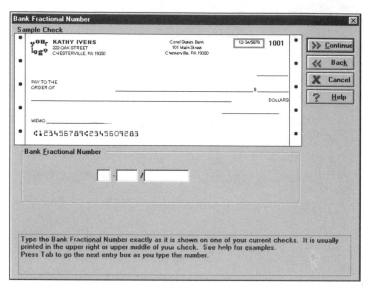

Figure 3-11 Copy the fractional number which usually appears in the top right-hand corner, below the check number.

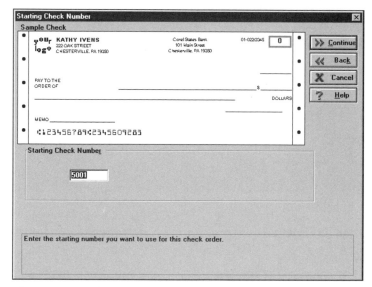

Figure 3-12 Choose your starting number carefully and insert it here.

10. Click Continue to proceed to the Signature Lines window.

11. Select the number of signature lines you want to appear on your checks.

12. Click Continue to move to the Verify Check Order dialog box seen in Figure 3-13.

TIP Because you will undoubtedly continue to use a checkbook to write checks while away from home, it is necessary to keep the numbers from overlapping. The best solution is to assign much higher numbers to the new computer checks. For instance, if your checkbook check numbers are in the under 2,000 range, you might assign the computer checks to begin at 5001. This way, you do not have a chance to duplicate numbers. This method also enables you to recognize the origin of the check by its number.

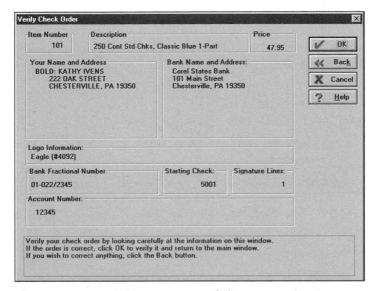

Figure 3-13 Look this one over carefully to ensure that ALL your information is accurate.

13. Click OK to complete the order or Back to change the order.

After you complete the order, an order form appears that displays the total and has instructions about adding your state tax and shipping fees. It also asks you to provide credit card information to pay for your order. You can print out the order and mail it (with credit card information or a check) or fax it (with credit card information).

Printing Checks

Once you have obtained your preprinted checks and entered all information in the checks to be printed, the only thing left to do is print them. The print process consists of two separate steps the first time you print. You first must set up your printer to accommodate your new checks. Then you must tell Quicken exactly which checks to print.

Basic printer setup

The initial printer setup includes deciding which printer to use, the type of checks you will be printing on, and various other settings. To set up your printer for the first time, follow these steps:

1. From the Quicken menu bar, select ⌈ File ⌉→⌈ Printer Setup ⌉→ ⌈ For Printing Checks ⌉ to access the Check Printer Setup window (Figure 3-14).

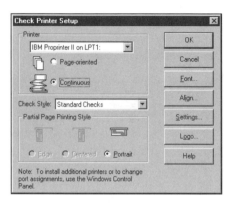

Figure 3-14 Quicken's printer setup options give you control over check printing.

2. From the Printer drop-down list, select the installed printer to use.

3. Press Tab to move the check type options.

4. Choose whether to use Page-oriented or Continuous checks by clicking the radio button to the left of your choice.

5. Move to the Check Style section by pressing Tab.

6. Select the style of check from the Check Style drop-down list.

7. Press Tab to move to the Partial Page Printing Style options, which enable you to determine the way partial sheets of checks can be fed into the printer.

TIP **The Partial Page Printing Style options may or may not be available, depending on your choice of check type, check style, and printer. If the option is not available, it appears grayed out and inaccessible.**

8. Select the available Partial Page Printing Style that is appropriate for your needs by clicking the radio button beneath the style.

9. Press Tab to move to OK.

If you're finished setting up the printer, click OK to save your changes and exit. If you want to use the optional printer settings found on the command buttons beneath OK, proceed to Advanced Printer Setup.

Advanced printer setup

The advanced printer settings give you additional flexibility in deciding how your checks print and how they appear. You can change the type and size of font, the resolution at which the checks are printed, and the alignment of the checks. You can even add a custom logo if you want.

FONT

To change the size or style of font used in printing your checks, follow these steps:

1. From the Quicken menu bar, select **File** → **Printer Setup** ›
   For Printing Checks to access the Check Printer Setup window.

2. Click the Font button that appears on the right-hand side of the window. This brings up the Check Printing Font window.

3. Using the scroll bar to view the available fonts, click the font you want to use for your checks.

TIP The U.S. Postal Service has moved into the computer age along with the rest of us and now uses electronic scanners to read addresses and sort mail. Therefore, to ensure that the scanners can read the mail without any hitches, use a clean, readable font without any fancy flourishes. Not only are the scanners unimpressed by a beautiful script, but they penalize you by holding up your mail until a mere human can figure out where it really is supposed to go.

4. Press Tab to move to the Font style.

5. Choose from the available styles by clicking the style of your choice.

6. Use Tab to move to the Size option.

7. Click the size font you want to use.

TIP As you select font, style, and size, your choice appears in the Sample box below the Font style window. Before you finalize your decision, check this sample to be sure it is what you expected.

8. Press Tab to move to OK.

9. Select OK to save your changes and return to the Check Printer Setup window. From here, you can either choose OK to exit printer setup altogether or select another option.

ALIGN

Making sure that your checks are lined up properly is extremely important. Quicken allows you to fine-tune the alignment automatically once you load the checks and line them up manually. The alignment options vary depending on the type of checks you're using.

SETTINGS

The Settings option enables you to make changes to settings that apply to your specific printer. It covers such things as paper size, page orientation, graphics resolution, and paper source. This option is different for each make and model printer. Refer to your printer documentation for more help.

LOGO

One of the nice things about being computerized is the flexibility it offers. You no longer need to have your checks preprinted with a logo. Instead, you can design your own and have Quicken print it every time you do a print run. In the event that you decide to redesign your logo, you do not need to order new checks; simply change the logo file Quicken uses. Follow these steps to use you own logo with Quicken checks:

1. Select File → Printer Setup → For Printing Checks .

2. From the Check Printer Setup window, select Logo to access the Check Logo dialog box (Figure 3-15).

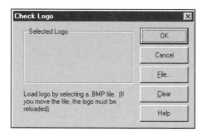

Figure 3-15 To use your own logo, simply tell Quicken where to find it.

3. In the Check Logo dialog box, click File.

4. Locate the logo file (it must be a BMP graphics file) and enter the filename in the File Name box.

5. Click OK to return to the Check Logo dialog box, where the logo now appears for you to preview.

6. If you have chosen the wrong logo, click File to choose another.

7. When you are satisfied with your choice, click OK to return to the Check Printer Setup window.

8. Choose another option or click OK to exit printer setup.

Choosing what to print

Once your printer is set up and the checks are properly aligned, you can move on the actual printing process. Of course, there is one final issue that needs to be resolved — exactly what are you going to print? Quicken realizes that, due to different circumstances, you may need to make some final adjustments. The place to do it is in the Select Checks to Print window (Figure 3-16), which you access by selecting File → Print Checks from the Quicken menu. The options offered here give you control over which checks to print, what checks you use, and even the starting check number. The options include the following:

* **First Check Number.** As you may have noticed, there is no place to enter the check number in the Write Checks window. The reason is quite simple. You select the beginning check number when you print checks for the first time, and Quicken automatically assigns the next available number for each check thereafter. In the event that you assign the next number to a manually written check, you can adjust the check numbers on the next print run.

* **Print.** The Print option allows you to print all the checks you have written, only checks that fall within a certain date range, or individual checks of your choosing.

* **Check Style.** This option indicates whether you are using standard, voucher, or wallet checks.

* **Checks on First Page.** Available only for standard and wallet checks, this option enables you to use a full sheet or a partial sheet of one or two checks only.

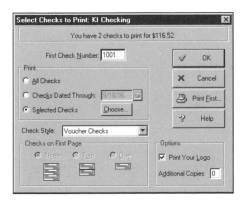

Figure 3-16 Quicken's flexible print options let you decide how and what to print.

* **Print Your Logo.** Check this option to have your logo printed on these checks. The option is not available unless you have created a logo and indicated during the printer setup that you want to use it on Quicken checks. In addition, it is only available on standard and voucher checks.

* **Additional Copies.** If you're using voucher checks, you can elect to print three additional copies with this option.

* **Print First.** This option enables you to print only the first check as a sample check so that you can be sure everything is lined up properly before printing the entire batch. (If the sample check works, you can print the rest. If it doesn't repeat the Print First, Quicken will adjust the check numbers).

Once you have set up your printer, selected your print options, and printed a sample check, you're ready to go. All that remains is to click OK in the Select Checks to Print window; Quicken does the rest.

BONUS

Here are some shortcuts and tricks for printing checks.

Postdating printed checks is easy

Because you can write checks to be sent at a later time, viewing a calendar often helps to determine when a check must be printed to arrive on time. Quicken conveniently provides a drop-down calendar for you. All you have to do is click the Calendar icon at the end of the Date field and choose your date. The Quicken Billminder makes sure that you don't forget to print and mail this check.

 X-REF Chapter 6 describes the Quicken Billminder in more detail.

Be a bargain hunter

Because Quicken has such a large installed user base, compatible checks and forms are available from a number of different sources. It may prove worthwhile to check out several other suppliers before making a purchase. The following vendors currently have home pages on the Internet from which you obtain information:

WEB PATH

* `http://www.pcchecks.com/pc.html`: PC Checks and Supplies On-Line Computer Supplies Catalog! Compatible with virtually all software programs.

* `http://www.checksforless.com/home.html`: FormSystems computer checks and forms.

* `http://www.forms.deluxe.com/`: Deluxe business forms, window envelopes and checks.

* `http://www.hotnew.com/checks/`: Designer checks, continuous and laser/ink-jet computer checks.

* `http://www.nebs.com`: Nebs office forms, window envelopes, and checks.

* `http://www.burroughs.com/continuous.html`: Burroughs Computer Checks and Forms.

Approach the buying of checks and forms via the Internet as you would any mail-order purchase. Be sure the firm you do business with is reputable, and *always* pay with a credit card. However, be careful giving your credit card number out over the Internet. It is not always a secure environment.

Have a New Year's Eve printing party

Here's a tax tip about check printing and tax deductions. Print and send the checks that offer a tax deduction by the last day of the year, even if the due date is later. If you pay quarterly estimated taxes to the state or the IRS, pay them before December 31, even though they have a due date of January 15. If it doesn't impact your cash flow, pay real estate taxes that are due in January by the end of December. Pile up those deductible checks and mail them.

Summary

Writing and printing checks is one of Quicken's best talents. The check-writing process is quite intuitive and reduces the amount of time spent manually writing and recording checks as well as addressing the envelopes. In this chapter, you learned how to write the checks, set up your printer, select your print options, and print the checks.

ENTERING SPECIAL TRANSACTIONS

IN THIS CHAPTER YOU LEARN THESE KEY SKILLS:

M ost of the time, the work you do in Quicken is straightforward and repetitious. The work was of the same nature when you used a manual checkbook: you did the same things the same way every week or every month. (Probably some of that boring, tedious, and tiresome work in a manual system made you consider moving to Quicken, so that you could automate your regular, repetitious transactions).

Then, once in a while, you have to do something different. You change your mind about sending a check you've already written, or you write a check for one amount and realize that it should have been for another amount. Maybe a check you sent got lost in the mail and you stopped payment on it. Perhaps you deposited a check and that check bounced. Whatever went wrong, you have to tell Quicken about it, or your reports won't be accurate.

In addition to problem-solving transactions, you can enter other transactions in Quicken that you probably weren't keeping track of in your manual system. For example, Quicken can help you track all the deductions in your paycheck, including how much you've contributed to your 401(k) fund. Or you can track nonmonetary items such as your frequent flier miles.

If you decide to use these features, the power that Quicken brings to your financial record-keeping adds information to your system that you couldn't track easily before. This chapter shows how Quicken can handle special transactions.

Voiding Transactions

Things go wrong. You enter a check and mail it, and it never gets there. You print a check and, before sending it, realize that it's for the wrong amount. You need to void this check in your Quicken system. To do so, select the transaction in your account register and press Ctrl+V.

Voiding a check automatically makes several changes (Figure 4-1):

✳ It removes the amount of the check from the Payment field.

✳ It removes each amount of a split transaction.

✳ It recalculates your balance.

✳ It puts an R (for Reconciled with bank statement) in the Clr field so that the missing check won't mess up your bank reconciliation process.

✳ It puts the word *VOID* in front of the payee's name.

| 10/22/96 | 114 | **VOID**Debbie Lewites | | *Payment* | R | *Deposit* | | 1,588 | 85 |
| | | Gifts Given | *Memo* | | | Enter | Edit ▾ | Split | |

Figure 4-1 A voided check is easy to recognize after Quicken makes changes to your register.

As mentioned in Chapter 3, you can't void an online transaction (well, you can, but it won't stop the check from going through the system, because you can't rip it up the way you can destroy a check in your possession). Instead, you have to use a stop payment process with your online banking service provider.

Follow the same steps to void a deposit. If you deposit a check and the check bounces, you have to void that deposit (you also should deal with the person who gave you the rubber check to teach him how rude it is to do that).

Don't confuse voiding a transaction with deleting a transaction. When you delete a transaction, all evidence of it disappears. The check number is missing, you have no audit trail, and, unless you have an excellent memory, you won't remember why a check number is missing.

TIP I tend to be fussy about audit trails because I like to be able to see (or figure out) exactly what happened after I voided a transaction. Actually, I *reverse* the check, I don't void it. This process isn't necessary to make everything work correctly, but it is useful, so I thought I'd share it.

Reversing a check means entering it again in the other direction. The check entry takes money out of the bank; the reversal puts it back in. All the details about the check remain on the register, however, and I can see the original amount of the check, the original date of the check, and the date I reversed it as well.

To reverse a check rather than void it, follow these steps:

1. Go to the next transaction line and enter the date of the reversal (usually today).

2. Enter the same check number as the original check.

3. Enter the same Payee.

4. In the Payment field, enter the amount preceded by a minus sign. Quicken moves the figure over to the Deposit column (which reflects what's happening — you're putting the money back into the bank).

5. Make sure that the category is the same as the original check.

6. Click the space in the Clr column. Quicken asks if you want to reconcile the account. Answer No, and a "c" appears in the Clr column. Placing a "c" in the Clr column indicates that you've cleared this check and flags an unusual situation during bank reconciliation, when the "c" can be changed to an "R."

7. Press Enter to finish this transaction. Quicken displays a message to indicate that you've duplicated a check number. Click OK.

8. Move to the original check and perform Step 6.

If this seems like more work than you want to do, there's an easier way to keep track of what you did. After you void a transaction, move to the Memo field of the voided transaction and write yourself a note. Indicate the original amount or any other information that will jog your memory about this transaction.

Entering Your Paycheck

Your paycheck represents more than just the amount you put into your bank account; it's full of money being held for you that, in fact, is your money.

The deductions for taxes are made for you and sent to the appropriate taxing authorities in your name. The government passed laws demanding that your employer provide this service for you instead of waiting until the end of the year and letting you send in the amount you owe. The government did this because it believes that many people won't send in the amount they owe (which is probably true), and because the government would rather have the money collect interest for it than have you earn the interest. Also, by "giving" this money to the government every pay period, you enable the government to pay its bills every week, including its own employee payroll.

You also may have money deducted from your paycheck for contributions to a pension account or a company savings plan (which frequently involve some matching funds from your employer). You may have a garnishment for child support or money you owe the government for prior taxes or a student loan. And your paycheck stub may indicate the number of vacation days you're earning. In a way, all of these items are your assets, and you can track them.

If you don't want to track your payroll deductions, just enter a normal deposit for the amount of your paycheck and don't read the rest of this section. To enter your paycheck and track all deductions, use the stub from your paycheck and follow these steps:

1. In the register for the bank account in which you deposit your paycheck, enter the date of deposit and then select DEP in the Num field.

2. In the Paid By field, enter the name of your employer.

 TIP **When you enter the employer's name, use the name exactly as it will appear on your W-2. This way, if you export your Quicken data to a tax preparation program, everything will be set up properly.**

3. Press Tab until you get to the Category field (skip the Deposit field) and click the Split button from the pop-up box.

4. In the Split Transaction window (Figure 4-2), select Salary for the Category, Tab to the Amount column, and enter your gross pay (not the amount of the check).

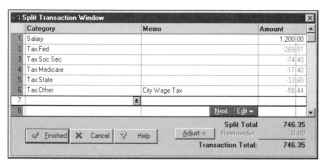

Figure 4-2 The Split Transaction window should end up looking like your paycheck stub.

5. Enter each deduction you want to track by entering the category and a negative number in the Amount column. Just enter a minus sign before you enter the number and, when you move to the next line, Quicken changes the entry so that it's red.

6. If you're tracking a 401(k) fund, and you've established an account for it in Quicken, instead of entering the category, choose Transfer and move the amount into your 401(k) account (later you can go to that account and enter your employer's contribution). Selecting Transfer brings up a list of accounts, and you can pick the right one for your 401(k) instead of assigning it to a category.

7. After you have entered all the deductions, the balance remaining should equal your net check, which is the amount of your bank deposit. If it doesn't, go back and make sure that you entered everything properly.

8. When everything is correct, click Finished. Because the original Deposit column wasn't filled out, Quicken wants to know if you're entering a payment or a deposit. Select Deposit and then click OK.

9. When you are returned to the register, click Enter to complete this transaction.

 TIP **If you want, you can enter the net amount of your check in the Deposit field before beginning the work of splitting the check. If you do, Quicken won't ask you whether or not the transaction is a payment or a deposit.**

To make your work in Quicken go even faster, after you've finished this transaction, make sure that it's selected in the register and press Ctrl+M to memorize the transaction. Then when you get your next paycheck, you can enter the same information with a click of the mouse by recalling the memorized data.

Entering Investment Transactions

The variety of investments available and the variety of ways in which you can set up your investments in Quicken make it difficult to discuss every possible transaction entry. So, I just discuss the way I'd handle an investment account for some stocks. The basic principles are pretty much the same for other investment types.

You can enter transactions in an investment account in two ways:

✳ Use the forms provided by the Easy Actions button — every available transaction type has a specific dialog box you can fill out to enter the transaction.

✳ Enter the transaction directly into the investment register in the same manner used for checks and other everyday transactions.

Using the Easy Action forms

The Easy Actions button displays a list of transaction types, and selecting any of them brings up a form that makes it easy to enter information about the transaction. To enter investment transactions with the Easy Action forms, follow these steps:

1. Go to the register for the investment account and click the Easy Actions button on the button bar. The available actions display (Figure 4-3).

Figure 4-3   All the usual transaction types for a stock investment are available from the Easy Actions list.

2. Choose an action — in this case, I'll sell some of my stock. Each action brings up a dialog box specific to the action.

3. The Sell/Remove Shares dialog box walks me through each step of the sale. Figure 4-4 shows the first page of the dialog box, where I've entered the name of the security I'm selling. The next dialog box asks for more details about the transaction.

Figure 4-4   The Sell/Remove Shares dialog box is a step-by-step assistant that prompts for each data detail.

4. Each transaction type has a dialog box, with its own set of information required to complete the entry. In each case, the paperwork from the investment or your broker provides the information that you use to complete the transaction.

This method of entering transactions is pretty reliable in terms of accuracy because the dialog boxes walk you through the details and offer explanations about the fields that must be filled in by you.

Using direct entry

If you're comfortable with investment transactions, direct entry is much faster. With this method, you just have to move to the next blank transaction line and fill in every field. A drop-down menu is available for choosing the transaction type (Figure 4-5).

Figure 4-5 Choosing an investment transaction type is the same as choosing a bank account transaction type.

Then you just have to fill out all the fields. Enter the price and the number of shares, and Quicken fills out the amount field — make sure that this amount matches your paperwork.

TIP **Quicken has a neat trick for entering investment transactions. You can enter the total amount of money involved in the transaction and enter the number of shares involved (sometimes the paperwork only shows that information), and Quicken calculates the share price for you.**

Tracking Nonmonetary Items

You can keep track of things that have value without adding that value to your system. For example, if you're racking up frequent flier miles, they have a value to you only if you use them for a ticket or an upgrade of a purchased ticket.

The same thing is true of the vacation days you accrue. They have no inherent value in the marketplace, so you don't want to use money to track them. If you did, that would change your net worth or your taxable income.

To track nonmonetary items, you have to start with an investment account:

1. Place your mouse pointer on the My Accounts icon on the Activity Bar to bring up the menu.

2. Choose Create a New Account and select Investment as the account type.

3. In the EasyStep dialog box, give the account a name that indicates its use — perhaps Mileage or Vacation.

4. Tell the account setup program that you're tracking a single security (the setup program will assume it's a single mutual fund).

5. Create a security for that account and give the security an equally descriptive name.

X-REF You can get more information about creating accounts in Chapter 7.

Now you're ready to begin tracking these items. You enter transactions directly into the account's register just as if you were entering any other type of transaction:

1. Enter the date for the opening number of items.

2. In the Action field, choose ShrsIn from the Action drop-down list. This is how you add shares (instead of money) to an investment account.

3. Enter the name of the Security.

4. Skip the Avg. Cost field and enter the number of items in the Shares field.

5. Click Enter.

You now have a total number for this nonmonetary item (Figure 4-6).

Date	Action	Security		Avg. Cost	Shares	Basis	Clr	Share Bal
	Memo					Mkt Value		
8/1/96	ShrsIn	Miles		*Avg Cost*	3,000	*Basis*		3,000 00
	Memo					*Mkt Value*		

Figure 4-6 Frequent flier miles are being tracked without affecting any financial information in the Quicken system.

Hereafter, whenever you fly, enter the number of miles you've earned (the airplane staff always announces it during the "find your nearest escape door" presentation while you're heading for the runway). Then you can compare your statements to your own records. When you turn in miles for a ticket or an upgrade, enter the transaction as a ShrsOut type, which removes the miles from the account.

 TIP If you're tracking vacation days, use the transaction approach that matches the way your employer offers the days. If you get a given amount of days per year, enter those days and then decrement the total as you use them. If you earn vacation days by working a certain amount of hours or days or weeks, enter the vacation days as you accrue them and decrement them as you use them. If you get compensatory time off for working holidays or weekends, you can track those days the same way.

Once you've entered your first nonmonetary account, you'll see how easy it is. Then you'll want to track all sorts of things. The principle here can be translated to any number of items.

BONUS

I f you don't understand the whole 401(k) process or you want to know what you should do if you don't have a set amount for every paycheck you receive, you're in luck.

Different paycheck every week? No problem

Do you get paid by the hour? Do you usually get bonuses or commissions in your paycheck? Is your paycheck different every week (or almost every week)? When you read the section in this chapter about having Quicken memorize your paycheck amount and the deductions, did you feel left out because you can't do that?

Here's how to join the "this is easy as pie" group that enters paychecks with memorized information:

1. Fill in all the categories on the Split Transactions window, but enter 0 for every amount.

2. Press Ctrl+M to memorize the transaction.

3. Next payday, enter the date and enter **DEP** in the Num field.

4. In the Paid By field, press the down arrow and select the memorized transaction with your employer's name.

5. Click the green check mark in the Category field.

6. The Split Transaction window opens with all the categories already filled in, and the amounts are blank.

7. Enter the amounts.

This process saves you all the work of typing in every category for your deductions. Pretty cool!

Some deductions on your paycheck stub are items that you should be tracking because they represent investments you're making in your future.

Understanding your 401(k)

Understanding your 401(k) and how it works is important, because it's your money, and the actions you take in your 401(k) account have consequences. The following is a brief overview of what's behind that 401(k) deduction in your pay.

The 401(k) program is a retirement savings plan that enables you to reduce your gross salary figure for federal income tax purposes by the amount placed into your retirement account. The amount by which you reduce your salary is limited to certain annual limitations and contribution percentages (which should be explained by your employer). The plan must meet strict eligibility and nondiscrimination tests.

By the way, federal income tax purposes means exactly that, and you'll see two different amounts on your W-2 form. The gross salary for your federal income tax is lower than the gross salary for Social Security and Medicare purposes, because these deductions aren't reduced by the amount of your 401(k) contribution.

Once the funds are placed into the account, you may not withdraw them until you retire (except for certain circumstances, which I explain next). After you withdraw them, they become taxable income. If you withdraw funds prematurely, the entire amount withdrawn is subject to federal income tax, plus a ten percent penalty tax over and above the income tax due.

Certain withdrawals, called *hardship withdrawals*, are permitted for certain medical or disability situations and for several other reasons. Some plans allow loans to be made to participants, the amounts of which depend on the current account balance. You need to discuss the particulars of your plan with your employer.

Some states do not allow salary reductions for 401(k) plans, and you will pay state income tax on your entire gross pay. Those states won't tax you, however, when you start taking benefits out upon retirement. The states that allow a reduction in state income tax, by lowering your gross pay by the amount of your 401(k) deduction, later tax your retirement income from the plan.

Summary

In this chapter, you learned about entering transactions that are a bit more complicated than entering a check or a standard deposit. These transactions never appeared in your manual checkbook. Instead, you probably kept notes or files in a cardboard box and spread papers all over the dining room table when you needed information.

Now a click of the mouse brings you this information, all sorted and totaled. You're going to make your accountant's life easier (and probably reduce his or her bill, because it will take much less time to figure out all that complicated investment gains and loss stuff).

CHAPTER FIVE

BALANCING YOUR CHECKBOOK

IN THIS CHAPTER YOU LEARN THESE KEY SKILLS:

Balancing your bank account means reconciling its figures against the figures on your bank statement. The task can be agonizing and is frequently one of the most frustrating things you do. The advantage you have since you've begun to use Quicken is that you don't have to contend with any math errors (I'm assuming that the bank's computer knows how to add and subtract; I know your computer and your Quicken software does).

One great side benefit of balancing your checkbook against the bank's statement is that you see all the transactions you forgot to enter into your Quicken bank register. Most of the time, these withdrawals are from ATMs, something I consistently forget to tell Quicken about. This chapter covers all the steps you need to take to make sure that your balance and the bank's balance are the same.

Entering Balance Information

The first step in reconciling your balance with the bank is to check the opening and closing balances and enter any adjustments the bank made to your account into Quicken.

Selecting the account

The bank statement that arrived in the mail is for a specific bank account, so open the register for that bank account in your Quicken window. Catch up with your transactions for that account by doing the following:

* If the bank statement shows any ATM withdrawals, enter those transactions.

* If the bank statement reflects a deposit that you didn't enter into your account, do that now.

* Check to see if a check number is missing, indicating that you wrote a check and neglected to tell Quicken about it. If so, enter it now.

Don't enter any bank charges or interest paid; those items are entered later. This clean-up process is only for transactions you made and forgot to enter. Now you're ready to match your records against the bank's records.

Entering the balances

From the account register, select Reconcile from the button bar. This brings up the Reconcile Bank Statement dialog box (Figure 5-1). The name of the account you're working on appears in the title bar.

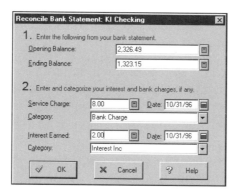

Figure 5-1 The Reconcile Bank Statement starts the account balancing process.

The first task is to complete the Reconcile Bank Statement dialog box:

1. Check the Opening Balance field against the opening balance on the bank statement (it may be called the starting balance). If a difference exists, change the dialog box to match the bank.

2. Enter the ending balance from the bank statement.

3. Enter any service charge that appears on your bank statement. If you have multiple charges, use the calculator to add them (click the Calculator icon next to the Service Charge field).

4. Enter the date the service charge was placed into your account. If you have multiple charges, use the date of the bank statement.

5. Enter the Quicken category for bank charges.

6. Enter any interest earned for this account.

7. Enter the date the interest was credited to your account.

8. Enter the Quicken category for interest income.

9. Click OK.

Quicken now has all the important figures from your bank statement.

Clearing Transactions

As soon as you click OK in the Reconcile Bank Statement dialog box, the reconcile window opens (Figure 5-2). This is where you tell Quicken about the transactions that have cleared. All the transactions that appear on your bank statement are cleared transactions. If the transactions are not on the statement, they are not cleared.

Checks are sorted by check number to make the process easier

The bank charges and interest you entered are marked as cleared

Deposits are listed in date order

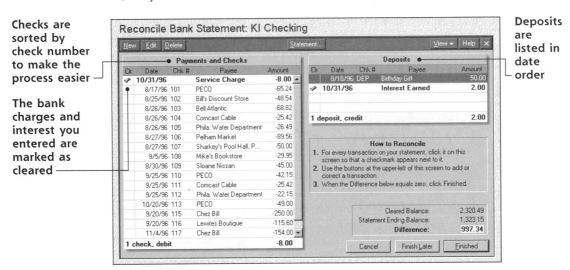

Figure 5-2 Transactions that appear on the statement are cleared transactions, and you have to notify Quicken.

The process of clearing a transaction is quite simple:

1. Click the transaction if it appears on the bank statement. A check mark appears next to the transaction to indicate it has cleared.

2. If you mark a transaction in error, click again to remove the check mark.

Here are some helpful hints for making this process smooth and easy:

✻ Instead of using the physical checks, use the list of check numbers on your statement. They appear in numerical order. An asterisk or some other mark usually appears to indicate a missing number.

✻ To clear a range of checks, click the first one and then hold down Shift and click the last one. All the checks in between are marked.

✻ If you find a transaction on the statement that you haven't entered into your Quicken software, follow these steps:

    1. Click New from the button bar, which brings up the account's register.

    2. Enter the transaction.

    3. Click the Reconcile tab to return to the reconcile window.

✻ If you want to delete a transaction, use Delete on the button bar.

✻ If you want to edit a transaction, use Edit on the button bar.

✻ If you want to change the way the checks are sorted, select View from the button bar and choose Sort by Date.

As you clear each transaction, the Difference amount in the lower-right corner of the reconcile window becomes smaller.

 TIP **Behind the scenes in your account register, Quicken places an R (for reconciled) in the Clr column of every cleared transaction.**

Reconciling Your Account

Once you've finished marking cleared transactions, the Difference figure should be 0.00. Sometimes it's not. Don't worry, there are ways to fix it. In fact, if this reconciliation is the first one for this account since you began using Quicken, chances are good that you're not looking at a zero balance in the Difference field.

If you want to stop working

If you've begun clearing transactions and you have to interrupt the process before you've finished reconciling, and a difference still remains, you can do so without having to start all over.

Select Finish Later to have Quicken maintain the marks you've made and hold everything the way it is at this moment. Later when you want to finish the reconciliation, bring up the register for this account and select Reconcile to pick up where you left off. Don't click Cancel, because nothing you've done will be saved and you'll have to begin marking cleared transactions all over again.

If the account balances

If the difference is zero, your account is balanced. Click Finished. Quicken congratulates you and offers a chance to create a Reconciliation Report.

You have the opportunity to print a Reconciliation Report when you've balanced your account. You do not have to do this, but you may want to view or save the information available in this report. It lists every transaction that was cleared and every check and deposit that did not yet clear the bank.

SETTING UP THE RECONCILIATION REPORT

To print a Reconciliation Report, click Yes. The Reconciliation Report Setup dialog box appears (Figure 5-3). Fill out the Setup dialog box as follows:

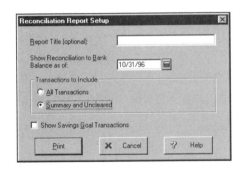

Figure 5-3 Complete the Setup dialog box to print a Reconciliation Report.

1. In the Report Title field, enter an optional title. If you don't enter a title, Quicken names the report *Reconciliation Report*. (I usually use the date as the title).

2. In the Show Reconciliation to Bank Balance as of field, enter the date for which this Reconciliation Report pertains. Usually that should be the statement date, but you may want to change it to the last day of your accounting period.

3. In the Transactions to Include section, select All Transactions to see details on every transaction. Select Summary and Uncleared to see only summary information about cleared transactions.

X-REF

4. If this account is linked to one of your savings goals, click Show Savings Goal Transactions. (See Chapter 10 for more information about setting up and using Savings Goals).

5. Select Print when you have finished filling out the Setup dialog box.

PRINTING THE RECONCILIATION REPORT

When you want to print the Reconciliation Report, Quicken displays the Print dialog box so that you can configure the print job (Figure 5-4).

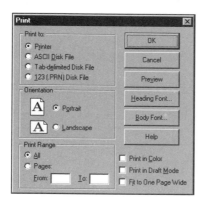

Figure 5-4 Tell Quicken how you want the report printed.

Configure the Print dialog box as follows:

1. In the Print to section of the dialog box, select the target for output using these guidelines:

* Printer sends the report to your printer.

* ASCII Disk File prints the report to a file and places it on your disk. This file can be brought into any word processor.

* Tab-delimited Disk File prints the report to a file and places it on your disk. This file can be used in a software application that can recognize delimiters. For instance, most word processors use tab delimiters to set up a report in columns; spreadsheet software uses tab delimiters to separate text into spreadsheet cells; and database programs use tab delimiters to sort the data into fields and records.

* 123 (.PRN) Disk File prints the report to a file and places it on your disk. This file can be used in Lotus spreadsheet software or any Lotus-compatible software. It is a comma-delimited file.

2. Select the orientation for the paper in the printer: For standard paper, Portrait prints vertically; Landscape prints horizontally.

3. In the Print Range section, decide how much of the report you want to print. Select All, or choose Pages and then specify the first and last page of the range.

4. Select Print in Color if you have a color printer. The following color attributes are added to the printed document:

   ✳ Report title, report date, and account names print in dark blue.
   ✳ Column titles print in light blue.
   ✳ Negative numbers print in red.

5. Select Print in Draft Mode to speed up printing. Quicken uses a built-in printer font to save the time needed to download Windows fonts. You cannot print in color if you select this option.

6. Select Fit to One Page Wide to scale down the report so it fits on a page. This is an effort to keep the report to one page, but if you have a great many transactions and have selected a detailed report, it saves pages but does not necessarily keep the report to one page.

7. Select Heading Font or Body Font to change the fonts for either item. The Report/List Font dialog box opens (Figure 5-5) so you can pick a font, a font style, and a size. Click OK after you have finished picking fonts.

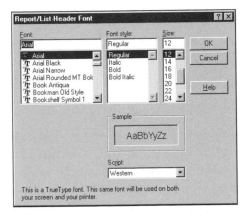

Figure 5-5 Change the font or the font attributes for any part of this report.

8. Click Preview to see an on-screen preview of the printed report.

9. Select Print to print the report.

If you're printing the report to disk, make sure that you remember the filename you used so you can find it when you want to open it in the software of your choice.

If the account doesn't balance

If you've checked everything and still cannot get a zero balance on the Difference line of the reconciliation window, you have to make some adjustments to balance your account. Later if you find the mistake, you can make a correcting entry and delete the adjustment you made during reconciliation.

To force the balance when the difference is not zero, follow these steps:

1. Select Finished.

2. The Adjust Balance dialog box appears because you need to make an adjustment to balance your account (Figure 5-6).

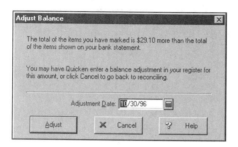

Figure 5-6 Quicken adjusts your balance to make sure you agree with the bank statement.

3. The adjustment amount is preset to match what's needed, and you cannot change the figure.

4. Change the date in Adjustment Date field to match the date of the bank statement.

5. Click Adjust to have Quicken make the adjustment transaction.

The following changes are made to your account register after you've used the reconciliation window:

* If you chose Finish Later and are still working on the reconciliation, the Clr column displayed a "c" for every transaction you've checked off, which means "cleared but not yet reconciled."

* If you chose Finish and your account is balanced, all the transactions that were cleared have an R (for Reconciled) in the Clr column.

* If Quicken had to make a balancing entry for an adjustment, you see the transaction, and it has an R in the Clr column.

Balancing your check register against the bank statement is one of the most important tasks you perform in Quicken. It's the only way to guarantee that you won't bounce checks.

BONUS

B e prepared, even with Quicken to assist you, to see that the first bank reconciliation isn't going to be a cakewalk. You have to balance everything in Quicken with the bank's totals. Unfortunately, the bank uses running totals that began way back when — beginning from when you first opened that bank account. The only Quicken users who have it easy are those who opened their bank account the same day they started to use Quicken (and you can probably fit all of those users in my dining room).

Hunting down those differences

Here are some things to look at as you search for an explanation for differences between the bank's numbers and your numbers:

* Do the number of deposits made (not the total amounts, just the frequency with which you made deposits) match?

* Does the total amount deposited match your records? Be sure you account for interest that the bank may have deposited.

* If you entered two deposited checks separately into your Quicken register but deposited them the same day, does your total equal the amount the bank recorded? The bank frequently shows one total even if you handed two separate deposit slips to the teller at the same time.

* Check every item you cleared in Quicken against the items on the bank statement, because sometimes you'll clear a transaction by accident.

* Do the number of checks (not the amounts, just the quantity of checks) cleared in Quicken match the number of checks returned with your statement? If your bank doesn't return the checks, match the number against the total number of checks listed on the statement.

* Go over your Quicken register carefully — entering an item more than once is not an uncommon mistake. Delete any duplicate items.

Creating fail-safe systems

Duplicating items in Quicken is a fairly common mistake. You can, however, create systems and protocols that can protect you against this. Duplicating a deposit is especially dangerous because if you're like me, if you think you have all that money in the bank, you'll spend it.

If you print checks with Quicken, you're less likely to have a duplicated expenditure, but if you carry a checkbook with you (for spur of the moment spending), you need a system to make sure that you enter any transactions, and enter them only once. You also need a system if you write all your checks manually and then enter them in Quicken.

Mark every manual check as soon as you enter it. Use the stub or manual register. In fact, use the column reserved for checking off a cleared check (you won't need it; you're using the cleared check column in Quicken). Or mark each check with a Q (for Quicken) when you enter it into your Quicken register. This system ensures that every check is entered and entered only once.

For deposits, get an envelope, a shoe box, or some other container for your copy of the deposit slip. Make it a habit to put every deposit slip into the container as soon as possible after returning from the bank. (I do a check of my pocketbook every few days and pull out all the deposit slips that are squished into it.) When you enter the deposit in Quicken, mark the deposit slip with a Q. Keep the deposit slip in the container. When the bank statement comes, the slip for every deposit noted on the statement can be stored elsewhere or thrown away.

For ATM transactions, don't throw that printed record into the trash container next to the ATM machine. Bring it home and treat it the same way described for deposit slips.

Summary

Quicken doesn't force you to perform reconciliations. No dialog box pops up and says, "Hey, you haven't opened the reconciliation window for this account, why not?" So, technically, you could use Quicken for all your check-writing needs without balancing your accounts.

But it's silly not to, because you should always know how much money you have in the bank. Bounced checks cost you embarrassment and service charges, both unpleasant things. Remember that balancing your account is much easier if you develop the habit of entering everything into Quicken — not just checks and deposits, but also cash withdrawals.

AUTOMATING QUICKEN TRANSACTIONS

IN THIS CHAPTER YOU LEARN THESE KEY SKILLS:

All too often, people new to computers are disappointed because they expect the computer to do everything with little or no guidance from the user. These users seem to think that they can set the machine up on the desk, plug it in, and watch it take care of everything automatically. When these users realize that they have to learn the software, type in all the information, and really work at the automating process, they begin to have second thoughts. In fact, I know of several, very expensive computers/paper weights sitting on the desks of people who apparently thought that the data would find its way into their computers by way of osmosis or psychic vibrations.

As much as I wish it worked that way, the harsh reality is that getting computerized still involves a great deal of manual labor. So, when a program actually does automate the process to some extent, it's nice. Quicken's *memorized transactions* and *scheduled transactions*, this chapter's focus, are features that save time and effort by reusing information after you input it the first time.

Understanding Memorized Transactions

Although I type well and relatively quickly, I still find it extremely tedious to enter information into whatever program I happen to be using. One advantage a computer has over you and me is the capability to instantly recall any piece of information it has stored. Therefore, it only makes sense that the computer should remember what you typed the last time and reuse that information the next time you need it. That description defines a memorized transaction precisely — the storage of transaction information in such a way that Quicken saves the information and compares it with new entries as you enter them. When it finds a match, it retrieves the information for you to reuse.

Memorized transaction types

Because transactions come in a variety of flavors, it is fortunate that Quicken allows you to include most of them in the Memorized Transactions category. The following transaction types can be stored as memorized transactions:

* **Register transactions.** Any transaction entered in a bank account register, except an online payment, is eligible to become a memorized transaction. This includes checks, transfers, ATM transactions, electronic fund transfers, and deposits.

* **Write Checks transactions.** The only transactions available in the Write Checks window are checks and online payments (if the account is set up for online banking). A check is the only one that can be a memorized transaction.

* **Loan transactions.** Payments made on borrowed money and payments received on loaned money can be memorized transactions.

* **Investment transactions.** Although investment transactions cannot be memorized automatically, they can be manually memorized, which is explained later.

* **Split Transactions with Percentages.** When you share expenses with a roommate or another person, split transactions with percentages come in quite handy. Every time you enter a new transaction, the amount applied to each category (roommate) is automatically calculated.

Automating with QuickFill options

QuickFill is the Swiss Army knife of automated data entry. With the appropriate QuickFill options selected, Quicken can do the following:

* Memorize new transactions
* Add memorized transactions to the Financial Calendar list (the place Quicken stores future transactions)
* Auto-fill transactions by matching existing entries as you type
* Add entries from the Financial Address Book to the Memorized Transaction List (an address book you can use to keep detailed information about payees)

To access the QuickFill options for all your work in Quicken, follow these steps:

1. From the menu bar, select Edit → Options → Register to open the Register Options dialog box (Figure 6-1).

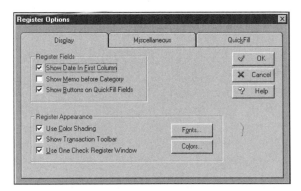

Figure 6-1 Quicken's wealth of options includes three groups for the register alone.

2. Click the QuickFill tab to access the QuickFill options (Figure 6-2).

3. Place a check mark (click) in the box to the left of the option you want to activate.

4. Click OK to save the QuickFill options settings and return to your work.

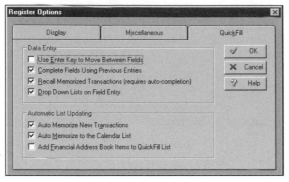

Figure 6-2 The QuickFill tab incorporates memorized transactions and related options.

The QuickFill options from which you have to choose include the following:

✳ **Use Enter Key to Move Between Fields.** Though not a memorized transaction option, this one offers an alternative means of moving through the Quicken fields without using Tab.

✳ **Complete Fields Using Previous Entries.** This option helps you take advantage of memorized transactions by searching for a match as you type an entry (such as a payee or a category) and filling in the field as soon as one is found.

✳ **Recall Memorized Transactions.** A delightful feature that works in conjunction with the previous option. Recall Memorized Transactions, if set to on, fills all the fields in the transaction with the information from the stored memorized transaction (for the particular Payee) as soon as you leave the Payee field.

✳ **Drop Down Lists on Field Entry.** For those fields with drop-down lists of choices (except the Payee field), selecting this option causes the drop-down list to open as soon as you move to the field.

✳ **Auto Memorize New Transactions.** If you have Quicken's Auto Memorize New Transactions option turned on, every new transaction you enter is automatically added to the Memorized Transaction List (with the exception of investment transactions). By default, the option is set to on.

✳ **Auto Memorize to the Calendar List.** Select this option to automatically add transactions entered elsewhere to the Financial Calendar Transaction list.

✳ **Add Financial Address Book Items to QuickFill List.** This option, which is available in the Quicken Deluxe version only, offers you the choice of having Financial Address Book entries automatically added to the Memorized Transactions List.

Creating Memorized Transactions

Entering memorized transactions is generally quite simple, especially if you have Auto Memorize turned on. A few variations exist, however, depending on where you happen to be in Quicken. Auto Memorize functions are available everywhere except in investment transactions and bank register deposit transactions.

New transactions

If you have the QuickFill Auto Memorize New Transactions option selected, the act of entering a transaction is all it takes to create a memorized transaction. Because Auto Memorize does not work on investment transactions and register deposits, you must convert them manually. The steps are the same as the steps for converting existing transactions that were created with Auto Memorize turned off. Read the "Existing transactions" section and follow the instructions to convert investment transactions and register deposits.

Existing transactions

If you create transactions with the Auto Memorize New Transactions option turned off and later decide to convert them to memorized transactions, the process is simple. The procedure is also the same to create new memorized transactions for investments and deposits, which are unaffected by the Auto Memorize New Transactions option.

To convert a transaction manually, follow these steps:

1. Open the appropriate register or window and move to the existing transaction you want to convert.

2. Right-click the Date field and select Memorize Transaction from the pop-up menu.

3. To be sure you really want to memorize the transaction, Quicken warns you that the transaction is about to be memorized and asks you to confirm. Click OK to complete the procedure and return to the register.

Split transactions with percentages

If Auto Memorize is turned on, the split transaction with percentages does not need to be manually converted to a memorized transaction. The split percentages, however, must be manually established. Split percentage transactions are ideal when certain expenses are shared proportionally between two or more people or categories. A good example is roommates sharing household expenses.

To set up a memorized split transaction with percentages, follow these steps:

1. Turn on the QuickFill Auto Memorize New Transactions option or create the split transaction and follow the directions for memorizing existing transactions found elsewhere in this chapter.

2. Enter the Date, Num, Payee, and Payment information as you would for any other transaction.

3. In the Category field, click the down arrow to activate the drop-down list.

4. Select Split to open the Split Transaction window.

5. In the Category field, create a new category for the first roommate's share of the expenses. (For more information on creating categories, see Chapter 8.) A category name that includes the roommate's initials and the type of expense makes it easy to track each person's share.

6. Tab to the Memo field and enter a brief description if you want.

7. Tab to the amount column that should contain the full amount of the payment.

8. In the Amount field, type in the percentage amount followed by a % sign. If the expenses are being split equally between two roommates, type **50%**.

9. Press Tab to move to the next line and begin the process over for the next roommate. Note that as soon as you move to the next line, the amount is recalculated using the percentage you entered.

10. To save the split and return to your work, click Finished.

Changing Memorized Transactions

Occasionally, you may need to change a memorized transaction. If you have misspelled a name or if a recurring bill amount changes, you will want to modify the memorized transaction so that it auto-fills with the correct information. How and where you edit a memorized transaction depends on the type of transaction.

Memorized Transaction List

The majority of memorized transactions appear in the Memorized Transaction List. You find checks, payments, deposits, transfers, ATM transactions, electronic fund transfers, loans, and split percentage transactions in the list.

EDITING MEMORIZED TRANSACTIONS

Although you can change the original transaction upon which the memorized transaction is based, the change will not affect the memorized transaction unless the change is made in the Memorized Transaction List.

To edit a memorized transaction, follow these steps:

1. Press Ctrl+T to open the Memorized Transaction List (Figure 6-3).

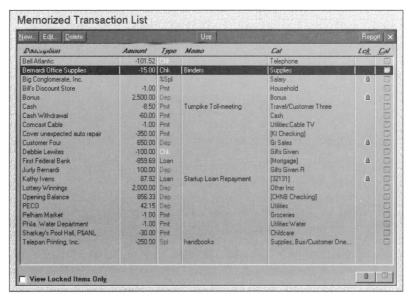

Figure 6-3   Use the Memorized Transaction List to manage your memorized transactions.

2. From the list, select the transaction to change.

3. Click Edit on the Memorized Transaction button bar to open the Edit Memorized Transaction dialog box like the one in Figure 6-4.

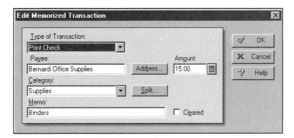

Figure 6-4   Change any information in the Edit Memorized Transaction dialog box.

4. Use Tab to move to the desired field and make the necessary changes.

5. After you finish editing the transaction, click OK to save the changes and return to the Memorized Transaction List.

LOCKING MEMORIZED TRANSACTIONS

One of the nice features of memorized transactions is that every time you enter another transaction that uses the same payee but has a different amount or category, the new transaction is saved as the memorized transaction, overwriting the old one. This capability is great, unless the transaction is a one-time variation that will revert to the original transaction the next time around.

To prevent a memorized transaction from being changed, you can lock it by following these steps:

1. Press Ctrl+T to open the Memorized Transaction List.

2. Highlight the transaction to lock.

3. In the Lck column, check to see if a Padlock icon appears. If one is there, the transaction is already locked.

4. If you do not see a Padlock icon in the Lck column, click in the Lck column on the highlighted transaction.

5. Once the Padlock icon appears, the memorized transaction is locked and will not be changed by future transactions with the same payee.

DELETING MEMORIZED TRANSACTIONS

Sometimes editing just isn't enough. When you no longer use a vendor, his or her memorized transaction is just taking up valuable resources.

The smart thing to do is to delete any obsolete transactions by following these steps:

1. Open the Memorized Transaction List by pressing Ctrl+T.

2. Select the transaction to delete.

3. Click Delete on the Memorized Transaction List button bar.

4. Be sure this is what you want to do and confirm your decision by clicking OK.

5. The memorized transaction (but not the original transaction) is removed.

Investment Transaction List

The only memorized transaction you won't find on the Memorized Transaction List is the investment transaction. It only appears on the Investment Transaction List. Unlike the other memorized transactions, you cannot edit or create reports on memorized investment transactions. About the only thing you can do is delete them.

To delete a memorized investment transaction, follow these steps:

1. From the Quicken menu bar, select ⎡Lists⎤→⎡Investment⎤→ ⎡Memorized Investment Trans.⎤ to open the Investment Transaction List (Figure 6-5).

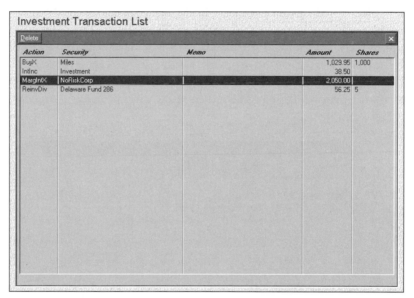

Figure 6-5   You can only view the Investment Transaction List or delete an item — no other options are available.

2. Select the transaction to delete.

3. Click Delete on the Investment Transaction button bar to remove the selected transaction.

4. If you're sure you want to delete this transaction, confirm by clicking OK in the Confirmation dialog box. As with all memorized transactions, deleting the memorized transaction does not affect the original.

Viewing Memorized Transactions

The reason that you invest the time and effort inputting data into Quicken is so that you can view it and use the data efficiently. There are several ways to view memorized transactions. The first, the Memorized Transaction List, is discussed elsewhere in this chapter. Other means of viewing memorized transactions include the Financial Calendar Transaction List and reports created in the Memorized Transaction List.

Financial Calendar Transaction List

To make it easy to create scheduled transactions, Quicken maintains a list of all memorized transactions in the Financial Calendar window. Although scheduled transactions are covered in detail elsewhere in this chapter, you should be aware of the part memorized transactions play in creating scheduled transactions. Memorized transactions appear in the Financial Transaction List, which is attached to the right side of the Financial Calendar (Figure 6-6). To view the Financial Calendar, select Schedule a Future Payment from the Bills icon in the Activity Bar.

Figure 6-6 Convert memorized transactions to scheduled transactions by dragging them from the Financial Transaction List to the Financial Calendar.

For more information, see the "Bonus" section at the end of this chapter.

Memorized Transaction List reports

As your Memorized Transaction List grows, you will occasionally need to weed out those transactions you no longer use. The reason is simple: Quicken has a limit of 2,000 memorized transactions. After you reach the limit, Quicken refuses to accept any more memorized transactions.

One way of determining whether or not a transaction deserves to remain on the list is to run a quick report and view the activity of that transaction.

To create a Memorized Transaction List report, follow these steps:

1. Press Ctrl+T to open the Memorized Transaction List.

2. Highlight the transaction on which you want to view the report.

3. Select Report from the Memorized Transaction List button bar.

4. The Payee Report (Figure 6-7) is created, providing you with a list of each of the transactions entered for this particular payee.

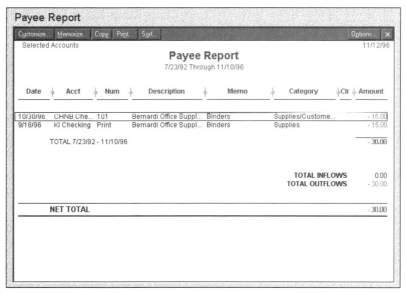

Figure 6-7   Generate a quick Payee Report from the Memorized Transaction List.

Because the report includes all your accounts, it makes it easy to see how much, if at all, you're using this transaction. From the information shown, you can decide whether a transaction is worth keeping as a memorized transaction.

Understanding Scheduled Transactions

Scheduled transactions are similar to memorized transactions in that they reuse information after your enter it once. Where they differ is in their capability to reuse the information without waiting for you to begin the process. Scheduled transactions are perfect for handling recurring bills that you pay the same time each month. Whether or not the amount is the same, you can schedule a recurring bill so that Quicken reminds you when it is time to pay and even goes so far as to automatically enter the transaction in the appropriate register. Your mortgage or rent payment, the utility bills, and monthly, quarterly or annual dues are all ideal candidates for scheduled payments.

Both regular account transactions and online payments are eligible to join the ranks of scheduled transactions. During the setup, you indicate which type of scheduled transaction it is.

To create a scheduled transaction, you need to provide Quicken with the necessary information. Just like your old tenth grade English teacher, Quicken wants to know who, what, when, and where.

To enter a new scheduled transaction, follow these steps:

1. Press Ctrl+J to open the Scheduled Transaction List (Figure 6-8).

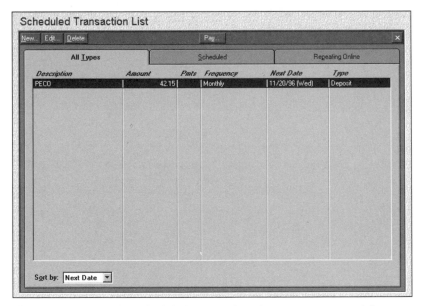

Figure 6-8 From the Scheduled Transaction List, you can create, delete, edit, or pay scheduled transactions.

2. From the Scheduled Transaction List button bar, select New to access the Create Scheduled Transaction dialog box.

3. Before you reach the Create Scheduled Transaction dialog box, however, you must first satisfy Quicken's natural curiosity and tell it whether this is a regular transaction or an online transaction.

4. Once you've selected the type of transaction, Quicken opens the Create Scheduled Transaction dialog box (Figure 6-9).

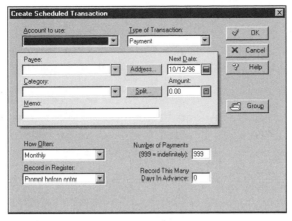

Figure 6-9 Designing a new scheduled transaction is simple with the Create Scheduled Transaction dialog box.

5. From the Account to use drop-down list, select the Quicken account in which to enter the transaction. Then press Tab to move to the next field.

6. Select the type of transaction from the Type of Transaction drop-down list. Tab to the Payee field.

7. Type the payee or select one from drop-down list. Note that when you select a payee from the drop-down list, the Category, Split, Amount, and Memo fields are filled in with information from the last transaction for that payee (as long as those fields had information in them for the original transaction). Move to the Address field by using Tab.

8. The Address field is available only if the transaction is a check to be printed. If this is a check and you want to include the address, click Address and fill out the information. Then Tab to the next field.

9. In the Next Date field, type or select from the drop-down calendar the date for the next scheduled payment. Press Tab to move to the Category field.

10. Enter the category or select one from the drop-down list. Then move to Split by using Tab.

11. If you want to split the transaction between two or more categories, click Split and enter the correct information. Tab to the Amount field and enter the amount of the transaction. If the amount changes each time, use an estimate and replace it with the actual amount when the scheduled transaction becomes due. Use Tab to move to the Memo field.

12. Enter a brief description of the transaction, if you want, and then Tab to Group.

TIP One way to reduce the amount of time you spend taking care of bills is to create *transaction groups*. This is an especially good idea if you print checks from Quicken. Bills that come due at approximately the same time of the month are well suited for transaction groups. Even if they're not due on the same date, paying them all at once is much simpler than paying the bills individually for several days running. Use the Group feature in the Create Scheduled Transaction dialog box to open the Create Transaction Group dialog box (Figure 6-10). Then fill out the following information:

* Enter the next scheduled date for this group of transactions.
* Select the Quicken account in which to enter the transactions.
* Indicate whether this is a regular or investment transaction group.
* Give the group a descriptive name.
* Indicate how often you pay this bill.
* Specify whether you want to be notified before the transactions are entered into the register.
* If this is a mortgage or other finite bill, enter the number of payments left.
* Specify how many days before the due date Quicken should remind you.

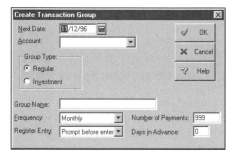

Figure 6-10 Transaction groups take the hassle out of paying bills.

TIP After you finish and click OK, a list of all available transactions appears. From the list, select the transactions you want to include in the new transaction group.

13. If you want to change the defaults in the four options at the bottom of the dialog box, Tab four times to reach the Frequency field. Select the frequency of this transaction from the drop-down list. Then Tab to the next field.

14. If this is a bill with a limited number of payments, indicate how many are left in the Number of Payments field. Move to the Record in Register field.

15. Decide whether or not you want Quicken to advise you before it automatically enters the transaction in the account register. Use Tab to move to the next field.

16. Enter the number of days in advance you want Quicken to remind you the transaction is due.

17. Click OK to save the scheduled transaction and return to the Scheduled Transaction List.

Changing Scheduled Transactions

Although I realize that the chances of your making a mistake are relatively slim, I would feel remiss in my job as an author if I did not make some mention of editing and deleting scheduled transactions. The truth is, even if you're perfect and never make a mistake, inevitably you will be faced with the need to change or delete a transaction.

Editing a scheduled transaction

When company names change or loan amounts decrease (wishful thinking) because of variable interest rates, you may have to edit the information for a scheduled transaction.

Not a problem; just follow these steps to edit a scheduled transaction:

1. Press Ctrl+J to open the Scheduled Transaction List window.

2. Highlight the transaction or group to modify.

3. Click Edit from the button bar to open the Edit Scheduled Transaction dialog box (Figure 6-11).

4. Tab to the fields that need to be changed and make the corrections.

5. Click OK to save the changes and return to the Scheduled Transaction List.

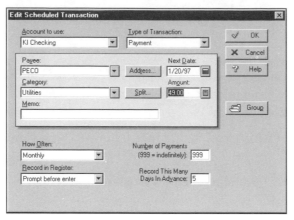

Figure 6-11 Change original transaction information in the Edit Scheduled Transaction dialog box.

Deleting a scheduled transaction

You will also encounter times when you finally pay off a loan or change mortgage companies, and you no longer have any use for a scheduled transaction. Deleting a scheduled transaction is even easier than creating one.

If the need arises, follow these steps to delete a transaction:

1. Press Ctrl+J to open the Scheduled Transaction List.

2. Select the scheduled transaction to delete.

3. Click Delete on the Scheduled Transaction List button bar.

4. If you are sure you want to delete this transaction, confirm your decision by clicking OK.

Using Quicken Reminders

Now that you have your transactions memorized and scheduled, the only thing left is to make sure you don't forget to write the checks and send them out. Before you get too excited, let me tell you that Quicken will write the checks (if you use computer checks) and even address them, but it won't lick the stamp or walk the envelope out to the mailbox. (Who knows, maybe the next version will.) It does, however, remind you when it's time to do all that. Quicken's Billminder feature, used in conjunction with Quicken Reminders, makes sure that you won't forget. Together they keep track of your scheduled transactions and tap you on the shoulder when it's time to take care of them. The only thing you have to do is set the options for both features.

Billminder

Quicken's Billminder is a handy feature that can pop up as soon as you start Windows and remind you of any scheduled transactions that are currently due. One nice thing about it is that Quicken does not have to be running for Billminder to do its job (Figure 6-12).

Figure 6-12   You can eliminate all those post-it notes stuck to your monitor when you use Billminder.

To set the options for Billminder, follow these steps:

1. Open Quicken.

2. From the menu bar, select Options → Reminders to access the Reminder Options dialog box (Figure 6-13).

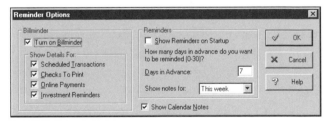

Figure 6-13   Your wish is Billminder's command in the Reminder Options dialog box.

3. To activate Billminder, place a check mark in the box next to Turn on Billminder.

4. The Show Details For section enables you to instruct Billminder to display either a summary or the details for each transaction due. Select those categories for which you want to see details and deselect those for which you want to see summaries.

Quicken Reminders

The bad news is that if you're like me and don't shut your computer down every night, the only time Billminder reminds you about bills that are due is when your machine crashes and you have to reboot. That's because Quicken, by default, sends you a Billminder note whenever you boot your computer. This is not a great way to keep the creditors happy (unless your machine crashes a great deal). The good news is that you can set the Quicken Reminders to display every time you start Quicken instead of each time you start your machine (Figure 6-14).

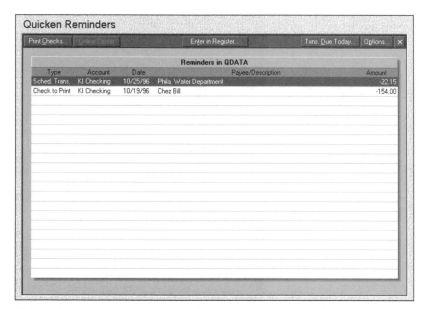

Figure 6-14 No matter how hard you try, Quicken won't let you forget (as long as you turn on Reminders).

To set up Quicken Reminders to suit your work habits, follow these steps:

1. From the menu bar, select **Options** → **Reminders** to access the Reminder Options dialog box.

2. Tab to the Reminders section and select Show Reminders on Startup to automatically activate the Quicken Reminders as soon as Quicken opens.

3. Tab to the Days in Advance field and enter the number of days before the due date you want to be notified.

4. Tab to the next field and select the time period from which to include Financial Calendar Notes.

5. Move to the Show Calendar Note field. To show Financial Calendar notes, put a check mark in the box.

6. Click OK to save the new settings and return to your work.

BONUS

One of the nice things about computer programs is that they offer you more than one way of accomplishing a task. Depending on your temperament, skills, and where you are in the program, you may find one way or the other easier.

Another way to add memorized transactions

If you happen to be working in the Memorized Transaction List and want to add a new memorized transaction, you do not need to return to register and follow the steps outlined earlier in this chapter.

You can create a memorized transaction right where you are by following these steps:

1. Select New from the Memorized Transaction List button bar to access the Create Memorized Transaction dialog box (Figure 6-15).

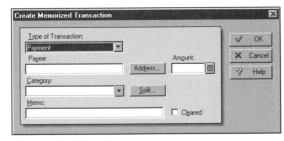

Figure 6-15 Add a memorized transaction anytime with the Create Memorized Transaction dialog box.

2. From the Type of Transaction drop-down list, choose the transaction type and then press Tab to move to the next field.

3. Enter the name of the payee or source (for deposits) in the Payee field and press Tab.

4. If the transaction is a check to print, you can add an address by clicking Address and filling in the appropriate information. To continue, press Tab.

5. Fill in the Amount of the transaction in the Amount field and press Tab.

6. From the Category drop-down list, select the category to which you want to assign the transaction and move to the next field by pressing Tab.

7. To split the transaction amount between two or more categories, click Split and fill in the necessary information. Then press Tab.

8. If you want, enter a brief description of the transaction in the Memo field.

9. If this transaction has already cleared the bank, place a check mark in the box to the left of Cleared.

10. Click OK to save the transaction and return to the Memorized Transaction List.

Schedule a transaction using the Financial Calendar

As I mention earlier in the chapter, you can create scheduled transactions by dragging and dropping in the Financial Calendar. Not only is it quick and easy, but it also lets you ensure that you allowed enough time for delivery.

To schedule a transaction from the Financial Calendar, follow these steps:

1. Place your mouse pointer on the Bills icon in the Activity Bar.

2. From the menu, select Schedule a Future Payment to open the Financial Calendar window (Figure 6-16).

3. Select a transaction from the Financial Transaction List (on the right side of the calendar).

 TIP If the Financial Transaction List does not appear in the Financial Calendar window, click the View button and select Show Memorized Transaction List.

4. Drag it to the desired date on the Financial Calendar to open the New Transaction dialog box (Figure 6-17).

5. Tab to the fields that need to be modified and make the necessary changes.

6. Click OK to save the scheduled transaction and return to the Financial Calendar.

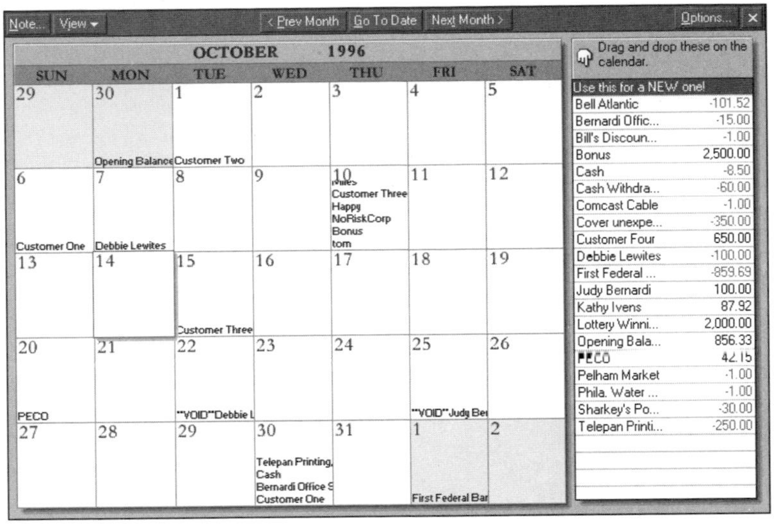

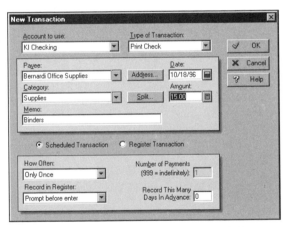

Figure 6-16 A visual representation often helps make scheduling easier and more accurate.

Figure 6-17 Because you're using an existing transaction, most of the information is already filled in for you.

Summary

Now that you know how to use Quicken's memorized and scheduled transactions to automate the checkbook process, you'll be done in no time. Unless you're trying to improve your typing skills by getting all the practice you can, make sure to set memorized transactions to on. Use scheduled transactions, and everyone will think you're extremely well organized and efficient. Might as well let them think whatever they want.

ADDING AND CHANGING ACCOUNTS

IN THIS CHAPTER YOU LEARN THESE KEY SKILLS:

The first time you used Quicken, you set up your bank account, which is the checking account you use to pay your bills. In regular language use, the word *account* usually means a bank account. For instance, I have a checking account, a savings account, and a money market account. I use each for different purposes, but I think of them collectively as my accounts.

When you use bookkeeping software such as Quicken, however, the word *account* has a broader meaning. In Quicken, an account is a way to track amounts and also a way to keep an accurate running total.

That's easy to understand with a bank account, and you'll want to add all your bank accounts to your Quicken file. But think about other amounts that may be important to track, such as the size of your mortgage, the value of your home, or money owed to you by other people. You can create accounts for these items. This chapter is all about adding accounts to your Quicken system.

Understanding Account Types

Creating a new account isn't difficult, but you do have to understand what type of account you're adding in order to create the account properly. If the account is not created with the correct criteria, the data you get from your Quicken software won't be accurate, which kind of kills the whole point. The types of accounts you can set up in Quicken are as follows:

* **Checking accounts.** Your main checking account is already set up in Quicken, but you may have additional checking accounts you want to track.

* **Savings accounts.** The money you save, instead of using to pay bills, is probably in a savings account. Actually, if you have a tin box that you've hidden behind one of the cinder blocks in the basement, you can call that a savings account and track it in Quicken.

* **Money market accounts.** If you have a money market account, you probably have a checkbook for it. You can use (or think of) this account as a savings account, a checking account, or both. No matter how you use it, you'll probably want to track the balance you keep in it.

* **Cash accounts.** This means cash, literally. You can track the money you take out of your wallet and hand to a clerk in a retail establishment.

* **Credit card accounts.** Whether it's a bank credit card or a local department store charge card, you can track your spending so the bill at the end of the month doesn't cause a shock.

* **Liability accounts.** It's a safe bet you owe money, whether it's a mortgage on your house or a loan for your automobile, and you can track the descending balances.

* **Asset accounts.** Assets are the things you own, such as your house and your furniture, and you can track their value.

* **Investment accounts.** If you've invested money in a mutual fund or stocks, you can use an investment account to track the performance and determine the current value.

Creating a New Account

Accounts are very easy to add, and you can add an account anytime you want to, even if you're in the middle of doing something else in Quicken.

Here's how to create a new account:

1. Place the mouse pointer on the My Accounts icon in the Activity Bar of your Quicken window.

2. When the pop-up menu appears (Figure 7-1), choose Create a New Account.

Figure 7-1 Choose Create a New Account to begin the process of adding an account to your Quicken system.

3. Quicken's automatic system, called the EasyStep Account Setup, opens and walks you through the process of creating the account.

Picking an account type

In the first EasyStep window (Figure 7-2), choose the type of account you want to create. After you've selected an account type, click Next to move to the next EasyStep window.

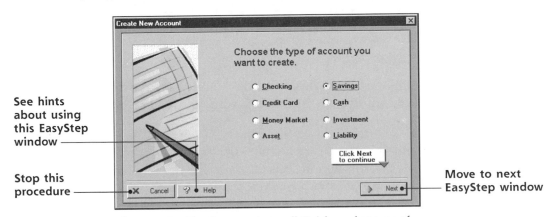

See hints about using this EasyStep window

Stop this procedure

Move to next EasyStep window

Figure 7-2 The first step is to tell Quicken what type of account you want to create.

TIP The rules are pretty strict for accounts, but there are a couple of places where you can use your own judgment. For example, if you have a money market account or a credit union account that pays interest and also lets you write checks, you may want to enter the account type as a savings account if that's how you really use it. If you write checks more frequently than you deposit money, you can treat it as a checking account.

Naming the account

In the next EasyStep window (Figure 7-3), you have to give your new account a name. In the box called Account Name, enter a name for this account. This name appears in all account listings and reports, so be sure to choose a name that will remind you which account this is.

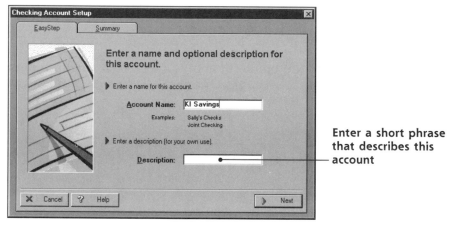

Enter a short phrase that describes this account

Figure 7-3 Enter an account name that has some meaning to you.

CAUTION The account name can be any combination of letters, numbers, and spaces. You cannot use any of the following characters, however: [ ] / : | ^

If you want, you can enter a descriptive phrase in the Description box. Although this entry is optional, it's a good idea to use this entry box for text that adds details to the information for this account. For instance, you can enter the account number. Even if it's not a bank account, you have an account number of some kind — a credit card number or a customer number from your mortgage company. Click Next when you have filled in all the information.

Deciding on a starting point

Next you have to decide on the point at which you want Quicken to track the account. To begin the process, Quicken wants to know if you have a recent statement for this account (Figure 7-4). You don't have to answer this accurately; you can design your answer to match the way you want to handle this account.

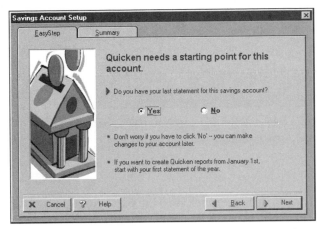

Figure 7-4 Decide whether to set up this account with an opening balance and a beginning date.

Here are the ramifications of the answers in this EasyStep window:

* If you answer No, Quicken applies a zero balance as of today's date.
* If you answer Yes, the next EasyStep window asks for the statement date and the balance.
* You can use any date you want for the statement date; it doesn't have to match a real statement.
* You can use any amount you want for the starting balance, as long as it matches the balance for the date you use as a statement date (you can use a date and balance from your checkbook stubs or you can call the bank and get today's balance).
* In truth, the balance doesn't matter because you can always go back later and adjust it.

Entering the starting date and balance

If you answered Yes to the question in the preceding EasyStep window, you see the window shown in Figure 7-5 (if you answered No, you see a message that reminds you that you're opening this new account with a zero balance because you chose not to enter a starting point).

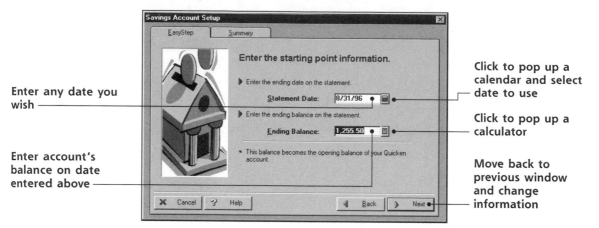

Enter any date you wish

Click to pop up a calendar and select date to use

Enter account's balance on date entered above

Click to pop up a calculator

Move back to previous window and change information

Figure 7-5 Enter the starting date and balance for this new account.

Follow these steps to complete this window:

1. Enter a starting date (remember, it doesn't have to be the date of your last statement).

2. Enter a starting amount. Don't enter any commas when you type in the amount, but you do have to enter a decimal point to separate the dollars and cents.

TIP **If the account balance is an even dollar amount, just type in the dollars, and Quicken automatically inserts a decimal point and two zeros.**

3. When you have finished entering data, click Next to continue the process.

Entering detailed information

The next EasyStep windows you see depend on the type of account you're creating. In this section, I discuss the various options for the different types of accounts. I start with bank accounts (checking, savings, money market) and Quicken credit card accounts. After that, I go over the different EasyStep windows you see for the other account types.

ENTERING DETAILED INFORMATION FOR BANK ACCOUNTS

If you're creating a bank account that you will use for online banking services (a checking or savings account) or if you have a Quicken credit card, the next EasyStep windows are designed to set up online banking services.

Quicken takes advantage of online services offered by banks and other financial institutions. In addition, some Quicken online services are available that you can use. Two types of online services are available that you can take advantage of if you have a modem:

* **Online banking**, which lets you download information about balances and transactions from your financial institution and transfer the information into your Quicken system

* **Online bill paying**, which lets you send payments to vendors by sending instructions about each payment over the modem to a bill-paying service or your bank (if your bank provides this service)

X-REF Information about setting up and using online banking and online bill paying are in Appendix A.

As you continue the account setup, you see the EasyStep window shown in Figure 7-6, where you can choose the type of online service you want to use for this account.

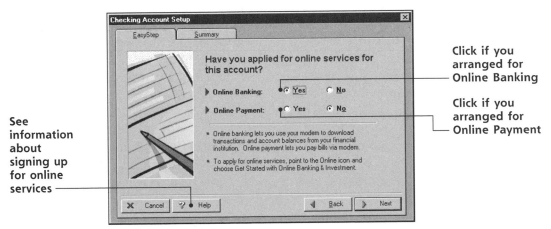

Figure 7-6 Indicate whether you've made arrangements for online services.

TIP If you haven't yet signed up for online services, you can answer No and then later, after you've made the necessary arrangements, change the information about this account to make it online-ready.

If you answer Yes to either service for the account you're creating, additional windows ask for detailed information.

The next EasyStep window is for entering information about your bank. Enter the name and the routing number of the financial institution you're going to use for online banking or online bill paying (Figure 7-7).

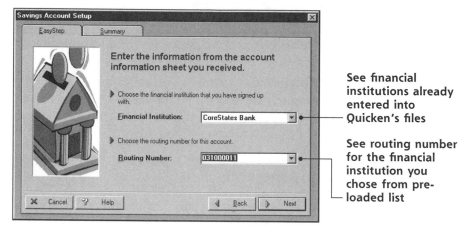

See financial institutions already entered into Quicken's files

See routing number for the financial institution you chose from pre-loaded list

Figure 7-7 The name of your financial institution and its Federal Reserve routing number are needed to use online services.

Quicken provides the names of many financial institutions, and your bank may be on this list. Click the arrow to the right of the Financial Institution text box and scroll through the list looking for your bank's name. If it's not there, enter the name manually.

You also have to enter the routing number for your bank. If your bank is listed in the Financial Institution list, click the arrow to the right of the Routing Number text box and that bank's routing number will be there. If your bank isn't listed, you can get the routing number from the information sheet you received when you signed up for online banking. Click Next when you have entered this information.

The next EasyStep window is for entering specific information about your account (Figure 7-8). Be sure to enter the account number as it is displayed in the information sheet from your bank. This may not match the account number you use when making deposits or withdrawals, because sometimes the "official" account number has more or fewer digits in it (due to the way the bank handles your account in its own system). The same is true for the type of account. For example, you and your bank may refer to your check-bouncing protection account by some fancy marketing name, but the official name of the account may be a Line of Credit Account. Enter an account type that matches the information sheet. Click Next when you have filled in the entries.

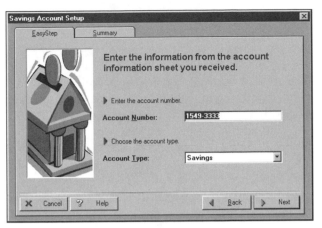

Figure 7-8 Enter the account number and the official account type from your bank's information sheet.

TRANSLATING THOSE NUMBERS THAT APPEAR ON YOUR CHECKS

If you're interested, here's the scoop on the routing number, which you can see on the bottom of all of your checks. Although it's not necessary to understand this to use the routing number, if you have a curious mind or are looking for a topic for cocktail chatter, this may be of interest. The routing number is a unique, nine-digit number assigned to every financial institution that operates in the United States. The digits in the routing number signify different pieces of information.

A routing number has its name because it makes it possible to route information from bank to bank. When you write a check and mail it to the payee, that payee deposits the check in his or her own bank (which could be anywhere). That check has to get back to your bank, so the money can be deducted from your account (which is called *clearing the check*). Eventually, the bank mails the check back to you with your statement.

Take a look at one of your checks, and you'll see a number indicating the routing number. In the upper right-hand side of the check is a number with a hyphen. Beneath this number is a line, and under the line is another number (it looks like a fraction, and, in fact, is called the *fraction* by people in banking).

The number on the left side of the hyphen is the identifying number assigned to the bank that clears the checks for the bank that issued the check. Not all banks clear their own checks; they pay other banks a fee to handle that chore. This number is not part of the bank's official routing number; it just tells the Federal Reserve where to send the check for clearing. The number on the right side of the hyphen is the unique identification number for the bank issuing the check (your bank). This number is part of the Federal Reserve routing number.

(*continued*)

TRANSLATING THOSE NUMBERS THAT APPEAR ON YOUR CHECKS (*continued*)

(Incidentally, if your bank does clear its own checks, the number for the clearing center won't necessarily be a duplicate of the bank's number, because the Federal Reserve issues the bank a special number designating the clearing center).

The number below the line is the Federal Reserve Center and division through which your bank's transactions are processed. This number is part of the Reserve routing number.

For instance, I live in Philadelphia, where the Federal Reserve Center number is 3. One of my banks is in Philadelphia County, which is designated area 10 of that Federal Reserve Center. The bank's unique number is 1. The fraction on my check reads as follows:

* 3-1 above the line (the clearing bank number — my bank's unique number)

* 310 below the line (the Federal Reserve Center and division)

We get the routing number by applying this formula:

XX YY ZZZZ A

where

XX = the Federal Reserve Center (single-digit centers have a leading zero)

YY = the district for that Federal Reserve Center (single-digit districts have a leading zero)

ZZZZ = the unique number for the bank (leading zeros are used to fill out the four digits)

A = the check digit, which is a (secret) mathematical calculation that uses the first eight digits of the routing number to ensure the accuracy of the routing number. That calculation results in the number 1 for this bank.

The check digit calculation is considered absolutely critical to the integrity of routing numbers, especially in the age of electronic transactions, because the receiving and clearing banks may not even see a paper check that can be verified and everything happens automatically. Therefore, this bank's routing number is 031000011.

Another bank I use has its headquarters in the suburbs of Philadelphia and has a routing number of 03130878. The 0313 indicates that this bank is also assigned to the Federal Reserve Center 3 but is in division 13. The bank's unique number is 878. The check digit calculation results in the number 4. Therefore, the bank's routing number is 031308784.

The next EasyStep window is for identification (Figure 7-9). If your online banking is only for personal banking, fill in your Social Security Number. If you're using online banking for a business account, fill in the *TIN* (*Tax Identification Number*). A TIN is also called an Employers Identification Number (EIN). It follows a pattern of XX-XXXXXXX. The first two XX digits represent your state, and a unique number is assigned for each state (for example, my TIN starts with 23, the number assigned to Pennsylvania).

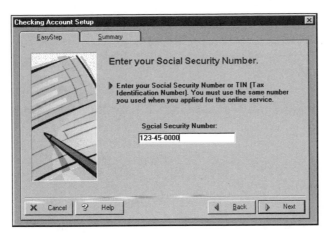

Figure 7-9 Your Social Security Number or business TIN
is your online identification.

TIP You must use the same identification number you used when you
applied to your bank for online banking. If this is a personal account,
there isn't any problem. If you mix business and personal transactions
in this account, however, you have to check your information sheet to
see whether you used your personal Social Security Number or your
business TIN. If your identification doesn't match the application, you
won't be admitted to online banking services when you dial in.

After all the information is entered (which may not be everything that's
needed, but you can go back and fill in missing information after you obtain it),
click Next. The last EasyStep window appears (Figure 7-10). This window contains the summary of all the information you've entered. You can change any
data that's displayed.

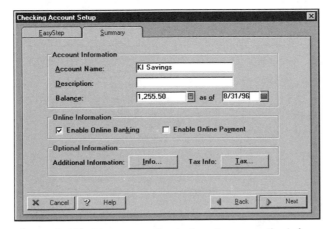

Figure 7-10 The summary window shows you the information
and gives you a chance to change any item.

The summary window appears whenever you create a new account, no matter what type of account you're creating. Detailed discussion about the summary is found later in this chapter, after I cover how to create all the account types available in Quicken.

If you enabled online banking, click Next to see the summary of the information you entered about your financial institution and your account (Figure 7-11). You can change anything that is incorrect.

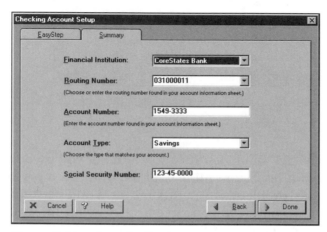

Figure 7-11   The online banking data is displayed so you can make sure that everything is correct.

Once all the information is correct (remember, missing information can be filled in later), click Done. This account is now added to your account register (Figure 7-12).

System is ready to enter a transaction for this account

Opening balance is the first entry for the new account

Account register has a tab for each account

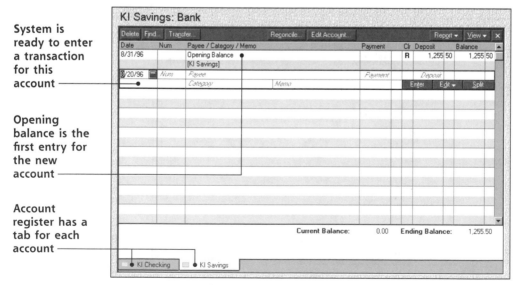

Figure 7-12   The account register displays the details for this new account.

Now let's look at the information you enter when you set up accounts that aren't bank accounts.

ENTERING DETAILED INFORMATION FOR CREDIT CARD ACCOUNTS

After you've filled in the basic information about the name, account number, and so forth, the credit card setup procedure has EasyStep windows for detailed information about each credit card.

You can enter the credit limit for your credit cards (Figure 7-13). Then, whenever you enter transactions into this credit card account, you can see how close you are to your limit. If your total gets dangerously close to your credit limit, you can switch to another credit card, apply for another credit card, or stop charging purchases. The last choice probably is the best advice.

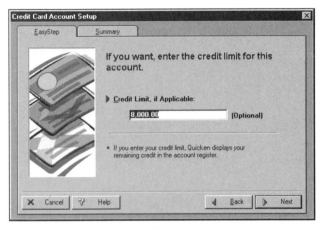

Figure 7-13   If you enter the credit limit, you can track your spending against it.

When you have entered all the information for this credit card account, click Done to place the account in your accounts register.

ENTERING DETAILED INFORMATION FOR ASSET ACCOUNTS

Asset accounts work a bit differently from bank accounts and credit cards. No bank or account number appears in the description of an asset account, only the name of the asset. For example, I have an asset account named Residence (I chose that name instead of "house" in case I someday figure out a way to afford another house that I'll track as "vacation home"). You can create an asset account for any type of possession you want to track: furniture, antiques, jewelry, cars, and so on.

Just as with bank accounts, however, Quicken asks if you want a starting point for this asset account. Instead of using a recent statement date and amount, you enter a date for which you ascertained the worth of the asset. Most of the time, you can use today's date and enter the amount the asset is worth. After you have entered the information, click Done to add the account to your accounts register.

ENTERING DETAILED INFORMATION FOR LIABILITY ACCOUNTS

Entering information for a new liability account is exactly like creating a bank account. You must enter the name, the statement date, and the amount of the liability as of that date. Then click Done. At that point, Quicken asks if you want to set up an amortization schedule for this liability. Answer Yes only if the liability is an amortized loan.

An *amortized loan* is a loan that is established so that interest is calculated on the remaining balance of the loan at the time of payment. That time of payment is set up as part of the agreement for the loan and is usually paid monthly. Each payment is split between interest and principal. Because a principal payment exists, at the next payment date, the amount of interest is less than it was on the last payment date (because the amount of the principal has been reduced). Your mortgage is an example of an amortized loan.

ENTERING DETAILED INFORMATION FOR INVESTMENT ACCOUNTS

An investment account is a way to track securities or other investments. An investment could be your stock portfolio, mutual funds, an IRA (Individual Retirement Account), Keogh, or 401(k).

TIP **You should establish as many accounts as those for which you receive statements. Tracking all your investments with one Quicken account is extremely difficult, if not impossible.**

LINKING A CHECKING ACCOUNT TO AN INVESTMENT
If you have an investment account that permits you to write checks against the investment's worth, Quicken creates a checking account and a link between the new checking account and the investment account. This feature is frequently available with brokerage accounts or money market funds (a money market fund is a mutual fund and is not the same as a money market account). When you enter a transaction in one of these linked accounts, the other account is also updated.

AMORTIZED VS. UNAMORTIZED LOANS

Almost all loans today are amortized. In the past, certain types of loans were not amortized, such as car loans or personal loans from banks. About 20 years ago, laws were passed to force lending institutions to stop using the loan calculations that had been used for car and personal loans. These calculations took the agreed-upon interest rate, declared a total interest amount based on that interest rate, and added that amount to the loan total. Then, as payments were made, the interest was paid off first, followed by the principal. It was possible to make several years worth of payments and then learn that the full principal amount was still due. Once that method of loan calculation was declared illegal, most loans became amortized loans.

Some exceptions exist, however, and it is possible to secure a loan that is not amortized. Those loans are called *interest-only* loans, because the agreement you sign guarantees that you pay the interest on a specific basis (usually monthly) and makes no demands about paying principal. The difference between an interest-only loan and the older, illegal loans is the fact that if you make a payment larger than the interest payment due, the difference is applied to principal. You are not required to pay off all the interest before you can make a principal payment. Credit lines and some home equity loans are frequently set up as interest-only loans. If you have a margin account with your broker, that account is most likely set up as an interest-only loan, and as dividends or other revenue are received in the margin account, any amounts that exceed the interest payment due are applied against the principal.

To create and link a checking account for an investment account that you're creating, answer Yes when Quicken asks if the investment account enables check writing. An EasyStep window opens to set up the account (Figure 7-14).

Figure 7-14   Create a checking account to link to your investment account.

You can establish a new account by entering the balance in the investment or use an existing account (which is usually not the appropriate choice, unless you have already set up a checking account that is attached to an investment and want to link it now). Click Next after you have entered the balance and selected an account.

TIP **If you're not sure whether you want to set up a linked account or use an existing account, respond No when Quicken asks if check writing is available for this investment. You can always create and link an account later.**

Now you have to tell Quicken the type of securities investment this account is tracking (Figure 7-15). The choices are as follows:

* **A variety of investments.** This could be the stocks and bonds you buy or the mutual or bond funds you're treating as a group.

* **A single investment.** This could be a single mutual fund, a single bond fund, or even a single stock.

Figure 7-15 Describe the type of investment you're tracking with this new account.

Choose an investment type and click Next. Quicken asks you if this investment is a tax-deferred account (a pension account, such as IRA, 401(k), and so on). Answer Yes or No and click Next to finish the creation of this account. A summary of your configuration appears, and you should click Done to tell Quicken you don't want to make any changes (or you can make changes and then click Done).

SETTING UP THE SECURITIES

After an investment account is created, you must set up the securities you will be tracking in the account. The EasyStep Security Setup begins (Figure 7-16). Click Next to begin entering information.

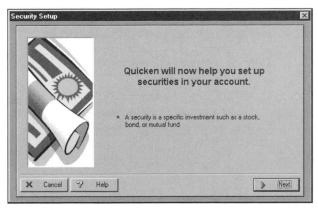

Figure 7-16 When you create an investment account, you have to provide information about the securities you'll be keeping an eye on.

First you have to name the security attached to this account and tell Quicken which type of security you chose (Figure 7-17). The choices for security types are Stock, Mutual Fund, or Bond, which are pretty self-explanatory. The ticker symbol for this item is optional, unless you're planning to track your stock by downloading information over your modem. If you are, you must enter the ticker symbol in this EasyStep window. Click Next when you have entered the data.

Security type this investment falls under

Name of security

Ticker symbol is necessary if tracking this security electronically

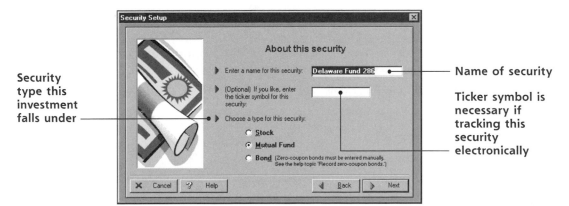

Figure 7-17 Enter the information about the security attached to this investment account.

You can enter additional information about the security and how you want to handle it with the next EasyStep window (Figure 7-18). The data you enter isn't for the purpose of tracking this security — its purpose is to add information that you can select and sort on when you build reports. After you have entered whatever information you desire, click Next.

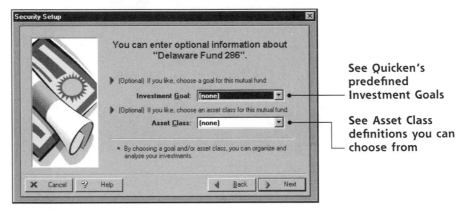

See Quicken's predefined Investment Goals

See Asset Class definitions you can choose from

Figure 7-18 Select optional classifications to organize your Quicken reports about your investments in a more detailed fashion.

The predefined investment goals are as follows:

* College Fund
* Growth
* High Risk
* Income
* Low Risk

If you want to use a goal of your own description, you can add it later by adding the goal while you are preparing your reports.

The predefined asset classes are as follows:

* Domestic Bonds
* Large Cap Stocks
* Small Cap Stocks
* Global Bonds
* International Stocks
* Money Market
* Other

ENTERING THE TRANSACTION HISTORY

Now you have to pick a starting date for tracking this security. You have three choices:

* **Today.** This option enables you to create the account and activate it immediately. You must go back and edit the account to enter all the previous data in order to have accurate records. The only reason to choose this option is if you're creating a number of investment accounts at this moment and plan to go back to enter detailed data soon (like tomorrow).

* **The end of last year.** This option permits the entry of data for the current year so far. This means you have some information for this year's taxes, but you must go back and edit the account to enter previous data to have accurate records about this security.

* **The date you purchased this fund.** This option permits entry of all the data about this security. Although this task is time-consuming, it is the only accurate way to track securities.

TIP It may seem tempting to make the tracking start date the end of last year, because it gets you through the tax preparation process for this year. This doesn't work at all, however, if you sell the security before the end of this year. You won't be able to calculate gains (or loss) properly without the complete history.

In fact, unless you're planning to hold on to this security forever and take it with you into your grave, eventually you have to enter the complete transaction history for this and every other security you enter into your Quicken software. Plan an evening when there's nothing interesting to watch on television, get out your shoebox (or whatever container you keep your investment statements in), and enter everything at once.

ENTERING THE COST BASIS

Now it's time to enter the number of shares you own in this security and the cost of each share (Figure 7-19). The number of shares and the cost for each is entered to match the choice you made in the previous EasyStep window for the starting point. That means you enter the number of shares you owned as of the date you chose, and you enter the worth of each share as of the date you chose.

Because it's easy to see that this information is not totally accurate if you aren't tracking the security since the first day you bought it, you'll understand why you eventually have to go back and enter all the information about this security's history.

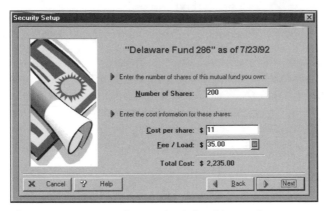

Figure 7-19 Enter the cost basis for this security.

TIP **The cost of the shares and the fee you paid to acquire them are the cost basis you use when you sell the securities. The formula for the profit you make when you sell the securities (called *gain*) is as follows:**

Net sales revenue (sales revenue less fees paid as a cost of selling) – cost basis = gain.

After you've entered the information about the security's cost basis, click Next. Quicken asks if you would like to add more securities to this account. Unless you're using one investment account to track all your securities (which isn't the most efficient way to do it), select No and click Next.

The investment setup process is complete, and you can see a summary of the information you've entered. Click Edit if you want to change anything.

After you finish entering the investment information for a security, the information is placed in the investment register. The investment account is placed in your accounts register.

Using the summary for all account types

No matter which account type you've created, when the process of creating the account is finished, a Summary dialog box appears (Figure 7-20). Different account types may have different items in the summary.

Once the basic information is entered, you can enter optional information about the account from this summary.

ENTERING ADDITIONAL INFORMATION

Click the Additional Information icon to see the dialog box shown in Figure 7-21. You can enter as much information as you think you'll need. The data you enter is for your own information only and has nothing to do with the bookkeeping functions performed by Quicken. Once you've finished entering data, click OK to close the dialog box.

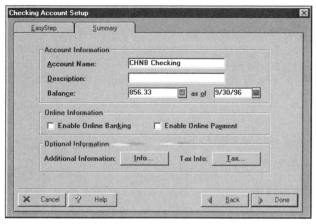

Figure 7-20 The Summary tab of the Setup dialog box is a chance to change any information you entered in the individual EasyStep windows.

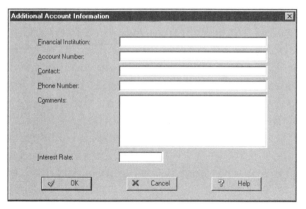

Figure 7-21 You can record data that's helpful to you (but unrelated to your bookkeeping chores) about every account.

ENTERING TAX INFORMATION

A Tax Info button is also available that opens a dialog box where you can configure the way specific transactions for this account can be handled for tax purposes (Figure 7-22). Information about setting up accounts for taxes is found in Chapter 13.

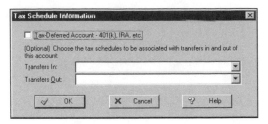

Figure 7-22 Transactions that affect your tax preparation can be tracked for every account.

Creating accounts the quick way

Once you understand the information required for each account type, you can move through the process of creating an account a bit faster. As soon as you start the process and see the first EasyStep window, click the Summary tab and fill in the fields instead of moving through each step one window at a time.

You'll find it easy to do this for some account types (especially bank accounts, which are less complicated than investment accounts).

TIP As you add more accounts, you'll develop a pattern for yourself about the kind of optional information you want to keep about each account type. For instance, I find it extremely useful to fill in a great deal of information in the optional information dialog box for my credit card accounts. If somebody steals my pocketbook, I can view my account list and call every credit card company with all the appropriate information at my fingertips. Or, if I am ordering merchandise over the telephone, I don't have to find my pocketbook to locate my credit card. I just view the account to see the credit card number and expiration date. Of course, my computer is near my telephone, so this is easy for me.

Viewing Accounts

You can view an account to see the transactions within it, or you can see a list of accounts. No matter how you want to view your accounts, you can always edit, change, or otherwise manipulate them.

Viewing account registers

Because the register is on your screen most of the time, it's easiest to take a peek at any account from there. This view of an account is the Account Register view. You can see the transactions for that account.

No matter which account you're working on in the register, you can take a quick look at any other account. The bottom of the register has a set of tabs. Each tab represents one of your accounts (Figure 7-23).

Use scroll bar to see additional accounts

Color-coded boxes represent account type

Click account tab to see that account

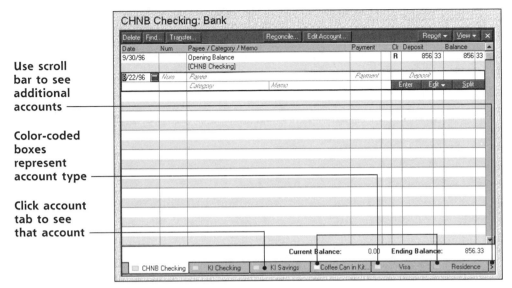

Figure 7-23 Tabs for every account are available below the register window.

Viewing the Account List

You can also look at a complete listing of all your accounts. To open the Account List window, use one of these actions:

✱ Press Ctrl+A.

✱ Choose **Lists** → **Account** from the menu bar.

✱ Hold your pointer on the My Accounts icon on the Activity Bar and then choose View all of my Accounts.

When the Account List displays (Figure 7-24), the All Types tab appears in the foreground, and you can see all your accounts.

A lightning bolt means this account is set up for online banking. A hand indicates that the account is a hidden account. Select or deselect View Hidden Accounts to view/hide hidden accounts. Use the buttons on the bar to make changes to a selected account. Use the tabs to view your account list sorted by type.

The columns on the All Types tab display information about each account. Table 7-1 lists the columns and the information displayed in each column.

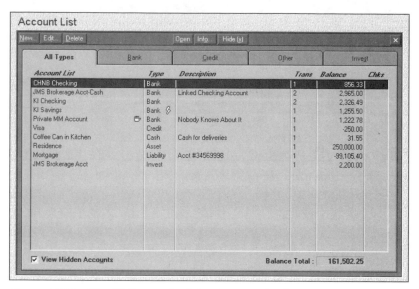

Figure 7-24 The All Types tab of the Account List shows every account.

TABLE 7-1 Interpreting the Account List Columns

Column	Displays
ACCOUNT LIST	Name of the account
TYPE	Account type
DESCRIPTION	Description you entered when you created the account
TRANS	Number of transactions in the account
BALANCE	Current balance of the account
CHKS	A check mark appears if there are checks waiting for printing; a lightning bolt appears if online payments are waiting to be sent.

You should note a couple of items in the All Types tab of the Account List:

* Some of the accounts have a minus sign in the Balance column. This indicates the account is a Liability type (or is an asset that is in the "red," such as an overdrawn bank account).

* Balance Total is the total of all the accounts that are listed. In effect, this number is the net total of all Assets and Liabilities, which can be viewed as a statement of Net Worth.

If you click any one of the other tabs, the Account List that displays includes only the accounts that match the account type noted on the tab (except that liability accounts and cash accounts are grouped in the tab called Other). All the column information remains the same as in the All Types tab, and the total you see is the total for all the accounts of this account type.

Changing Account Information

You can use the buttons on the Account List button bar to create or manipulate accounts. New opens the EasyStep window that begins the Create Account program discussed earlier in this chapter. All the other buttons manipulate existing accounts, so you have to select (highlight) an account before you can use the button to change it.

Edit button

If you select an account from the list and click the Edit button, a window opens that displays the information for the selected account (Figure 7-25). You can make changes to the information currently attached to that account (the information you entered when you created the account).

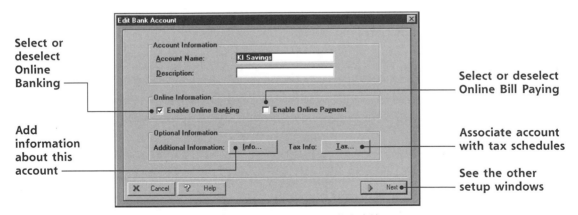

Figure 7-25   Use the Edit Bank Account dialog box to make changes to the account setup information.

Delete button

Deleting an account is not usually a good idea, because all the information about transactions that are connected to that account also disappears. If you created an account incorrectly, however, and there are no transactions are against it yet, it's perfectly okay to delete it.

If transactions do exist on the account, and you're thinking about deleting it because you don't want those transactions to be displayed or used in totaling information when you run reports, you may want to try hiding the account instead.

To delete an account, select it from the list and click Delete on the button bar. Quicken wants to make sure that you are really, really, sure about doing this. A confirmation dialog box displays, and you have to type **yes** in the Type "yes" to confirm field and click OK to confirm the deletion. If you just click OK, the account is not deleted.

Open button

If you select an account and choose Open from the button bar, your register opens with that account displayed in the Register window. You can see the transactions connected to this account, or you can enter a new transaction. After you're finished working on the account, click the Accounts tab to return to the Account List.

Info button

Click the Info button to see the Additional Information page for the selected account. This button is a quick way to view the information you entered when you created the account or to enter information you didn't know about during the account creation process.

Hide button

The Hide button is a toggle, which means it changes the current state of the selected account. If an account is not hidden, select it and click Hide to hide it. If an account is already hidden, select it and click Hide to unhide it. When you hide an account, the following things happen to that account:

* The account does not show up on the Account List (unless you select the View Hidden Accounts option).

* The account does not appear on the account tabs at the bottom of the register (this doesn't occur until after you have quit Quicken and started again).

* The account (and its transaction amounts) can easily be excluded from reports, because a question pops up in all reports about whether or not you want to include hidden accounts.

BONUS

Tracking Stocks

Tracking stocks or other investments is a bit more complicated than tracking bank accounts, but doing it correctly is important. Otherwise, when you sell, you may end up paying more taxes than are due or failing to pay the correct taxes and shelling out a lot of money for penalties later on. There are some basic tenets to understand about your stock investments, and getting the concepts straight will make it easier to track them.

When stocks are purchased, the amount spent on them is what is known as the *cost basis*. If you sell them, the difference between the money you receive and the cost basis is your gain. If you owned the stock less than one year, it's a short-term gain; if you held the stock more than a year, it's a long-term gain.

When stock splits, the original cost basis has to be reallocated among all the holdings after the split. For instance, you own 100 shares of XYZ company, which you purchased for $5 per share. The cost basis per share is $5, and the aggregate cost basis for your holdings is $500.

If the stock splits two-to-one, the aggregate basis is unchanged. The per-share basis, however, is now $2.50. If you sell some or all the shares at this point, you must use that per-share cost basis.

When you keep track of stocks, you should use a layered approach. That is, track each purchase of a group of shares separately. If you buy 100 shares at $6 per share, then you buy 100 additional shares at $7 per share, track the shares as layers. Each layer of shares consists of those shares purchased at the same time for the same price.

Your Accounts Are Your Balance Sheet

The account types available in Quicken represent the accounts used in a balance sheet. A balance sheet is a collection of accounts that represent what you own (assets) and what you owe (liabilities). The difference between those totals is your net worth.

Traditionally, accountants set up a balance sheet with the asset accounts on the left side of the page and the liability accounts on the right. Each asset and liability is listed individually with a total at the bottom of the list.

The mathematical formula is as follows:

Total Assets – Total Liabilities = Net Worth

You don't have to remember that formula, because Quicken has a Net Worth report that you can run whenever you want to determine your net worth.

Most of the time, the total of asset accounts is higher than the total of liability accounts. If your liabilities exceed your assets, the net worth number will be a minus, which means you may want to take a careful look at your spending habits or get another job.

Summary

You can run Quicken with only the bank account you created when you first started using the software. You can pay bills and track the money you're spending on various categories of expenses without adding any additional accounts.

Creating accounts for all the assets and liabilities you want to track, however, makes your Quicken system more useful to you. It means that you can keep an eye on what you own and what you owe, and you'll always know what you're worth.

UNDERSTANDING CATEGORIES

IN THIS CHAPTER YOU LEARN THESE KEY SKILLS:

A s you use Quicken's register to enter transactions, you choose a category to assign to each transaction. Categories provide a way to subtotal your expenditures so that you can see what you're spending your money on. Quicken provides some built-in categories, and for many people, those categories work for most transactions. After using the software for several months, the reports you view or print begin to show you a picture of your spending habits.

You may decide that some reports give you more information than you need to know about your spending. Perhaps you don't care whether your vacation expenses are reported with separate totals for lodging and airplanes; it only matters that you always spend more than you'd planned.

For some reports, however, you may find yourself wanting to know more. Knowing the category isn't enough; you want to know the details. For example, maybe you don't think knowing the total amount of money you've spent on life insurance is sufficient. Knowing how much of that total was for your insurance and how much was for insurance on your spouse or children also is important to you.

You can change the way Quicken keeps track of the details of your income and expenditures. Once you understand categories, subcategories, and supercategories, you can design your own tracking systems. In this chapter, you learn about all these categories and how to use them to enhance the level of information you can track in Quicken.

Using Categories

When you first set up your Quicken software, certain categories were placed into your data file. The number of categories and their names differ depending on the way you answered the setup questions. For example, if you answered Yes to the question about whether you own a home, categories specific to home ownership were added to your file.

The categories available to you are kept in a list called the Category & Transfer List in your Quicken data file.

Adding categories

You can add new categories whenever you need them. You have two ways to accomplish this:

* You can add a category while you're entering a transaction.
* You can add a category directly to the Category & Transfer List.

ADDING A CATEGORY DURING TRANSACTION ENTRY

While you're entering a transaction into your register, if the category list that pops up while you're in the Category field doesn't have a classification that fits this transaction, you can add one.

You can add a category during transaction entry a couple of ways. To add a category directly to the Category field, follow these steps:

1. Begin typing the name of the new category into the field (as you enter each character, Quicken looks for a match in the existing category list).

2. When you have finished typing the category name, press Tab to move to the next field.

3. Because Quicken could not match the category you entered to an existing category, it asks if you want to enter a new category (Figure 8-1).

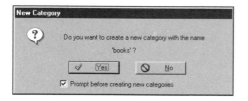

Figure 8-1 Quicken double-checks to make sure that you realize you entered a category that doesn't exist.

4. Answer Yes to add the new category. The Set Up Category dialog box displays so that you can add this category to the Category & Transfer List (Figure 8-2).

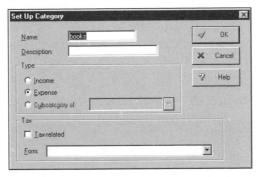

Figure 8-2 The Set Up Category dialog box fills in the information it has.

5. The information filled in by Quicken (the name you entered and the Type, which Quicken assumes from the type of transaction you're entering) is sufficient to add the category to your system. You can fill in one or more of the remaining fields in the dialog box, however, as follows:

  ❋ If you want, you can enter a description of this category.

  ❋ Select Subcategory to make this category a subcategory of an existing one. Then click the down arrow to the right of the Subcategory of field to see a list of existing categories. Select the parent category you want to associate with your new category. See the discussion on subcategories later in this chapter for more information on this subject.

  ❋ Select Tax-related if this category impacts your taxes. Then click the down arrow to the right of the Form field and select the appropriate tax form.

6. Click OK after you have finished setting up this new category.

You can also add a new category during transaction entry by displaying the drop-down list of existing categories and selecting Add Cat. The Set Up Category dialog box appears, but no information has been filled in yet. Enter the name and type of category and fill in any additional fields as described.

ADDING A CATEGORY DIRECTLY TO THE CATEGORY & TRANSFER LIST

Adding a category is just as easy to do when you're not in the middle of entering transactions. You can add a category directly to the Category & Transfer List at any time by using these steps:

1. Press Ctrl+C to bring up the Category & Transfer List (Figure 8-3).

Click a tab to see listing for that tab's category type

Use buttons to perform actions on items in list

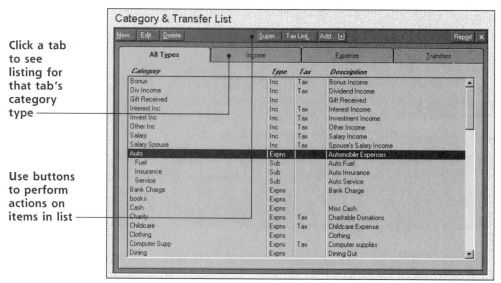

Figure 8-3   The Category & Transfer List displays all the categories in your system.

2. Select New from the button bar.

3. Fill out the Set Up Category dialog box as described earlier.

TIP   The Category & Transfer List is exactly what its name implies — a list of all your categories and all the accounts available for transactions that are transfers (the asset and liability accounts). If you scroll through the All Types tab, after Quicken lists the categories, you see the list of transfer accounts. Or you can click the Transfers tab to see only those accounts. When you're transferring money from one account to the other, no category is needed — instead, you need the account to which the money is being transferred. Because this selection is required during a transfer transaction, those accounts are listed along with the categories, and they appear in the category drop-down list.

ADDING PRESET CATEGORIES

Quicken provides a number of categories in its file system, and the categories in your system depend on the way you answered the setup questions when you first started using Quicken. If you answered No to questions about marriage, home ownership, or children, the categories needed to track information about those details weren't added to your system. If things change, you may want to add those categories to your file so they're available when you enter transactions.

You don't have to add those categories from scratch; you can just move them into your system by following these steps:

1. From the Category & Transfer List window, click the Add button to bring up the Add Categories dialog box (Figure 8-4).

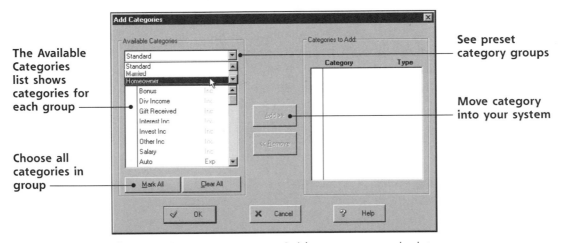

Figure 8-4 You can move any Quicken preset categories into your own file system.

2. Choose a category group from the Available Categories box. The categories for the selected group display in the box below.

3. Select each category you want to move into your own category list. As you click a category, a check mark appears to the left of the category name.

4. When you have chosen all the categories you want to use in your own transactions, choose Add. The selected categories are listed in the right side of the dialog box in the section named Categories to Add.

5. Click OK when you are finished. The categories are added to your Category & Transfer List.

TIP If you want to use all the categories in the group, choose Mark All, and a check mark appears next to each item. If you want to include all but one or two of the categories, select Mark All and then click the items you don't want (clicking a selected item deselects it).

Deleting or changing categories

You can delete categories, change the names of categories, or change other options in categories to make your Quicken system more efficient:

* If you have categories you aren't using and you know you never will, you can delete them. This makes scrolling through the category list a bit faster and more efficient when you are entering transactions.

* If you want to rename some categories in order to be more precise or to fit your spending patterns better, you can do so easily.

* If you want to change the tax information of a category, you can add, delete, or change a tax link.

* If you want to change the category type of an existing category, you can do so.

All of these actions are performed in the Category & Transfer List window.

To delete a category, follow these steps:

1. In the Category & Transfer List window, select the category you want to remove.

2. Select Delete from the button bar.

3. Quicken displays a little warning message telling you that you're about to delete a category permanently. Click OK to delete the account (or click Cancel if the warning scares you off and you want to think about it).

The category is removed from your system. If any transactions had been assigned to this category, they are changed to a category of "unassigned."

To change a category's information, follow these steps:

1. In the Category & Transfer List window, select the category you want to change.

2. Choose Edit from the button bar. The Edit Category dialog box displays (Figure 8-5).

3. Change the name, description, type, or tax information as you want and then click OK.

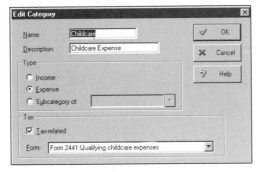

Figure 8-5 The Edit Category dialog box.

Understanding investment categories

Investment categories are handled differently. They have a different naming scheme and different rules:

* The first character of all investment category names is an underscore.
* You cannot delete an investment category if you have an investment account in your accounts list.

When you first install and set up Quicken, no investment categories are established. As soon as you create the first investment account, however, the investment categories are added to your Category & Transfer List.

Investment categories have the same category types as other categories: Income and Expense. However, all other aspects of investment categories are unique. Table 8-1 shows the available investment categories in Quicken. The categories that have been placed into your system are those needed for the specific investment accounts you've created.

TABLE 8-1 Categories for Investment Accounts

Category Name	Type	Tax Related?	Description
_DIVINC	Income	Tax	Dividend
_INTINC	Income	Tax	Investment Interest Income
_INTINC TAXFREE	Income	Tax	Tax Free Interest Income
_LT CAPGNDST	Income	Tax	Long Term Capital Gain Distribution
_RLZDGAIN	Income	Tax	Realized Gain/Loss

(continued)

TABLE 8-1 Categories for Investment Accounts (*continued*)

Category Name	Type	Tax Related?	Description
_ST CAPGNDST	Income	Tax	Short Term Capital Gain Distribution
_UNRLZDGAIN	Income		Unrealized Gain/Loss
_ACCRUED INT	Expense	Tax	Accrued Interest
_INTEXP	Expense	Tax	Investment Interest Expense

Using Subcategories

A *subcategory* is a way to separate the totals for a category into subtotals. A number of subcategories are built into the Quicken preset categories. For instance, the Auto expense category has subcategories for fuel, insurance, and service. When you use subcategories, the category to which the subcategory is attached is called the *parent*.

When you're entering transactions, the drop-down list for categories shows subcategories indented under their parent categories (Figure 8-6).

Figure 8-6 You can easily identify a subcategory because it's indented.

After you enter the transaction, the Category field shows the parent category and the subcategory separated by a colon (Figure 8-7).

| 8/26/96 | 104 | Comcast Cable | | 25 | 42 | | | 1,968 | 47 |
| | | Utilities:Cable TV | Service 8/14-9/15 | | | | | | |

Figure 8-7 Transactions assigned to a subcategory also display the parent category.

Adding subcategories

Once you decide you want to subtotal the transactions for a category, you can create the necessary subcategories. For instance, suppose that you want to track your insurance expenses by subcategories. You may want to separate out health insurance, life insurance, and insurance on your household goods. Or perhaps you pay separately for basic homeowners insurance and special insurance policies for valuables such as jewelry or antiques.

To add a subcategory, follow these steps:

1. From the Category & Transfer List window, choose New to bring up the Set Up Category dialog box.

2. Enter a name and optional description for this subcategory.

3. In the transaction type section of the dialog box, select Subcategory of.

4. Click the arrow to the right of the Subcategory of box and scroll through the list to find the category you want to use as the parent of this new subcategory (Figure 8-8).

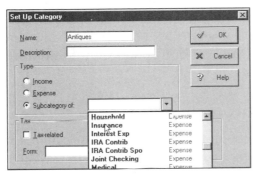

Figure 8-8   Choose the parent category for the new subcategory you're creating.

5. If this subcategory is a tax deduction (or taxable income if the parent category is an income category), select Tax-related and then choose a tax form from the drop-down list in the Form box.

6. Click OK after you have finished. Hereafter, you see this subcategory when you enter transactions.

Once you've learned how easy it is to create a subcategory, you will use them frequently. Every time you say to yourself, "I wish I knew how much I was spending on that," you can find out. Lots of times, when you wonder about where your money is going, finding out that information is helpful for creating reasonable budgets for next year's spending.

Incidentally, you can create subcategories for subcategories. Use the same approach as described previously, and when you fill out the name of the parent category in the dialog box, use a subcategory instead. For instance, you may want to add sub-subcategories under the subcategory Service, which is under the category Auto. That way you can track what you spend on normal maintenance (oil changes and other routine service) and how much you spend on repairs for things that break. When you use sub-subcategories, the Category field of your register separates each level of category with a colon, displaying this format:

Parent:Subcategory:Sub-Subcategory

Deleting a subcategory

To delete a subcategory, select it in your Category & Transfer List and then choose Delete. Instead of asking you to confirm the deletion, Quicken asks if you want to merge the subcategory with its parent. This means that every transaction in your system assigned to this subcategory will be changed to reflect the parent subcategory instead.

If you say No, the subcategory is deleted and any transactions that are assigned to it are marked as having no category. If you say Yes, all the transactions in your system are searched and every one that uses this subcategory is changed to reflect the parent category instead. This process can be time-consuming (the more transactions in your system, the longer it takes). If you have transactions that you want to track assigned to the subcategory you're deleting, either don't delete the subcategory (click Cancel) or delete it before you're ready to go for coffee or a meal. You certainly don't want to sit in front of your computer waiting for the process to finish.

Changing a subcategory

You can change the definition of a subcategory by selecting it in your Category & Transfer List and choosing Edit from the button bar. Then you can perform one or more of these actions:

* Change the name
* Change the description
* Change the parent to which the category is attached
* Change the tax options

You can also change a subcategory into a category. Just select Income or Expense instead of Subcategory of.

Using Supercategories

A *supercategory* is a way to simplify some of the reports for which you ask, because you can group categories together to see a grand total. Supercategories can also help you create simple budgets that rely on totals of similar categories.

For instance, you may want to create a report or a budget in which you merely need to see what amounts you're spending on broad categories such as "house stuff." You could pull together into one supercategory everything you spend on your house, including maintenance and utilities. Another supercategory might be "frivolous stuff," in which you include entertainment, dining out, and purchases of things that aren't necessities. Of course, your definition of frivolous may be different from mine — I personally consider dining out a necessity.

Using supercategories is a two-part exercise: (1) design the supercategories you need and (2) then assign categories to them.

Adding, removing, and changing supercategories

Quicken has established some supercategories for you, and you can add your own supercategories to that list and remove any supercategory you don't think you will use. You can also change the name of any existing supercategory.

To work with supercategories, go to the Category & Transfer List window and select Super from the button bar. This displays the Manage Supercategories dialog box seen in Figure 8-9.

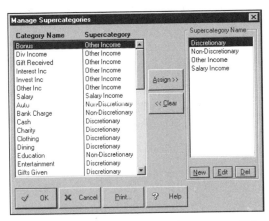

Figure 8-9 You can remove, change, or add to the preset supercategories.

ADDING A SUPERCATEGORY

To add a supercategory to your system, follow these steps:

1. Choose New from the Manage Supercategories dialog box. The Create New Supercategory dialog box opens (Figure 8-10).

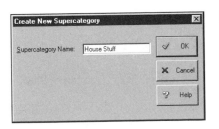

Figure 8-10 Creating a new supercategory is incredibly easy!

2. Enter a name in the Supercategory Name box.

3. Click OK. Quicken returns you to the Manage Supercategories dialog box, and the new supercategory is on the list.

DELETING A SUPERCATEGORY

If you want to remove a supercategory (either one of the preset ones or one you added), just select (highlight) the appropriate one and choose Del. Poof, it's gone! That's all there is to it, and it's so easy, it's dangerous. Quicken doesn't ask "Are you sure?" or warn you that you're about to delete a supercategory that may be used for existing reports. Of course, if you delete a supercategory and change your mind, adding it back is quite easy, using the steps noted previously.

CHANGING A SUPERCATEGORY

You can change the name of an existing supercategory (one of your own or one of the preset items) by selecting it and choosing Edit. The Edit Supercategory dialog box appears with the current name highlighted (Figure 8-11).

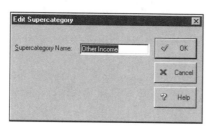

Figure 8-11 You can change the name of any existing supercategory.

To enter a new name, just start typing. The first character you type removes the current name (that's how it works whenever any text is highlighted in a Windows dialog box).

To make a minor change to the current name, use the right arrow or left arrow to remove the highlight. Then move to the place where you want to add a character (or a space) or delete a character. When you finish making changes, click OK to return to the Manage Supercategories dialog box.

Assigning categories to supercategories

Once you've established the supercategories, you can assign or reassign categories. To do this, use the Manage Supercategories dialog box and follow these steps:

1. From the Category Name list box, select the category you want to assign or reassign.

2. Select the supercategory to which you are assigning the category.

3. When both items are selected (highlighted), click Assign (Figure 8-12). Then click OK to close the dialog box (or click Clear if you change your mind).

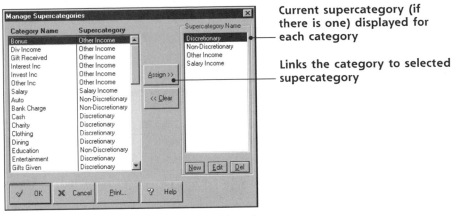

Current supercategory (if there is one) displayed for each category

Links the category to selected supercategory

Figure 8-12 The selected category is assigned to the selected supercategory.

You can select multiple categories and assign them to a supercategory simultaneously:

1. Select the supercategory you want to use.

2. Select the first category you want to assign to this supercategory. Then hold down Ctrl while you select additional categories.

3. Select Assign to assign all the selected categories at once. Then click OK to close the dialog box.

TIP If you want to assign multiple categories and they are contiguous, a shortcut is available that's faster than holding down Ctrl and selecting each category one at a time. Select the first category in the group and then move to the last category in the group. Hold down Shift while you select the last category. All the categories between the first and last are selected.

Running Category Reports

For a quick look at the total transactions for a category, select a category from the Category & Transfer List and then click the Report button on the button bar. The Category Report window opens with the totals for the selected category, along with information about the transactions assigned to the category (Figure 8-13).

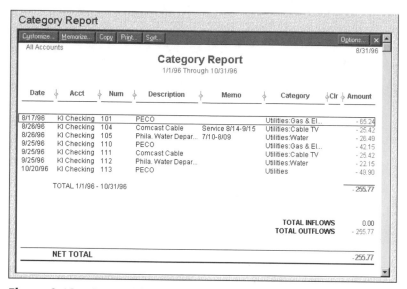

Figure 8-13 Get a quick report on a category with one click of the mouse.

You can do a great many things with Quicken reports to learn more about the information displayed or to change the way the information appears on-screen. With a Category Report, however, the intent is to see the totals for the selected category, and it doesn't make sense to go through any complicated configuration options. When you build more complicated reports, you will want to try all the customization options available with the Customize button.

You may have certain things you want to do with this report, however, and you can use the buttons on the button bar to accomplish them:

* Click Memorize to give this report a name and add it to the memorized reports in your system. Later, you can look at your memorized reports by choosing that option in the Reports menu (**Reports** → **Other** → **Memorized Reports**).

* Click Copy to copy this report to the Clipboard. Then you can open another Windows software program and paste this information into it.

* Use the Print button to get yourself a hard copy of the report (*hard copy* is the jargon used by computer folks for a printed document).

* Use the Sort button to rearrange the order in which the items are displayed.

Category Reports are quick peeks at information about a selected category and they're a good way to answer the question, "How did I spend that much money on that?".

BONUS

Categories can be powerful, and you can use your circumstances (and your imagination) to employ them effectively.

Duplicate categories can be useful

It may sound illogical, but sometimes you may find it useful to have two categories that cover the same category but have different entry types — say, one is income and the other is expense.

I find this useful in a number of situations. My sister and I occasionally chip in together to buy gifts for other family members. If I write the check for the gift (assigning the check to Gifts Given), when I receive my sister's check for her half, I enter it with a category of Gifts Given R (the R is for reimbursement). Of course, if my sister lays out the money, when I send her a check, I apply it to Gifts Given. Either way, my Quicken reports reflect the same total for gift giving.

If you think about it, a number of categories probably exist for which you could use a reimbursement category. Perhaps you regularly eat out with friends or family who write a check for their share of the meal (especially if you used a credit card to pay the tab). Married couples who don't operate their lives from a joint bank account and arrange the bill-paying equitably between them using individual bank accounts sometimes have to reimburse each other for some household expenses.

If you have a category for which you receive an occasional reimbursement, consider creating another similar category that has an income type.

Attention, homeowners

If you're a homeowner, rush to your Category & Transfer List and immediately create a category named Permanent Improvements. Tracking the amounts you spend on your house for permanent improvements to your home is important. A permanent improvement is generally described as "something that wasn't there before." Adding a room, a fireplace, a closet, or a shower qualifies as a permanent improvement.

Permanent improvements are added to the cost basis of your house and may become important when you sell it. Under current law, when you sell your house, you must pay tax on the gain (the difference between the cost and the sale price) unless you purchase another residence for at least as much as the amount for which you sold this one. You have two years to buy your next residence. Specific figures such as the minimum amounts for those gains are involved in the calculation, and you should check with an accountant to see what the current law provides.

Not everyone buys a larger, more expensive house when selling a residence, and people in this group can be liable for taxes. If you want to downsize when the children are grown and gone by purchasing a smaller house that costs less than what you received for your previous home, keeping track of permanent improvements can save you money when you calculate your tax liability.

If you are over 55 years of age, you can take a one-time exemption from this tax, again with limitations. You should check the current rules regarding the limits of exemptions. This is a boon for homeowners who don't want to be bothered with the upkeep of houses (especially once the children have gone out on their own). They sell their residences and move into apartments.

Summary

In this chapter, you learned about categories, subcategories, and supercategories. You can use this knowledge to make your Quicken system more sophisticated and more powerful. In fact, if you're really a detail freak, there's almost no end to the amount of infinitesimal information you can get, as long as you set up Quicken to deliver it.

CHAPTER NINE

ENTERING BUSINESS TRANSACTIONS

9

IN THIS CHAPTER YOU LEARN THESE KEY SKILLS:

SETTING UP QUICKEN FOR BUSINESS REPORTS
PAGE 162

UNDERSTANDING AND USING CLASSES   PAGE 162

ENTERING BUSINESS TRANSACTIONS   PAGE 165

REPORTING ON BUSINESS FINANCES   PAGE 169

I f you run a small business or have a business income in addition to your salary, you can use Quicken to track your business as well as your personal income and expenditures. In fact, on a customer-by-customer or job-by-job basis, you can use Quicken to track where your business income comes from and where your business expenditures are spent.

You have to prepare carefully for business bookkeeping, and not all of that preparation is connected to Quicken. For example, you should get separate credit cards for your business expenses and get out of the habit of writing checks to cash if any business expenses are involved in the transaction. In fact, cash and business aren't concepts that belong together. Don't take cash from customers and don't spend cash for business expenses except for tolls, parking, and other incidental expenses — and get a receipt.

The most important thing to remember is that to get the information you need about whether your business is making money, you have to have very precise record keeping. Of course, that concept also goes a long way toward saving you aggravation if the IRS ever asks you any serious questions. This chapter covers some Quicken features that help you achieve that precision as you learn how to track business transactions.

Setting Up Quicken for Business Reports

You have several choices for the way you use Quicken for business. You can set up a separate file system in Quicken and use that for business. Your original, first file system (the one you set up when you originally installed the software) can continue to be the file for keeping your personal records. This means you have to open and close the files as you move between your personal and business record-keeping tasks.

Or you can keep one set of files and use it for personal and business records. Within that file set, you can set up separate bank accounts to reflect your real bank accounts. I'm assuming that you have a separate bank account for your business, but if you don't, you should open one. This is the most common choice for Quicken users because it's also the easiest way to work.

Or if you really want to live on the edge, you can track all your personal and business income and expenses in one Quicken file and in one bank account. Doing so is not illegal; it's just not smart business. But if you're careful about every transaction, you can make it work, even when the IRS comes calling with questions.

Understanding and Using Classes

Classes are Quicken features that provide additional analysis over and above the information you get from categories and category reports. You can use classes to enhance the amount of detail you get about your transactions.

For example, suppose that you own two cars. Every time you pay your bill from the gasoline credit card or the local mechanic, you can assign the amounts to whichever car was responsible for the expense. Create a class for the Jaguar and a class for the Alfa Romeo (I live in a fantasy world). Your regular reports from Quicken tell you how much you spent on fuel, and when you need to know specifically what it costs to keep the Jaguar on the road, you ask for a class report. This capability becomes more important for business use, especially if you use the Jag for personal errands and the Alfa for visiting customers.

Or you can create classes for each customer. When you do work for a customer, you can track your expenses (tolls, telephone, whatever) by the normal Quicken categories and then, at the end of the month, run a class report to see those expenses on a customer-by-customer basis. Then send each customer an invoice for reimbursement.

The way you use classes completely depends on the type of business you have and the way you need to keep records. You have to plan your classes to match your needs.

TIP Before you create classes, create the reports you want to see on a piece of paper. Play with that scheme, asking yourself what you really need to know. Once you've created a bunch of reports that match your needs, create the classes you need to make those reports.

Creating classes

You can create the classes you need before you begin using them or create them as you need them. You'll probably end up doing both.

To set up a class, whether you are in the middle of a transaction or are just setting up Quicken for your own use, follow these steps:

1. Press Ctrl+L to display the Class List (Figure 9-1).

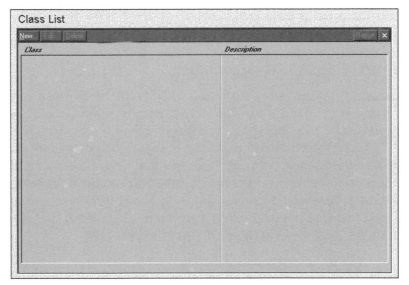

Figure 9-1 The first time you use the Class List, only the New button is available.

2. Select New to bring up the Set Up Class dialog box (Figure 9-2).

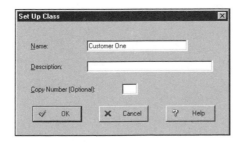

Figure 9-2 Establishing a class is a simple, short process.

3. Enter the name for this class. This name appears in all the reports you create. (Pay no attention to the width of the field; Quicken only lets you enter 15 characters).

4. Enter an optional description, which appears in column headings in the reports you create. If you don't enter anything here, Quicken substitutes the name.

5. If you live in Canada, you can use the Copy Number field to separate tax records for individuals and then use it for reporting with Quick Tax.

6. Click OK after you finish entering information.

Begin to create the next class and continue to create all the classes you need. Remember, if you need more classes, you can add them during transactions.

 TIP **If you want to keep up with computer jargon, the capability to add basic information while you work (such as adding a class while you're entering a transaction) is called *on-the-fly entry*.**

Using classes as subclasses

You can also subclassify your business transactions. For example, you may want to track each project for each customer or separate customer transactions between sales of products and services rendered.

Quicken makes it easy to do this because each and every class you establish can be either a class or a subclass. You don't have to predetermine its use; just place a colon between a class and another class to have the second one treated as a subclass. For instance, the Class List in Figure 9-3 shows classes that can easily be used as subclasses by making a project a subclass of a customer (or vice versa).

Notice the following things about this Class List:

✳ A class exists for each customer.

✳ You must track a class for each project or contract, and those classes must be subclassed specifically under their connected classes. The description indicates the connection between the project and its customer, so that the user doesn't have to remember which is which.

✳ Different types of work (sales and service) have classes that can be used as subclasses for any customer.

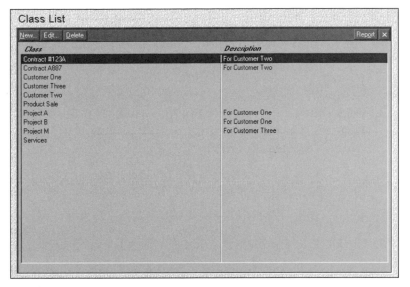

Figure 9-3 A Class List set up for easy subclass use.

Your own Class List may include only connected subclasses or only generic subclasses. Or you may use the description field differently — perhaps noting the contract's worth.

Entering Business Transactions

E ntering a business transaction really isn't any different from entering personal transactions. The only variation is the additional information you need to produce the required business reports, which you determined when creating classes.

Checking and adding categories

Before you enter any business expenses (or revenue), you have to make sure that all the available business categories are going to appear on your category pop-up list when you enter transactions. If you told Quicken you wanted to use the software for business during the setup process, the categories are there.

If you didn't say Yes to business expenses during setup, you have to bring all the business categories into your system before you enter transactions.

To do that, follow these steps:

1. Press Ctrl+C to bring up the Category & Transfer List.

2. Click Add from the list's button bar to display the Add Categories dialog box (Figure 9-4).

3. Click the arrow to the right of the Available Categories field and select Business. The business categories are displayed in the box below the Available Categories field.

4. Select Mark All to select all the business income and expense categories. Check marks appear next to each business category.

5. Select Add to add these categories to your system.

6. Click OK to complete the addition of these categories.

Now when you see the pop-up list for categories during transaction entry, the business categories are included. You can, of course, always add more business categories to suit your needs.

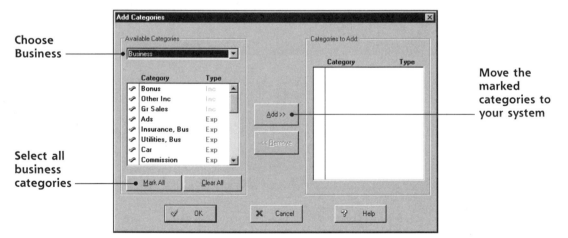

Choose Business ⎯⎯

Move the marked categories to your system

Select all business categories ⎯⎯

Figure 9-4 Add categories for business transactions if you didn't tell Quicken about business use during the original setup of the software.

TIP After you select Mark All, scroll through the list of business categories and deselect any you know you won't be using. You can deselect by clicking the category, and the check mark disappears. In fact, you can select and deselect any category by clicking on it — it's a toggle. After you eliminate any categories you won't need, click Add. This way, you won't have to scroll through a long category list that includes unnecessary options.

Entering a business expenditure

Now that your classes are established, you can use them when it's appropriate. Here's how to enter a check and assign a class (watch for Step 6 — that's the important step):

1. Call up the bank account you're using for business.

2. Enter the date for the transaction.

3. In the Num field, enter the check number.

4. Move to the Payee field and enter the name of the payee.

5. Move to the Payment field and enter the amount.

6. Move to the category field. Enter a category. Then enter a forward slash (/) and the class name attached to this transaction. To subclassify, type a colon (:) and enter the second class.

7. Type a note in the Memo field (this step is optional, but I find it useful for business expenses).

That's all there is to it. The forward slash gave Quicken the signal that you're tracking this transaction by class. Your transaction has all the information embedded in it to produce the reports you need (Figure 9-5).

| 10/30/96 | 101 | Bernardi Office Supplies | | 15 | 00 | *Deposit* | | |
| | | Supplies/Customer One | Binders | | | | | |

Figure 9-5 The forward slash between the category and the class tells Quicken to keep track of this transaction for both reporting configurations.

 TIP If you don't remember the name of the class, after you enter the category, press Ctrl+L to see the Class List and then double-click the class you want to use. Quicken inserts the forward slash and the class name.

Entering a business cash receipt

The jargon for depositing money from a customer is *cash receipt*, which means you received a payment.

You enter a cash receipt in Quicken in the same manner as you enter a deposit in your personal bank account:

1. Move to your business account.

2. Enter the date of the deposit in the Date field.

3. Type **DEP** in the Num field.

4. In the Paid By field, enter the name of the customer who gave you the check.

5. Enter the amount of the check in the Deposit field.

6. In the Category field, enter an income type (usually Gr Sales, which is a business category for gross sales).

7. Type a slash and then enter the class.

8. If you want to attach a subclass to this cash receipt, add a colon and then enter the name of the subclass.

9. Type a note in the Memo field if you want (perhaps the invoice being paid, if one exists).

10. Press Enter to finish the entry.

Entering a business split transaction

Just as with your personal transactions, you can split a business transaction. There are more ways to split it, however. In a personal transaction, you usually split an expense to divide it between categories by choosing Split when the list of categories displays. In a business transaction, you can assign the entire amount to the same category and split it among classes.

Everything is the same as entering a standard expense except that you have to fill out the Split Transaction window (Figure 9-6).

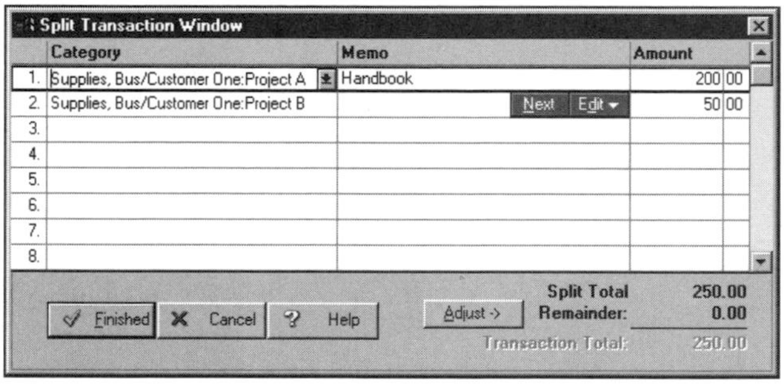

Figure 9-6 Split a transaction between classes.

Of course, you could also split an expense transaction among categories, among categories and classes, and among categories, classes, and subclasses. Your choice determines whether you use a colon (categories), a slash (classes), or both.

You can also split an income transaction between classes. If you're using classes for customers, you would never have one check from multiple customers. However, you could conceivably get one check from a customer for multiple projects.

Reporting on Business Finances

Ou can create reports on a variety of criteria for your business income and expenditures. This way, you can keep an eye on more than just whether or not you're making money. You can see whether you're making money with one type of service and losing money on another. Or you can see which customers generate the most income.

Viewing Register Reports

Register Reports are a good way to see an overview of activity. You can get a quick report from the register of the business bank account:

1. Click a transaction that contains either the Payee/Paid By entry or the category on which you want information.

2. Select Report from the register's button bar.

3. Choose a report on either the Payee/Paid By field or the Category field. The report is displayed on the screen.

For example, select a transaction that has revenue from a customer with the income category of Gr Sales (there may also be a class and subclass). You can get a report on the Paid By entry (in this case, a customer), as Figure 9-7 shows.

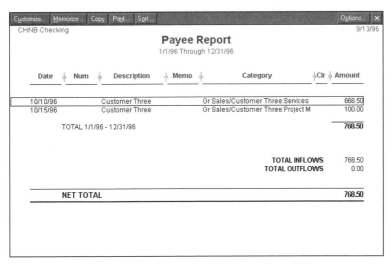

Figure 9-7   A quick report on this Payee/Paid By field is available from the register.

You can also get a report on the category (in this case, Gr Sales), as in Figure 9-8.

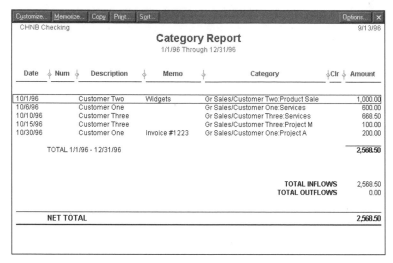

Figure 9-8 An itemized report on a category is available instantly.

If you select an empty transaction line, you can choose Register Report from the Reports button and get a report on the activities for the bank register (Figure 9-9).

Figure 9-9 A general report of the activity for this register doesn't provide much information about the individual items.

Customizing a Register Report

You can build on this Register Report and get more specific information. To do so, select Customize from the register's button bar. The Customize Register Report dialog box displays (Figure 9-10).

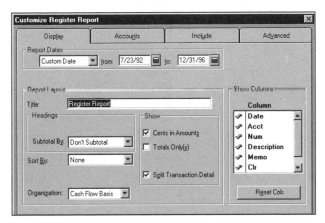

Figure 9-10   You can change the way the register's report displays information by customizing it.

DISPLAY TAB

Start with the Display tab:

1. Use the Report Dates field to select the date range. The available choices include various months, quarters, and years. You can select Custom Date and insert a from and to date of your own choosing.

2. Use the Title field to change the name of the report if you're planning to print or memorize it.

3. In the Subtotal By field, you can specify a date range (months, year, and so on) or Category, Class, or Payee. All the items in the element you select will be subtotaled. For a business report, subtotaling by Class is a good idea.

4. In the Organization field, select Income & Expense (organized on those items) or Cash Flow (organized in the order in which money was spent and received).

5. In the Show section, you can opt whether you want to show the Cents in Amounts (or just dollars), Totals Only, and Split Transaction Detail.

6. In the Column box, select or deselect the columns you want to display (some aren't terribly important, and you may want to get rid of them for this report).

INCLUDE TAB

The next tab in this dialog box is the Accounts tab. Because you're running your business from a separate business account, you shouldn't have any need to use this tab to add more accounts to the report. Therefore, move to the Include tab (Figure 9-11) to set the values available there:

1. Select the dates you want to include for these options.

2. Click the Categories or Classes button to choose whether you want to see a list of categories or classes from which to select.

3. Select the individual categories or classes you want to include in this report. You can select Mark All or Clear All and then select individual categories or Classes.

4. Use the Matching section to specify the specific items you want to match for the fields listed. Note that you can even match on text that's in a Memo field (now that you know that, you can plan to use the Memo field efficiently).

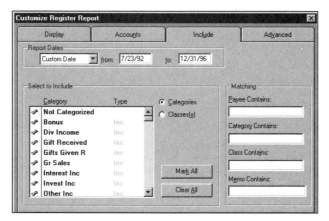

Figure 9-11 Decide on the elements you want to include for this report.

When you have finished making selections on the Include tab, click the Advanced tab.

ADVANCED TAB

In the Advanced tab (Figure 9-12), make changes as needed.

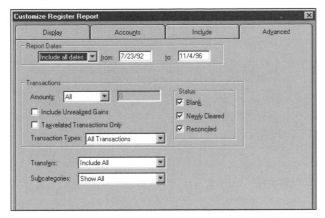

Figure 9-12 Fine-tune your report criteria with the
Advanced tab.

To make changes, follow these steps:

1. You have yet another chance to change the dates in this dialog box, but if you didn't change them so far, you probably won't change them here.

2. In the Transactions section, if you want to include or exclude transactions based on the amount of an individual entry, choose Amounts and then select All, less than, equal to, or greater than. Specify an amount if you choose anything but All.

3. The Unrealized Gains and Tax-related Transactions selections are irrelevant for business reports.

4. Select the Transaction Types you want to include, choosing from Payments, Deposits, Unprinted Checks, or All Transactions.

5. Select the bank statement status of the transactions you want to include (Blank, Newly Cleared, or Reconciled).

6. Choose whether you want to include Transfers.

7. Choose the way you want to select Subcategories, selecting to Show All, Hide All, or Show Reversed (subcategory in front of category).

GENERATING THE CUSTOMIZED REPORT

Once you have made all your selections, select Create to generate this report. When it displays (Figure 9-13), decide whether you want to select Customize again and fine-tune it a bit more.

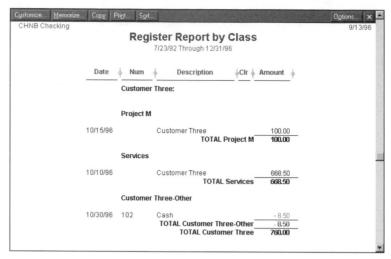

Figure 9-13   The report is totaled and sorted the way it's needed.

When the report looks just the way you want it, you can print it or memorize it by clicking the corresponding buttons on the button bar. If you choose Memorize, the Memorize Report dialog box asks you for some information (Figure 9-14):

1. Enter a new title if you don't like the one Quicken chose.

2. Those date choices are back again!

3. You can enter an optional description to remind yourself of the way you set up this report.

4. Select an optional icon (which will be placed next to the report's name in the report listings so that you can click on it to get this report).

5. Click OK after you have entered all the information.

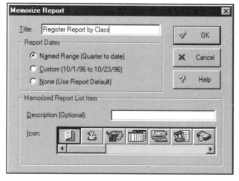

Figure 9-14   Select a title and icon and save this report for the future.

To see this report in the future, select Reports → Other and then choose Memorized Reports. You will see this report listed in the Memorized tab of that dialog box (Figure 9-15).

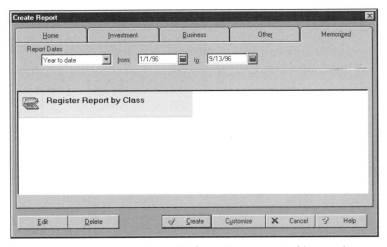

Figure 9-15 The report is available anytime you need it once it appears in the Memorized tab.

Creating other business reports

If you open Reports → Business, you see a listing of available business reports (Figure 9-16).

Figure 9-16 Quicken provides some business reports that you can customize to fit your own circumstances.

The smartest thing you can do before you dive in and create transactions, design reports, and run your business finances in Quicken is to show your accountant everything you plan to do. Your accountant may have some suggestions and even have some good ideas for the way reports should be built.

BONUS

S ome decisions you make about how to handle your business finances may require a bit of setup so that Quicken is ready to do things your way.

Start a whole new Quicken file for your business

If you decide to create an entirely separate file for your business use, here's how to do it:

1. Choose File → New from the Quicken menu bar.

2. Quicken asks whether you're sure. Say Yes so that Quicken knows you want to create a new set of files for a new purpose.

3. Make sure that New Quicken File is selected and click OK.

4. In the Create Quicken File dialog box that displays, enter a name for this new file (if for your business files, name it Business).

5. Click OK.

At this point, Quicken walks you through the setup for new files, which is like the setup process you completed when you first started Quicken and established your first file. You create a checking account and then can move on to create all the other things you need, such as categories, classes, bank accounts, and so on. In effect, you're starting all over, but you haven't deleted your original file; you've just added another one.

To move between files, select File → Open and select the file with which you want to work. Your original file is named Qdata.QDB unless you changed it when you first installed Quicken. The title bar at the top of your screen shows the name of the file with which you're working.

Pension yourself off

Self-employed individuals should remember that they can create pension plans for themselves. The law treats plans established by individual proprietors the same way it treats plans established by corporations. The term *employee*, as defined by the IRS, includes a participant in a plan of an unincorporated enterprise who is a partner or a sole proprietor of that enterprise.

The term *compensation* can also mean the earned income of a self-employed person. When the IRS uses the term *employer*, it can also mean a sole proprietor, and the IRS interprets that sole proprietor as his or her own employer. The IRS also considers a partnership to be the employer of each of the partners. Talk to your investment counselor about a Keogh plan or another form of pension plan to provide tax deferrals and retirement income.

The law has some limitations about whether self-employed individuals can get the tax deduction for their pension contributions (depending on the other pensions available and other IRS restrictions), so you should also check this out with your accountant.

Summary

Using Quicken for a small business, even if in conjunction with how you're using it for personal finances, is a good idea if you're careful to separate business transactions from personal ones. Open a separate business account and don't pay personal bills from it. Don't put business cash receipts into your personal account. Keep detailed records about all business transactions, because almost everything is tax-deductible as a business expense. This chapter showed how to put the power of Quicken to work for your business.

PLANNING AHEAD WITH QUICKEN

THIS PART CONTAINS THE FOLLOWING CHAPTERS:

Quicken has some flashy, expandable features, and there's no doubt that it can help you fine-tune your finances to a level that an accountant would envy. But Quicken isn't famous for creating more accountants. It's famous for helping everyday people do the same things they've done before — only more quickly and easily.

Randy and Sharon Spotswood are self-proclaimed normal, everyday people. Both have important jobs in a large hospital, and with a little girl and another child on the way, two main segments dominate their life — work and family. These two segments intersect when it comes to household finances: Taking the money they've worked so hard for and turning it into maximum benefit to the family.

That's where Quicken has helped. Randy considers himself an average user, but Quicken has had a better-than-average impact on their finances. "I have never looked forward to balancing the checkbook," Randy says. "Reconciling our checkbook used to be a time-consuming, frustrating event that usually had me pulling hairs out of my balding head. But since I started using Quicken, dealing with our checkbook has become much less frustrating."

Of course, Quicken is no magic elixir. Quicken can't tell Randy to remember the checkbook, and it can't remind Sharon to record her ATM withdrawals. Diligence is the responsibility of the user. After seeing what Quicken can do, however, Randy and Sharon found diligence was much easier to inspire.

Recording all of their transactions and purchases in Quicken has given Randy and Sharon a great look into where their money goes. For example, Randy says, "if I want to see what percentage of last year's income was spent on insurance, I access our Quicken personal account, click the Graphs icon, and select income versus expenses." What awaits him is a colorful display of their finances in bar and pie graphs. "All I have to do is look for the insurance category on each graph to determine the percentage. Quicken helps me find this kind of information in a hurry."

Having this type of information at their fingertips helps Randy and Sharon determine the best course of action for the family's money. It might seem like a frivolous expense here and there doesn't really matter, but when it turns into a big slice in a pie chart, reality hits home, and Quicken has done its job.

Randy and Sharon haven't ruled out using Quicken for more advanced features. They simply haven't needed to yet. "Perhaps sometime in the near future," Randy says, "I'll use Quicken for online banking, but for today, I'm just happy to use it when checkbook reconciliation time rolls around."

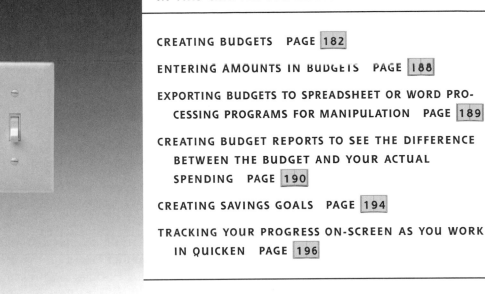

CHAPTER TEN

BUDGETS

IN THIS CHAPTER YOU LEARN THESE KEY SKILLS:

What are you spending money on that you cannot live without? Of course, rent or mortgage payments fit into this category. But how much are you spending on clothing or entertainment? Or even on food? What do you toss into the shopping cart at the supermarket that isn't edible? Or necessary?

Why do each of my children think that a CD player with enormous speakers in the bedroom is a birthright? Why do I need three of those just because there are three children? Why are there multiple television sets in your house?

What do you want that you can't afford (even if you don't need it, you really want it)? What can you reduce your spending on to get it?

If you had to guess how much you're spending on every category for which you write a check or pass along cash, how accurate would you be when you compared it to the actual figures shown in Quicken? Most people don't really know.

The solution to all of this, tracking your money and trading off your spending on some items to purchase other items, is found in budgeting your money. Quicken provides a slew of ways to create and live with budgets, which is the topic of this chapter.

Creating Budgets

You have a couple of ways to approach the process of creating a budget, and they all start with the same procedures. The differences are in the way that the dollar amounts get into the budget:

* You can use AutoCreate, which creates a budget using the data in your registers.

* You can create a budget of categories with no amounts and enter the amounts you want to use for budgeting (the zero-filled budget method).

* You can copy another budget and then make the changes you need to use this budget for a different set of budgeting standards.

 WEB PATH **Get budgeting tips at Eastern Michigan University's Web site at** http://www.emich.edu/public/fin_aid/finaid5/finaid5a.html.

Autocreating a budget

The easiest way to create a budget is to let Quicken do a great deal of the work. This method is called *AutoCreate*. It produces a budget based on the income and spending recorded in your registers. Because this budget requires transaction entries, you can't use AutoCreate if you're doing your budget and you've just started using Quicken. Either wait a couple of months and then create the budget with AutoCreate or use the zero-filled budget method (discussed later in the chapter).

CREATING AND NAMING THE BUDGET

The budgeting process begins with the Create Budget features in Quicken, during which you set up the basic information. The whole thing is quite easy to accomplish:

1. Place your mouse pointer over the Planning icon in the Activity Bar.

2. When the menu pops up, click Budget My Spending.

3. The Budget window displays (Figure 10-1).

4. Click New on the Budget window button bar to bring up the Create Budget dialog box (Figure 10-2).

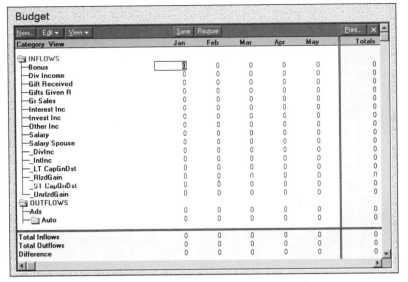

Figure 10-1 All the categories in your system are listed so that you can begin creating your budget.

Figure 10-2 To start a budget, you just have to name it and then decide which process you want to use to create it — in this case, I'm using AutoCreate.

5. In the Name field, give the budget a title. If you're creating your first budget, Quicken automatically names it Budget 1 (the second budget you create is Budget 2 and so on). You can leave the name or change it to anything you want.

6. In the Description field, you can optionally add some information to remind yourself about this budget's use. Any time you work in the Manage Budgets window in Quicken, you will be able to see this description.

7. Select Autocreate Budget and then click OK to finish this portion of creating the budget.

Steps 1 through 6 are the steps you take to create any type of budget. In this case, you're telling Quicken to create the budget automatically (although you do have some decision-making power about the way this budget will be created, which I explain in the next section).

PICKING THE DATES AND AMOUNTS

Because you've chosen Autocreate Budget, the Automatically Create Budget dialog box appears (Figure 10-3). Now you can begin to set the configuration that Quicken uses to create this budget for you:

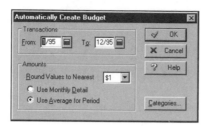

Figure 10-3 Choose your budget's configuration with the choices offered on the dialog box.

1. Choose the date range you want Quicken to use when your current data is gathered.

 TIP By default, Quicken uses the entire last year as the budget date range, which means that all your recorded transactions throughout the year will be used. If you didn't use Quicken last year, you have to change the dates to this year. But even if you did use Quicken last year, you still may want to use more current figures. If you're creating your budget early in the year, last year's figures will probably work best. But if you're starting around September or later, the current spending patterns available in this year's figures may be better. You know whether your spending changed a great deal this year, so make your decision about the date range with some careful thought about your own financial data.

2. In the field labeled Round Values to Nearest, tell Quicken how you want to round off the pennies (you don't need exact figures for a budget), choosing from $1, $10, and $100.

3. Select Use Monthly Detail if you want Quicken to copy all the actual figures for the months specified into your budget. Select Use Average for Period if you want Quicken to calculate monthly averages for every category and bring those averages into your budget.

 TIP If you use Monthly Detail, that doesn't mean you have to do a monthly budget. You can do a quarterly budget or even a yearly budget, and Quicken totals monthly amounts to match the way you create the budget. If you use Average for Period, the same principle applies. Quicken takes the monthly average, multiplies it three times, and enters the result as a quarterly average.

PICKING THE CATEGORIES TO USE

You can decide which categories you want to use for budgeting by clicking the Categories button. The Select Categories to Include dialog box appears, listing all the categories in your system (Figure 10-4):

Figure 10-4 Choose the categories you want to budget.

1. Scroll through the category list and click any category you want to exclude (because all the categories are marked, clicking unmarks a category — click an unmarked category to put the mark back).

2. If you want to use a limited number of categories, a faster method is to select Clear All and then click the categories you want to select.

3. Click OK once you have finished. Quicken returns you to the Automatically Create Budget dialog box.

4. Click OK to finish creating this budget.

Quicken fills in the blank budget with the budget figures. The first thing you should do is choose View from the budget's button bar and then click Zero Budget Categories. The check mark next to that menu item disappears, meaning that you've deselected it (to restore the check mark and bring back the zero budget categories, click again). This eliminates all the budget lines that have no figures and makes it much easier to read your budget (Figure 10-5).

You can change any figures in the budget that you want. When you're satisfied that you have the budget you want to use, choose Save from the button bar.

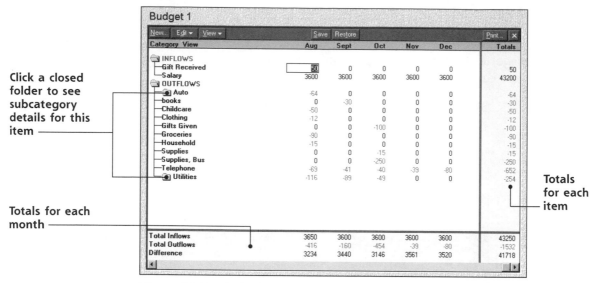

Click a closed folder to see subcategory details for this item

Totals for each month

Totals for each item

Figure 10-5 The budget displays the transactions and totals them.

Creating a budget from scratch

If you don't have enough existing transactions in your system to create a realistic budget, or if you want to make yourself a budget using figures you've decided on (that do not match your real expenditures), you can create an empty budget:

✷ If you already have a budget and the new one is an additional budget, display the current budget and choose New from the button bar to start a new one.

✷ If you don't yet have any budgets, place your mouse pointer over the Planning icon on the Activity Bar and, when the menu pops up, select Budget My Spending.

Either way, you see the Create Budget dialog box (Figure 10-6).

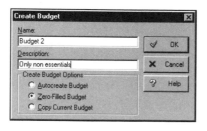

Figure 10-6 This budget is zero-filled, so there won't be any figures inserted in the item lines.

1. Enter a name for this budget (or use the default name provided by Quicken).

2. Enter an optional description.

3. Select Zero-Filled Budget to tell Quicken you don't want to take any figures from your existing transactions.

4. Click OK to see your Budget window (Figure 10-7).

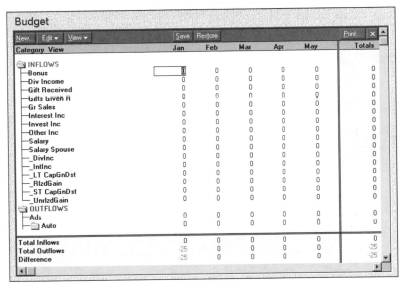

Figure 10-7 The budget is displayed, and you can begin to fill in your figures.

Once you've created the zero-filled budget, you can enter the figures you need.

Budgeting by supercategory

When you view your budget, it displays your categories. In fact, the words *Category View* appear just below the button bar. The budget is showing you figures that are organized and displayed by category (and subcategory).

If you created supercategories, you can use them for budgeting, which gives you a more general overview of your spending. Supercategories are groupings of categories, and you can create as many as you want.

X-REF **See Chapter 8 for information about setting up supercategories.**

If you created supercategories that make sense to budget for (such as discretionary versus necessary spending or household versus personal spending) it's frequently a good idea to base a budget on them.

To create your budget using supercategories, follow these steps:

1. Click View on the Budget window's button bar and click the Supercategories listing to place a check mark next to it.

2. The budget displays your supercategories, and the words *Supercategory View* appear below the button bar (Figure 10-8).

Folders represent supercategories — click a closed folder to see categories

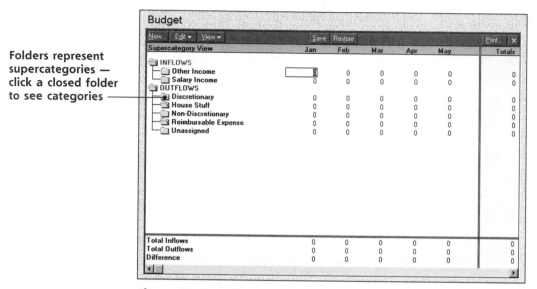

Figure 10-8 Budgeting by supercategory is an often-useful alternative.

3. Enter a budget amount for a supercategory if you want to match your spending for its categories against a grand total.

4. Click a closed supercategory folder to enter a budget amount for individual categories if you want to budget your spending by category.

5. Move a category into a different supercategory by dragging it from its present supercategory to the new one (to drag, place the pointer on the category and then press and hold the left mouse button while you move the pointer to the new supercategory, then release the mouse button).

The supercategory budget is a great approach for people (like me) who don't want to worry about the nickel and dime stuff and prefer to say "here's my budget limit on discretionary spending."

Entering Amounts in Budgets

E ven if you autocreate your budget and have it filled with figures from your current spending patterns, you're going to want to enter amounts for specific categories or supercategories. And, of course, if you created a zero-based budget, you have to fill in all the amounts for the categories or supercategories for which you've decided to budget.

Here are the guidelines for entering amounts:

* Click an amount (which highlights it and places a box around it to indicate that it's been selected for editing) and enter a new amount.

* To undo a new amount, press Esc to restore the cell to the amount that was in the cell before you changed it.

* To fill a row (for instance, to duplicate the amount in one month to all the remaining months), click the amount you want to use and then select `Edit` → `Fill Row Right` from the button bar. All the cells to the right of the original amount are filled in with the same amount.

* To save the new figures, select Save from the button bar.

* To undo the changes, select Restore from the button bar. This puts the budget figures back to where they were the last time you saved the budget.

Exporting Budgets to Other Programs for Manipulation

Once you've created one or more budgets, you can move the information to another program to manipulate the figures. This way, you can change certain figures without actually changing your budget. It's a way to say "what if...". If the Budget window isn't on your screen, do the following:

1. Place the mouse pointer over the Planning icon on the Activity Bar.

2. Select Budget My Spending from the pop-up menu. The last budget you worked on displays in the Budget window.

3. To change to another budget, select `View` → `Other Budgets` from the button bar and select a budget from the list that displays.

The export process really involves the use of the Windows Clipboard, which gives you a great many choices about the way you want to use the budget information. To export the budget, follow these steps:

1. Select `Edit` → `Copy All`. The contents are placed on the Windows Clipboard.

2. Open the Windows software application you want to place your budget in.

3. In the software window, choose `Edit` → `Paste`.

4. The budget is imported into the software (Figure 10-9), and you can do whatever you want with the numbers.

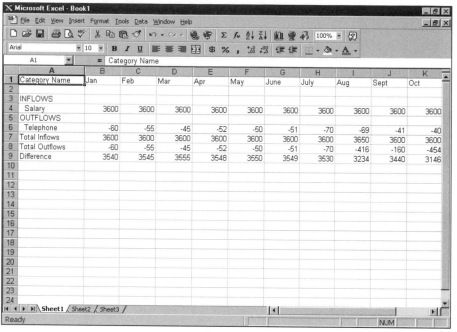

Figure 10-9   The budget has been exported to a spreadsheet program and all the tools available in that program can be used on the budget figures.

You can also export a budget to a word processor, a presentation program, or any other Windows software application that you want to use to play around with the figures.

Creating Budget Reports

The only way to see how you're doing at meeting your budget goals is to compare the budget figures with your actual expenditures (and income, if you're including revenue items in your budget). Two types of budget reports are available in Quicken: the *Budget Report* and the *Monthly Budget Report*.

The Budget Report is a very basic report. It looks at all the accounts and all the categories and displays the differences between your budget amounts and your transaction amounts. The Monthly Budget Report does the same type of calculations, but it looks only at your bank accounts (including any accounts you've set up for cash or credit cards) and subtotals the figures by months.

Creating a standard Budget Report

The standard Budget Report is a useful overview of your spending versus your planning.

To create a Budget Report, follow these steps:

1. From the Reports menu, move your mouse pointer to Other to see the submenu.

2. Select Budget to see the Create Report dialog box (Figure 10-10).

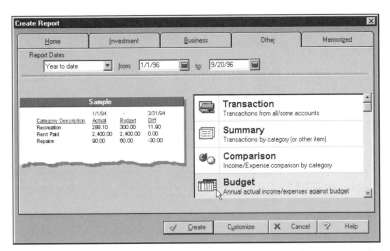

Figure 10-10   The Create Report dialog box has a Budget Report choice available to make the whole process very easy.

3. Click the icon to the left of the title for the Budget Report.

4. Quicken searches through the transactions (the more transactions you've entered, the longer this takes, but it should take less than a minute) and then grabs the information from your budget.

5. The data is displayed as a comparative study between your budget and your actual transactions (Figure 10-11).

Once the report is displayed, you have a number of options available through the use of the buttons on the report window's button bar:

* Select Customize to change the format (the date range, the categories, and so on) of the report.

* Select Memorize to save this report.

* Select Copy to place the contents of the report on the Windows Clipboard and then paste it into another Windows software application.

* Select Print from the button bar to save a hard copy of this report.

Often, however, a quick glance at the on-screen display tells you what you want to know.

Budget Report

Budget Report

| Customize... | Memorize... | Copy | Print... | | Options... | × |

All Accounts   9/20/96

Budget Report
1/1/96 Through 9/20/96

Category Description	1/1/96 Actual	- Budget	9/20/96 Diff
Discretionary			
Clothing	12.32	12.00	- 0.32
Gifts Given	0.00	0.00	0.00
Household	15.16	15.00	- 0.16
TOTAL Discretionary	27.48	27.00	- 0.48
Non-Discretionary			
-Other	18.75	19.00	0.25
Childcare	50.00	50.00	0.00
Groceries	89.56	90.00	0.44
-Other	2.31	0.00	- 2.31
Telephone	68.82	479.33	410.51
-Other	0.00	0.00	0.00
Utilities:Cable TV	25.42	41.66	16.24
Utilities:Gas & Electric	65.24	93.00	27.76
Utilities:Water	26.49	40.66	14.17
TOTAL Non-Discretionary	346.59	813.65	467.06

Figure 10-11   You can easily see where you're under budget, over budget, or right on target.

TIP   If you place your mouse pointer on any of the figures in the Actual column, the pointer shape changes to a magnifying glass with the letter *z* in it. The *z* stands for zoom, and clicking the figure zooms you into the transactions that made up that total, so that you can see all the gory details about how you spent that much money on that category.

Creating a Monthly Budget Report

If you'd prefer to see a comparison of your budget against your actualities on a month-by-month basis, Quicken has the Monthly Budget Report all configured for you.

To create a Monthly Budget Report, follow these steps:

1. Select **Reports** → **Home** → **Monthly Budget** from the Quicken menu bar.

2. When the Create Report dialog box displays, click the icon to the left of the report entitled Monthly Budget.

3. The Monthly Budget Report displays, and you can use the horizontal scroll bar to move through the months and see the amounts (Figure 10-12).

4. The same button bar options are available for you to choose from as those described for the Budget Report.

| | | 9/20/96 | 1/1/96 | | 9/20/96 |
Category Description	Budget	Diff	Actual	Budget	Diff
OUTFLOWS					
Discretionary					
Clothing	0.00	0.00	12.32	0.00	- 12.32
Gifts Given	0.00	0.00	0.00	0.00	0.00
Household	0.00	0.00	15.16	0.00	- 15.16
Travel	0.00	0.00	0.00	0.00	0.00
TOTAL Discretionary	0.00	0.00	27.48	0.00	- 27.48
Non-Discretionary					
-Other	0.00	0.00	18.75	0.00	- 18.75
Childcare	0.00	0.00	50.00	0.00	- 50.00
Groceries	0.00	0.00	89.56	0.00	- 89.56
-Other	0.00	0.00	2.31	0.00	- 2.31
Telephone	0.00	0.00	68.82	0.00	- 68.82
-Other	0.00	0.00	0.00	0.00	0.00
Utilities:Cable TV	16.66	16.66	25.42	16.66	- 8.76

Monthly Budget Report — Monthly Budget Report, 1/1/96 Through 9/20/96. Bank,Cash,CC Accounts. 9/20/96

Figure 10-12 You can easily see when you went overboard and when you exercised restraint by viewing your spending against your budget plans on a monthly basis.

One advantage of looking at the Monthly Budget Report is that it frequently makes it easier to explain the differences to yourself. Perhaps you can justify the July expenses that were over budget by explaining that you were on vacation and couldn't stand the thought of driving by all those gift shops. Or, in November, the pre-holiday sales at the local department stores were so good that you did all your holiday shopping in one fell swoop. Use whatever excuse works for you.

Creating a budget graph

You can get a quick idea of the difference between your budget and your actualities by looking at a graph that displays that information.

To create a budget graph, follow these steps:

1. Select **Reports** → **Graphs** → **Budget Variance** from the Quicken menu bar.

2. When the Create Graph dialog box appears, click the icon to the left of the report, titled Budget Variance.

3. Wait a few seconds for Quicken to gather the data and make the calculations.

When the graph displays, you can easily see where your actualities don't match the budget plans you made. If anything seems really out of line, place your mouse pointer on the bar in question, and Quicken responds with an exact figure for you (Figure 10-13). Click the bar to see the details of the transactions that got you to this point.

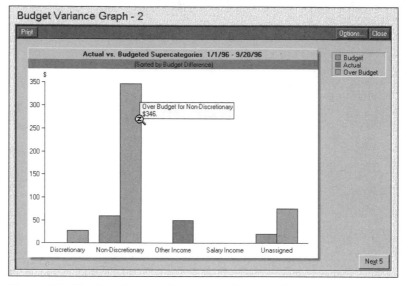

Figure 10-13 Somehow it all seems much worse when you see one bar on a graph towering over the others.

Creating Savings Goals

Another type of budgeting is setting a goal for savings. A savings goal is a way to budget cash for purchases.

To create a savings goal, follow these steps:

1. Select [**Features**] from the Quicken menu bar and then point to Planning.

2. Choose Savings Goals from the submenu to bring up the Savings Goals window.

3. Select New to display the Create New Savings Goal dialog box (Figure 10-14).

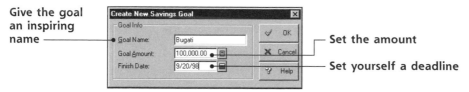

Figure 10-14 Set a goal for saving money so that you can buy the luxury or necessity for which you've decided it is worthwhile to save.

4. Enter a goal name for this savings objective (which becomes the name for the savings goal account created to track this goal).

5. Enter a goal amount (click the calculator if you need to add figures — don't forget the tax).

6. Enter a finish date (click the Calendar icon if you want to select a date with your mouse).

7. Click OK to finish the process and return to the Savings Goals window, where your goal has been entered (Figure 10-15).

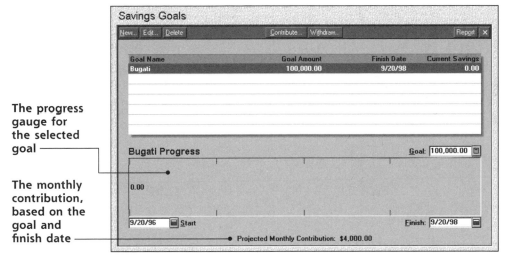

The progress gauge for the selected goal

The monthly contribution, based on the goal and finish date

Figure 10-15 The savings goal is listed and you're on your way!

All that remains to do is to put money into this savings goal account. To do so, follow these steps:

1. Select Contribute from the Savings Goals window button bar.

2. In the Contribute to Goal dialog box (Figure 10-16), enter the bank account dedicated to this goal, in which the money is placed. Click the arrow to the right of the From Account field to see a list of your accounts.

3. Enter the date of this bank deposit.

4. Enter the amount of this deposit.

5. Click OK when you have finished contributing to your goal.

TIP **Unfortunately, reality dictates the presence of a Withdraw button on the Savings Goals button bar. If you have to remove money earmarked for this goal in order to pay bills, use the Withdraw function to tell Quicken how much you've removed.**

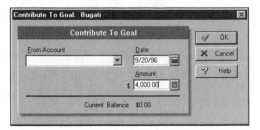

Figure 10-16 You have to tell Quicken when you put money in the bank to contribute to this goal.

Tracking Your Progress

Y ou can track the progress of your ambition to meet a budget or save for a goal. The progress-tracking function revolves around a nifty feature called the *progress bar*, which sits at the bottom of your Quicken window. It looks a little like the gas gauge on your dashboard (except it's horizontal).

To put a progress bar on your window, follow these steps:

1. From the ⌷ Features ⌷ menu, point your mouse to ⌷ Planning ⌷.

2. Choose Progress Bars from the submenu.

3. The progress bar appears at the bottom of your Quicken window (Figure 10-17).

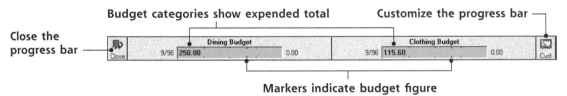

Figure 10-17 You have no way to avoid your budget goals with a Quicken budget progress bar staring you in the face.

When the progress bar is on display, you can change the display by clicking the icon called Cust (short for customize). When the Customize Progress Bar dialog box appears, select the options you want to use (Figure 10-18).

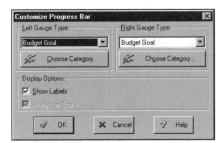

Figure 10-18 You can decide for yourself how you want to use the progress bar by changing the options.

Customize the progress bar by using these guidelines:

1. For each gauge (Left or Right), to specify a type of bar, choose among the following:

   * A defined Savings Goal. You must have defined a savings goal to use it on a progress bar.

   * A Budget Goal, which is a budget figure for a category on which you want to keep a close eye. You must have defined a budget.

   * Supercategory Budget Goal, which is a budgeted amount for a related group of categories. The goal on which you're keeping an eye is the grand total for all the categories in the supercategory. You have to define a budget and a supercategory to use this type of progress bar.

2. Select a type of goal for each gauge. You can have the same type of goal on each side of the progress bar or use each gauge for a different type of goal.

3. For a budget goal, click Choose Category and then pick a category from the list that displays.

4. For a supercategory goal, click Choose Supercategory and then pick a supercategory from the list that displays.

5. For a savings goal, click Choose Goal and pick a savings goal from the list that displays.

6. Select None if you don't want to use that gauge at this time.

7. In the Display Options section of the dialog box, select Show Labels to have the goals title appear above each gauge.

8. Select Always on Top to keep the progress bar visible regardless of the Quicken window in which you're working.

9. Click OK when you have finished configuring your progress bar.

If you place your mouse over either gauge, the pointer changes to a magnifying class. Double-click the gauge to display the Budget window or *Savings Goals* window.

BONUS

Now that you know how to set up a budget as well as savings goals, only one small problem remains — how do you stay on the budget and achieve those savings goals? Like most things in life, a relatively large gap exists between budget theory and budget practice. Buying that health club membership is a great deal easier than getting in there every day and working out. Budgeting is no different. It sounds great until you have to start doing it. You know you want the results; it's just that the price seems stiffer when you begin paying it. To ease the pain of budgeting (you're on your own with the health club), here are some tips on how to keep your spending in line with your proposed budget. The best way to approach it is to examine your expense categories.

Housing expenses

Because housing is one of the major expenditures for individuals and families alike, it seems the best place to start. Whether you rent or own your home, there are things you can do to reduce your monthly expenditures.

As a renter, you can do a number of things to improve your cash flow and reduce your expenses:

* Look into the possibility of buying. The current market offers low interest rates and low down payment requirements in many areas. It may be no more expensive and possibly even cheaper to own than to rent.

* Most states require landlords to extend a ten-day grace period to tenants, which means that a landlord rarely gets the rent on time. Offer to pay your rent on or before the actual due date for a $10 to $20 monthly rate reduction.

* If you're at all handy, offer to take care of minor repairs in return for a reduced monthly rate.

* If you're single, consider getting a roommate to share the expenses.

Owning a home offers many advantages; however, it also can be a strain on the finances, with taxes, insurance, and upkeep added to the monthly mortgage payment. To reduce the overhead of owning a home, try some of these tips.

* If interest rates have dropped substantially since you first purchased the home, consider refinancing at a lower rate.

 WEB PATH **For loan, mortgage, and credit card rates as well as related information, check out this Web site:** `http://www.bankrate.com`.

* If you took advantage of a low down payment option and are paying a monthly PMI (Private Mortgage Insurance) fee, you may be able to eliminate it by having your house reappraised. If the value of your property has risen to the point where the loan-to-value ratio meets the lending institution's requirements, you can cancel the PMI.

* If real estate in your area is down, it may be a good time to have the local tax assessor reassess your property. If the value has dropped, you may be eligible for a reduction in your taxes.

Household expenses

I like to throw everything necessary for running the household under this category, including food, clothing, and utilities. To save on expenses related to utilities, try these options:

* Make your house energy efficient by insulating, weather stripping, and performing regular maintenance on heating and air conditioning units.

* Use computerized thermostats to control heating and cooling by time periods. There's no point in maintaining a "comfortable" temperature when no one's around to enjoy it (except the utility company).

* Buy energy efficient appliances.

* Make sure that you're getting the best long-distance telephone rates available. Most providers offer several plans but do not necessarily make them widely known.

WEB PATH ➡️ **Fone Saver offers domestic rate comparisons for the major long distance providers. Its Web site is at** `http://www.wp.com/Fone_Saver/ld.html#ATT_SS`.

To save on food expenses, take advantage of the growing number of wholesale clubs and buy in bulk. Not only do you reduce the cost of the items, but you also cut down on transportation expenses and time by shopping less frequently. To save on clothing-related expenses, try these tips:

* Buy items of clothing that match what you already own to make your wardrobe more versatile without buying entire ensembles.

* Avoid buying those things that require dry cleaning.

* Buy "classic" styles that will be fashionable for a while. Avoid faddish items that come and go before the season is even out.

* Give old clothes to a charitable organization and request a receipt. You can then write them off as a charitable donation on your tax return.

Budget window shortcuts

Quicken provides some shortcuts that you can use to move around the Budget window quickly, as the following chart shows:

Key(s)	Movement
TAB	Moves right one amount at a time
RIGHT ARROW	Moves right one amount at a time
ENTER	Moves right one amount at a time
LEFT ARROW	Moves left one amount at a time
ESC	Removes an entered amount and replaces it with the original amount
UP ARROW	Moves up one row in the same column
DOWN ARROW	Moves down one row in the same column
PAGE DOWN	Moves down through the window to show the next window-sized section
PAGE UP	Moves up through the window to show the next window-sized section
HOME,HOME	Moves to the cell farthest left in the current row
END,END	Moves to the last cell in the current row
CTRL+HOME	Moves to the first row of the budget
CTRL+END	Moves to the last row of the budget
CTRL+ARROW	Moves the budget one window-sized page in the direction of the arrow

Summary

In this chapter, you learned how to create several planning devices for yourself, namely budgets and savings goals. The ability to keep an eye on budgets and compare their figures to your actual spending means you can adjust your spending (or your budget) as frequently as needed. Tracking your savings goals lets you plan more realistically.

FORECASTING CASH FLOW

F orecasting is the capability to project the future based on the past. For financial forecasting, this means looking at your financial history to see if there's a way to predict your financial future.

Quicken has built-in forecasting features that analyze your revenues and expenses. By using the information gained from those figures, you then can make fairly accurate predictions about what kind of bank balances you can expect to have at various points in the future. For example, if you're wondering what would happen to your financial picture if you decided to eat out three times a week and see a movie once every two weeks, you can look at the long-term effects of these new spending habits. Or you could look at a shorter time period by forecasting your financial worth after you pay for your daughter's wedding. (Who made that rule about the bride's parents paying? As the mother of three daughters, I'd love to meet that person.) This chapter explores Quicken's forecasting capabilities and how to make them work for you.

Understanding Forecasts

Once you have some transactions in your Quicken system (at least a couple of months' worth, although more is better), Quicken can use your figures to forecast your finances. Quicken also uses your transactions to create budgets, but the differences between budgets and forecasts are substantial.

A *budget* is a way to create amounts and then track those amounts against your actual spending. The figures Quicken uses to create the budget are the transactions you've entered into your bank account registers. A *forecast*, on the other hand, is a projection of the balances you should expect to see in your bank accounts, considering the way your money is flowing today. The forecasted balance is a combination of forecasted revenues and expenditures. The forecast figure is derived from scheduled transactions, estimated amounts that are gathered from your future transactions, and your real, completed transactions. In the end, the forecast data is usually a combination of known items and estimated items:

* *Known items* are regular scheduled transactions that occur on a specific date. They're found in your Scheduled Transaction List and in regularly occurring transactions that Quicken finds when it examines your bank register.

* *Estimated items* are averages of the amounts Quicken finds when it examines your register and your budgets. These items are averaged by being spread out over the period of time for which you want to forecast.

Creating a Forecast

When you create your first forecast, Quicken produces a *Base Scenario* for you to view. You can manipulate the way the forecast looks at your figures and see what happens if anything changes. Before you can do that, however, you have to create a forecast.

Creating a Base Scenario forecast

The Base Scenario forecast is a standard forecast that uses the existing information in your system. You can configure the way that information is used during the creation process.

To create a forecast, follow these steps:

1. Choose `Features` from the file menu and then choose `Planning` → `Forecasting`.

2. The Automatically Create Forecast dialog box appears (Figure 11-1).

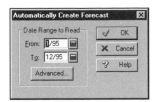

Figure 11-1 If you have transactions from the previous year, the Automatically Create Forecast dialog box goes into autopilot and creates a forecast.

3. By default, Quicken wants to use all of last year's figures to create this forecast (which makes sense). If you used Quicken during all or part of last year, you don't have to change the date fields.

4. If you didn't use Quicken in the preceding year, change the dates to reflect the date range for which the transactions exist that Quicken needs to view.

5. Click Advanced to tell Quicken more about how you want the forecast developed in the Advanced AutoCreate dialog box (Figure 11-2).

Choose item(s) you want created

Choose source of estimated amounts

Specify categories to include in forecast calculations

Choose accounts to include in forecast calculations

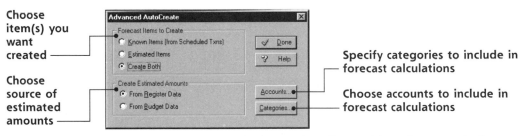

Figure 11-2 Customize the forecast by telling Quicken what to use in the calculations.

6. In the Forecast Items to Create section, select one of these options:

 ✳ Known Items, which uses items from your Scheduled Transaction List.

 ✳ Estimated Items, which uses estimated amounts from examining the transactions on your register or looking at your budgets.

 ✳ Create Both, which uses both of the preceding options.

7. In the Create Estimated Amounts section, select one of these options:

 ✳ From Register Data, which tells Quicken to look through your register and take an average of what it finds for each category.

 ✳ From Budget Data, which uses the budget you've created for this account.

TIP Don't choose to forecast from a budget unless you've created a budget that has the same categories you want to use for forecasting.

For a standard forecast, that's all you have to do. If you want, however, you can change the accounts or the categories you want to forecast:

1. Click Accounts to see the Select Accounts to Include dialog box (Figure 11-3).

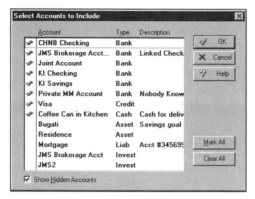

Figure 11-3 Select the accounts you want to include in your forecast.

2. Select or deselect accounts by clicking them.

3. Click Categories to see the Select Categories to Include dialog box (Figure 11-4).

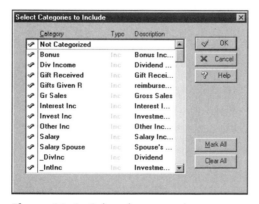

Figure 11-4 Select the categories you want to include in the forecast.

4. Select or deselect categories by clicking them.

5. Click OK in each dialog box to return to the Advanced AutoCreate dialog box. Then click Done.

6. After you're returned to the original Automatically Create Forecast dialog box, click OK.

Quicken uses the configuration options you set as it looks at the information in your file. It creates a forecast called Base Scenario and displays it in the Base Scenario window (Figure 11-5).

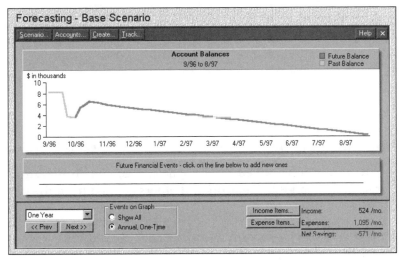

Figure 11-5   The forecasting report is displayed, with plenty of options for manipulating it.

The graph itself displays your projected account balances for the future, using these conventions:

* A yellow line shows past balances.
* A blue line indicates a projected positive balance.
* A red line indicates a projected negative balance.

You can hold the mouse pointer on the graph over any date, and the projected balance for that date appears. This window has several elements that you can use to play around with the forecasting figures. Remember that changing figures in a forecast never affects real data, so playing "what if" and viewing the results is safe.

Saving the Base Scenario

If you want to use this as a base forecast and measure other forecasts you create against it, you should save the Base Scenario:

1. Click Scenario from the button bar to see the Manage Forecast Scenarios dialog box (Figure 11-6).

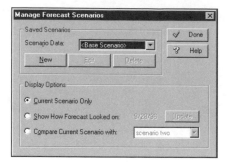

Figure 11-6 Save the Base Scenario before you change it or create another scenario.

2. Click Done to save the Base Scenario.

3. Ignore the other fields on the dialog box for this Base Scenario.

Now that you've saved the Base Scenario, you can change items to see the difference between this scenario and others created from the changes.

Creating Multiple Forecasts

You can use the Base Scenario window to make changes to any available field. You can change just one thing and then create a new scenario or make multiple changes before creating a scenario with those changes. Once you have multiple scenarios, you can compare the results of your changes by comparing the scenarios.

Changing the Forecasting window

The Forecasting window has plenty of elements, and you can change any of them to play "what if" games. What if your income changed, or your expenses, or you looked at different accounts or categories? You can create scenarios that answer those questions. This section examines the fields on the Forecasting window.

DATE RANGE

The Date Range field offers several options for changing the contents of the forecast (and therefore changing the graph):

* Click the arrow in the Date Range field to select a different date range (choose among One Month, Six Months, One Year, or Two Years).

* Click the Prev button to see the forecast for the previous date range (if you selected One Month as the date range, you see the previous month; if you selected One Year as the date range, you see the previous year, and so on).

* Click the Next button to see the forecast for the next date range.

As you make changes in the date ranges, you will see the graph change.

EVENTS ON THE GRAPH

You can opt to Show All events on the graph or only Annual, One-Time events. If you're looking at a long date range, such as a year, choosing annual events probably is better, so that the graph doesn't get too busy. You will still get a fairly accurate forecast. To see all the known regularly scheduled events in your accounts, select Show All.

INCOME ITEMS

The monthly average for income is displayed for you. This figure is used for forecasting. If you click the Income Items button, the Forecast Income Items dialog box displays (Figure 11-7).

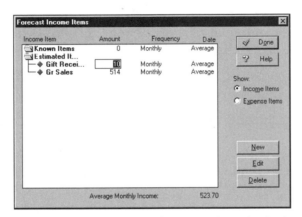

Figure 11-7 Manipulate the income items in the forecast to see the results of the changes.

You can create, edit, or delete income items. The changes you make are only for the forecast and don't affect your real Quicken transactions.

CREATING A NEW INCOME ITEM FOR THE FORECAST
To put another income item into the forecast's calculations, follow these steps:

1. Click New to display the Create New Income Item dialog box (Figure 11-8).

2. Enter a description of the item.

3. Enter the amount (click the Calculator icon if you need to perform any calculations to reach the amount).

4. Enter the frequency for this item. Click the arrow to see a drop-down list and then select a frequency. The choices range from Only Once to Weekly, with several choices in between.

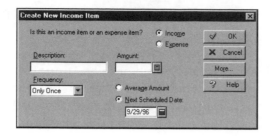

Figure 11-8 Create a new income item to change the forecasting calculations without really entering anything in your Quicken file.

5. Select Average Amount to create an estimated item. This means the item will be considered an average amount spread out over the period of time you selected in the Frequency field.

6. Select Next Scheduled Date to create an item that is forecasted on the date you enter.

7. Click More to open a category dialog box so that you can enter a category for the new item (this step is optional because the item is a forecast, not a real transaction).

8. Click OK when you're finished. Quicken returns you to the Forecast Income Items dialog box.

If this new item is the only thing you want to add to the forecast, click Done.

EDITING AN INCOME ITEM

You can change an existing income item to see the effect on the forecast:

1. Select the item you want to change.

2. Click Edit to see the Edit Income Item dialog box (Figure 11-9).

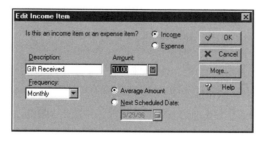

Figure 11-9 Make any changes you want to this income item to see how they affect the forecast.

3. Make changes to any of the fields and then click OK to return to the Forecast Income Items dialog box.

The changes you make are for the purposes of forecasting; you're not changing your real Quicken transactions. If you're finished working on income items for the forecast, click Done.

DELETING AN INCOME ITEM

If you want to remove an income item from the forecast calculations, select it and click Delete. You're not deleting the item from your transactions, only from the forecast calculations.

EXPENSE ITEMS

From the Forecasting window, you can click the Expense Items button to add, edit, or delete expense items. The processes are exactly the same as those described for income items. Remember that you're not changing your transaction records — you're only changing the figures that the forecasting feature uses.

FUTURE FINANCIAL EVENTS

Directly below the graph is a line (above it is the instruction to click the line to add a new financial event). If you click that line, the same dialog box appears as just described for creating new income or expense items. Fill out the dialog box as described earlier.

Saving the new scenario

Once you have changed anything in the scenario, you can save it. Choose Scenario from the button bar to bring up the Manage Forecast Scenarios dialog box (Figure 11-10).

To save a forecast with any scenario, follow these steps:

1. Select New.

2. Enter a name for the new scenario.

3. Click OK.

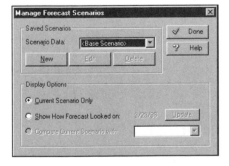

Figure 11-10 You can save a forecast with any scenario.

    You can continue to add items, delete items, or make any other changes you want. You can repeat the preceding steps to save the forecast configuration every time you complete the desired changes.

Changing Forecasting Data

You can change the way data is used in a forecast without adding or deleting any items. The most significant change you can make is to switch between forecasting from known items to estimated items. This section discusses changing from known to estimated items and vice versa. (See "Understanding Forecasts" earlier in this chapter to refresh your memory on the difference between known and estimated items.)

Looking at known items

When you use known items, your forecast graph is a little bumpier because no averaging takes place to smooth things out. Sometimes that may be a good way to look at a forecast. For example, you can add a couple of known items (some financial events that you expect to take place) to the Base Scenario and save the forecast. The Forecasting window for that forecast has an additional element. There is a marker for every known item (Figure 11-11).

You should note two things about markers for known items:

* The markers are color-coded (which Figure 11-11 doesn't show, of course) so that income items are green and expense items are red.

* If a known item is anything except a one-time item, a marker is placed for each time it occurs. Monthly items have a marker every month, weekly items have four markers under each month's date, and so on.

Click a marker to see information about it (Figure 11-12). Click the New, Edit, or Delete button to make a change.

Click a marker for details about it

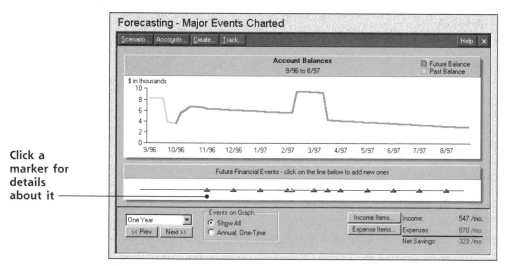

Figure 11-11 A forecasting graph with known items has markers for the items.

Add another known item to scenario — | — Change any detail for this item

Click to remove item

Figure 11-12 Information about a known item is available with a click of the mouse.

Changing between estimated and known items

There are times when you want to see known items in a forecast so that you can tell where your peaks and valleys are in bank balances. For other forecasts (created for other reasons), you will want to use estimated items to get a broader look at the long term.

A fast way to change the type of forecast is to switch between known and estimated items in a current forecast instead of creating a new forecast from scratch. Then just save the forecast with the switched item types as a new forecast. (For the following example, I change expense items, but you use the exact same procedures for income items.)

To change an estimated item to a known item, follow these steps:

1. In the Forecasting window, click the Expense Item button to bring up the Forecast Expense Items dialog box (Figure 11-13).

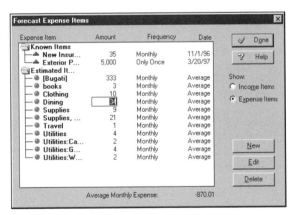

Figure 11-13 Known and estimated expenses are displayed separately.

2. Select the amount of the item you want to change.

3. Click Edit. The Edit Expense Item dialog box displays (Figure 11-14).

4. Click the Next Scheduled Date button and specify the next date for which you will incur this expense.

5. Select a frequency for this expense by clicking the arrow and selecting an interval (choose from One-Time, Weekly, Monthly, and so on).

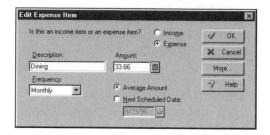

Figure 11-14 Change the frequency and specify a next scheduled date to switch this item to a known item.

6. Click OK to return to the Forecast Expense Items dialog box.

7. Repeat the steps for any other expenses you want to change to known items.

8. Click Done when you're finished.

You can, of course, reverse this process and change known items to estimated items. Just select Average Amount in the Edit Expense Item dialog box.

Comparing Forecasts

Once you've created several scenarios, you can compare the way your balances look between any two of them:

1. Display one of the scenarios.

2. Click the Scenario button to bring up the Manage Forecast Scenarios dialog box, and pick a scenario to compare with the one displayed in the Forecasting window.

3. In the Display Options section, select Compare Current Scenario with.

4. Click the arrow to the right of the field and choose a scenario for this comparison.

5. Click Done.

The window displays a graph that shows both scenarios (Figure 11-15).

You can also compare a scenario that you've changed (either once or several times) to the way it looked before you made those changes. Just choose Show How Forecast Looked on and specify a date. The graph lines show your projected account balances with the current configuration and the projected account balances with a new configuration that takes into consideration the date you specified.

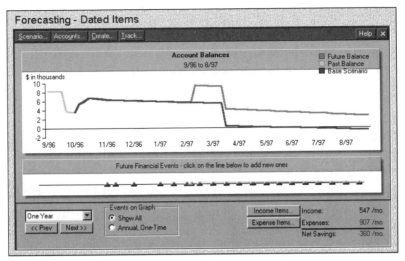

Figure 11-15 The projection lines in this forecast graph are color-coded to indicate which scenario is which.

BONUS

One of the best uses of forecasting is to help plan for future expenses, especially if those expenses are extremely high.

Planning for major expense

You may be worrying about paying for college for your children. Or perhaps you need to pay for a wedding.

You can create a forecast that lets you know what your bank balances will be in the future, given certain known facts. When you make your first forecast, it reflects your current situation. If you're putting a certain amount of money into a savings account every week or every month and you're not withdrawing money from that account, the forecast shows you the account's balance in the future. Then you can create a forecast that lets you know what your bank balances will be if you change your saving scheme or change your spending habits.

When you make income and expense changes in the forecast, those changes don't affect your real transactions, so you can safely play around with the numbers. This is called playing "what if" games. What if you stopped eating out three times a month and only treated yourself to a restaurant twice a month?

What if you put an additional $25 into the savings account and also stopped eating out?

As you create each scenario, you can name and save it and then compare it against other scenarios you've created.

Planning for retirement

You can create a forecast to help you plan for your retirement. Your income will probably change after your retirement, but so will your expenses. This situation is ideal for forecasting.

Set up your income based on what you expect to receive from Social Security and pensions. Set up your expenses based on the changes you anticipate. If you're spending a great deal of money on family health insurance premiums, after your retire, you will reduce that expenditure as you only need to purchase medi-gap insurance.

Then create different scenarios to see what happens if you sell your house and pay rent or decide to travel now that you don't have to go to work every day.

Summary

The capability to project account balances and see the flow of cash in and out of your accounts is especially useful if you're trying to figure out when you can afford a major expense (or if you can ever afford it). This is one way to see a graphical estimate of your cash flow under a variety of circumstances.

CHAPTER TWELVE

PLANNING FOR FUTURE CASH NEEDS

IN THIS CHAPTER YOU LEARN THESE KEY SKILLS:

UNDERSTANDING QUICKEN'S PLANNING FEATURES
PAGE 216

PLANNING FOR COLLEGE   PAGE 218

PLANNING FOR RETIREMENT   PAGE 223

PLANNING FOR OTHER LARGE EXPENSES   PAGE 228

12

P icture this: you're spending a quiet evening at home watching television, and your family wanders into the family room to join you. As she takes a seat, your daughter announces she's decided to apply to the best colleges in the country to ensure that she'll get into medical school. You see dollar signs floating in the air in front of the TV screen. Your son enters the room proclaiming he's decided to become a rocket scientist. More dollar signs float past. Your spouse sits on the couch next to you and, during the next commercial, starts talking about the vacation home that the two of you should get after retirement, where you can relax in between trips to Europe.

Think you'll be ready to write those checks when the time comes? Not without some good planning. Even with good planning, you will probably have to get some loans, make some sacrifices, and suffer through some cold sweating in the middle of the night. But you have no chance of making any of this happen without getting a good handle on your resources and planning for major expenditures. Luckily, Quicken has features that can help you with this process.

WEB PATH ➡ Watch for the "Best of the Web" buttons in the Planners discussed in this chapter.

Understanding Quicken's Planning Features

Quicken comes with several built-in tools to help you plan your financial future. Some of these features let you jump from a software window to relevant pages of expert advice that you can display on your screen. Others are programs that ask you to enter information and then help you use that information to plan ahead.

Although this chapter won't cover all the available planning topics, I cover a couple of major events: planning for college and planning for retirement (the two most common financial traumas). What you learn about using Quicken to plan for these events you can apply to all other topics in Quicken's planning features.

Expert advice

Your Quicken CD-ROM is filled with financial advice. Three well-regarded experts have contributed to files that you can access with a click of the mouse:

* *Jane Bryant Quinn* is a well-known financial columnist for many magazines and newspapers.
* *Marshall Loeb* has given advice to millions through magazines, radio commentary, and books.
* *Eric Tyson* is a critically acclaimed writer and lecturer.

The advice from these experts is specific and to the point. You will be able to read the text and listen to the advice (assuming that you have a sound card and speakers attached to your computer).

To get advice on planning, click Advice and select Planning & Prioritizing or Life Events. Pick a topic and then move through the other topics and examples by clicking the linked text (green text is linked to another advice page) or by clicking the More Topics button. Figure 12-1 shows a typical advice window.

TIP If you're using Quicken in Windows 3.*x*, your screen looks a bit different, but the information is all there.

The topics in Planning & Prioritizing include the following:

* Retirement planning
* College planning
* Your savings plan
* Planning for emergencies
* Managing loans & debt

* Using planning resources
* Prioritizing

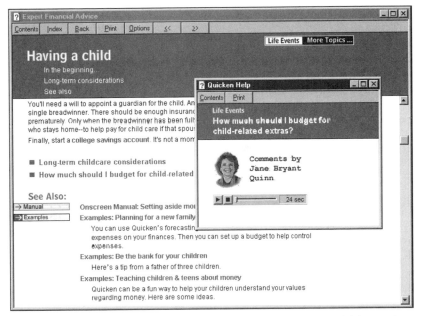

Figure 12-1 Advice from A to Z about a financial topic is available anytime.

The topics in Life Events include the following:

* Marriage
* Having a child
* Getting a divorce
* Financial responsibility for aging parents

Prioritizing your goals

One area with which Quicken can help you is setting up priorities. Prioritizing is jargon for "What am I willing to give up to get something else?" You will find this much easier to do if you have an expert kick off your thinking process for you.

To see what the experts have to say, follow these steps:

1. Select Advice.

2. Choose Planning & Prioritizing.

3. Select Prioritizing from the Chapter Topics list.

4. After the Prioritizing advice window appears, pick a topic (Figure 12-2).

TIP If you're using Quicken in Windows 3.*x*, your screen looks a bit different, but the information is all there.

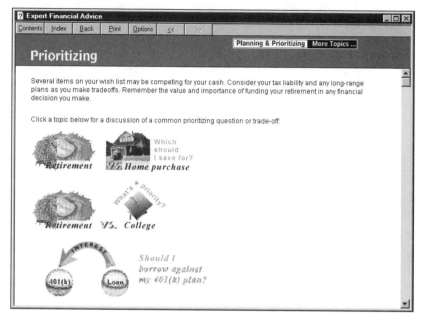

Figure 12-2   Decisions, decisions. Let an expert help.

Planning for College

As expensive as you might think it is to raise children, you ain't seen nothin' yet. A college education could cost you more money than the total you spent on that child from birth through high school graduation. Most of us have no way to meet the expense of college without a great deal of planning. Quicken's built-in college planning can assist.

To use Quicken's built-in college planning feature, follow these steps:

1. Place your pointer on the Planning icon in the Activity Bar to pop up the Planning menu.

2. Select Use Financial Planning Calculators to see the Financial Planners dialog box that features the five Quicken planners (Figure 12-3).

3. For this discussion, select College and then click OK.

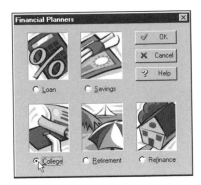

Figure 12-3 Quicken offers plenty of help when you need to plan for one of these financial goals.

Filling in the planning calculator

To start planning, Quicken provides a College Planner that acts as a calculator (Figure 12-4).

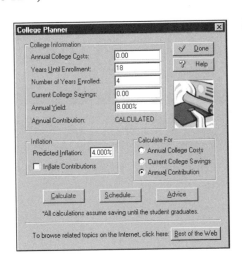

Figure 12-4 The College Planner calculates the total you need by taking the information you have and filling in the blanks.

The interesting thing about the College Planner is that it's willing to work with you and changes the way it works to do so. You tell it what you know and it returns the answer for the item you don't know. If you know what you can afford to contribute, it tells you what the cost will be on top of that contribution. If you know the cost, it tells you how much you have to be prepared to contribute.

DECIDING THE CALCULATION TYPE

The first thing to do is to tell the College Planner how you want it to calculate the figures. You do this in the Calculate For section of the dialog box:

* If you know how much you'll be able to contribute each year and have already begun saving for college, select Annual College Costs to have Quicken tell you the college expense you can afford (then you can pick a school that comes close).

* If you know the annual cost of the college and you know how much you can contribute from your income, select Current College Savings to have Quicken tell you how much you have to save to make up the difference.

* If you know the cost and you have begun saving, select Annual Contribution to have Quicken tell you how much additional money you will have to find each year.

FILLING IN THE BASIC FIGURES

Now you can begin filling in the basic college information (the fields that are blank change depending on the choice you made in the Calculate For section of the dialog box). Press Tab to move from field to field as you fill in these amounts:

1. If the Annual College Costs field is blank, fill in that number. Don't know? Can't guess? Click Advice to see some helpful information (Figure 12-5).

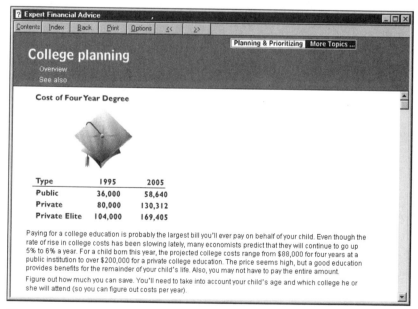

Figure 12-5 The experts have done some research for you — divide the totals by four to estimate the annual cost.

TIP If you're using Quicken in Windows 3.x, your advice screen looks a bit different, but the functions are the same.

2. The Years Until Enrollment field is your ticking time bomb — how many years away is freshman orientation camp for your child? You can assume the child will be 18-years-old at the time, so do the math.

3. The Number of Years Enrolled figure depends on your child's ambitions, unless the child is very young, in which case it depends on your ambitions. An associate degree is two years, a standard undergraduate degree is four years, and you can add on as many years as you think this child will need if you're planning on graduate school.

4. Your current college savings should be entered if it's blank, and that means as of today.

5. Annual Yield is the earning rate for the money you're saving. If you've put that money into a bank savings account, enter that figure (and then talk to an investment advisor about moving it into something more aggressive). If the money is in a fund, enter the average yield you've had for that fund. If the money is split among varying investment objects, enter an average yield.

6. Annual Contribution, if it's blank, is the place to announce how much you'll be able to contribute each year.

ADJUSTING FOR INFLATION

In the Inflation section of the dialog box, fill in the predicted inflation. This is a guess about the yearly inflation rate for the cost of college (which has been larger than the general inflation rate for many years). Quicken assumes 4 percent, but you should check the newspapers and financial magazines to get a figure. You don't have to enter the percent sign. If you assume that you'll have to adjust your yearly contribution to keep up with the inflation rate, select Inflate Contributions.

Viewing the calculated figure

As you enter each figure and press Tab to move on, the College Planner calculates the missing ingredient for you. The calculated figure continues to change as you enter information (Figure 12-6).

TIP   If you fill in a field and want to play "what if," instead of pressing Tab, click Calculate to see the current calculated figure. Then make changes and try again.

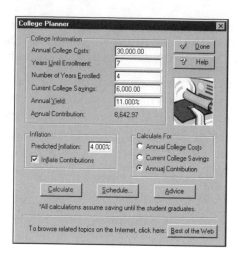

Figure 12-6 Based on the information given, the calculated contribution for this family is more than $8,600 a year.

Viewing your schedule

Whatever the amount of the calculated figure for which you asked, Quicken tells you how to reach it. Select Schedule to see what you have to do. For example, as Figure 12-7 shows, an 11-year schedule is needed when 7 years remain until enrollment at a 4-year college. Once enrollment begins, both deposits and tuition payments are scheduled. You can print the schedule by clicking the Print button on the button bar.

Year	Deposit	Tuition	Balance
0	0.00	0.00	6,000.00
1996	8,642.97	0.00	15,302.97
1997	8,988.69	0.00	25,974.99
1998	9,348.24	0.00	38,180.47
1999	9,722.17	0.00	52,102.49
2000	10,111.05	0.00	67,944.81
2001	10,515.49	0.00	85,934.24
2002	10,936.11	0.00	106,323.12
2003	11,373.56	39,477.95	85,571.69
2004	11,828.50	41,057.07	61,239.73
2005	12,301.64	42,699.35	32,881.46
2006	11,525.87	44,407.33	0.00

Figure 12-7 This is the schedule for a calculated contribution.

Dialing out for dollars

At the bottom of the College Planner dialog box is a Best of the Web button. Click it to find out where on the Internet you can go to get information about funding college education (Quicken warns you that clicking this button closes the College Planner and asks you to say it's OK).

The Quicken Live window opens to help you prepare for your trip to the World Wide Web (Figure 12-8). Scroll through the window to find the Web site that looks most helpful.

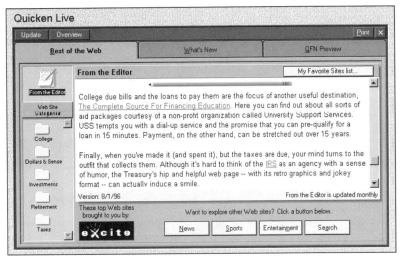

Figure 12-8 Plenty of information about Web sites is available before your modem dials out, to make it faster and easier to navigate once you're on the Internet.

Click From the Editor to go to the From the Editor section, which offers general advice about discovering financial info on the Web. Click a folder to see Web sites specific to the Quicken planning categories. Click My Favorite Sites list to add a current site and reach it again with one-click access.

Now that you have all the information, all you have to do is figure out how to come up with the money.

Planning for Retirement

Similar to the planning process for college, the retirement planning you can do with Quicken consists of entering the information you know (or the information you have some control over) and letting Quicken calculate the unknown. It starts with the Retirement Planner:

1. Place your pointer on the Planning icon in the Activity Bar to see the pop-up menu.

2. Select Use Financial Planning Calculators .

3. Select Retirement from the Financial Planners dialog box.

Filling in the planning calculator

The Retirement Planner that appears when you select this option has a number of fields to fill out and also provides several choices for the calculation you want Quicken to make (Figure 12-9).

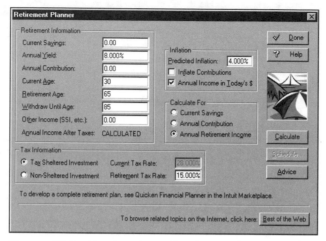

Figure 12-9   You can play "what if" games to determine the best route to a comfortable retirement.

The most important thing about the Retirement Planner is that it is tied into a retirement investment, such as a 401(k), an IRA, or another similar tax-deferred investment. If you have multiple retirement investment accounts, you must run the Retirement Planner calculation process separately for each one.

DECIDING THE CALCULATION TYPE

For the Retirement Planner, the choices for calculation are as follows:

* Current Savings, which tells Quicken to calculate what money you should have put away, given your annual contribution and the annual retirement income you expect.

* Annual Contribution, which tells Quicken to calculate how much you have to contribute to your retirement account, given your current savings and the amount of annual retirement income you expect.

* Annual Retirement Income, which asks Quicken to calculate what you should expect, given your savings and annual contribution to this investment.

FILLING IN THE BASIC FIGURES

Once you've decided on the calculation you need, begin filling out the planning calculator:

1. In Current Savings, enter the amount of money already in this investment.

2. In Annual Yield, enter the interest rate you're getting for this investment.

3. In Annual Contribution, enter the amount you will contribute to this investment each year.

4. In Current Age, enter your age, as of today.

5. In Retirement Age, enter the age at which you expect to retire.

6. In Withdraw Until Age, enter the age you think you'll be when you stop withdrawing the money from this investment.

TIP **The Withdraw Until Age field is, of course, asking you to guess how long you'll live. To make sure that you've covered all bases and don't end up outliving your money, enter a large number in this field. Assume that you will be healthy and will outlive everybody and everything (including your capital).**

7. In Other Income, enter any Social Security payments you expect to receive when you retire. Use the annual figure, not the amount of the monthly check.

8. In Annual Income After Taxes, enter the annual amount you expect (or would like) to receive from your investment when you retire.

WHAT'S THE TAX STATUS OF THE INVESTMENT?

In the Tax Information section of the planner, identify the investment's tax status and tax consequences to you:

* If this investment is a true pension investment, select Tax Sheltered. If you have an IRA or a Keogh investment, these are both tax-sheltered.

* If you have a standard, non-pension investment you're using to build capital and income for your retirement, select Non-Sheltered Investment.

* In Current Tax Rate, enter your tax rate for your current income.

* In Retirement Tax Rate, enter the tax rate you expect to apply when you retire.

ADJUSTING FOR INFLATION

You should let Quicken adjust the figures for the effects of inflation during the calculation, so fill in the optional Inflation section of the planner just to be safe:

* Predicted Inflation is assumed to be 4 percent. If you have information or instincts telling you that you should change that figure, enter your figure (you don't have to enter the percent sign).

* Select Inflate Contributions to calculate your contributions with an increase assumed every year because of the inflation rate you entered.

* Select Annual Income in Today's $ if you want Quicken to calculate your retirement checks in the face of the inflation rate you entered. Because that will lessen the power of your retirement dollars, considering inflation means the amount calculated for your income will be less than if you didn't take inflation into consideration. Clear the selection box to calculate retirement income without taking the eroding effects of inflation into consideration.

Viewing the bottom line

As you enter figures and press Tab to move to the next field, the calculated field changes to reflect the figures (Figure 12-10).

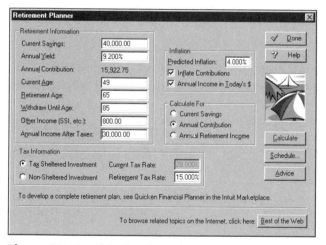

Figure 12-10 This planning calculation was for the annual contribution needed to meet the goals entered.

Now you know what the goal is. Remember that you can play "what if" and change some figures to see the effect on the calculated field.

Viewing your schedule

Once you've established the figures so they seem accurate and reasonable, you can determine what it's going to take to get where you want to go. Select Schedule to see what you have to do (Figure 12-11). Remember that you can always go back and change some of your expectations to change the calculation and see a new schedule.

Age	Deposit	Income	Balance
60	24,512.34	0.00	505,175.00
61	25,492.84	0.00	577,143.94
62	26,512.55	0.00	656,753.73
63	27,573.05	0.00	744,748.13
64	28,675.97	0.00	841,940.93
65	0.00	64,342.41	849,137.58
66	0.00	66,916.11	854,185.84
67	0.00	69,592.76	856,775.65
68	0.00	72,376.47	856,563.91
69	0.00	75,271.52	853,171.28
70	0.00	78,282.39	846,178.67
71	0.00	81,413.68	835,123.37

Figure 12-11 The deposits that have to be made go on for years before the income is collected, so I scrolled through the schedule to see some good news.

Internet info

To learn about some of the helpful sites on the Internet, click the Best of the Web button and click the Retirement folder. Check out the topics and note the Web sites you think would be helpful (Figure 12-12).

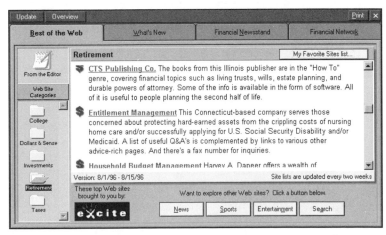

Figure 12-12 There's more to a peaceful retirement than collecting pension checks, and help is available on the Web for all the plans you have to make.

Calculating other pensions

If you have other pension investments, repeat the process for each of them. This way, you know just how much you have to plan on investing or can count on receiving (depending on the calculation you asked Quicken to do).

TIP If you have multiple pension investments, don't use the same figures in your entries as somebody with one pension. If you want to end up with $30,000 in income, don't ask each pension to provide that. Instead, go for proportionate goals. If one pension investment account is approximately a third of the other, use that ratio as you work.

Planning for Other Large Expenses

S everal other Financial Planning Calculators are available from the Planning icon on the Activity Bar. The process you use is similar to those for the two common planners described in this chapter.

Loan Planner

You can use the Loan Planner to come up with a manageable debt strategy. The planner lets you choose whether you want to calculate the amount of the loan you can handle or the size of the payments (Figure 12-13).

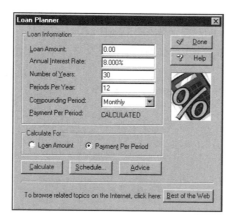

Figure 12-13 Enter the figures and let Quicken calculate the unanswered question.

The Loan Planner is an excellent "what if" tool. If you're thinking about buying something that has to be paid off (perhaps a car or a vacation), run the facts through the planner first.

Refinance Planner

Interest rates down? Lots of equity in your house, and you're ready for a pocketful of cash in exchange for some of it? Whatever the reason, when you're ready to refinance your mortgage, get a handle on the real savings and real costs. Select the Refinance Planner to work out the numbers and have Quicken calculate the answers you need (Figure 12-14).

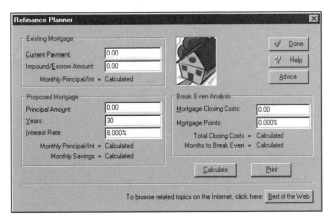

Figure 12-14 There's no sense in refinancing if you're not going to break even before you move.

Remember that the point of refinancing isn't to lower the interest rate of your mortgage, it's to save money in the long run. If settlement costs, points, and other expenditures add up to a hefty figure, you may not really save money.

Savings Planner

Great! You've decided to put money into some form of savings or investment account on a regular basis. What do you want to know about the results? Quicken can calculate a regular contribution to get you to your goal or let you know how much you'll have if you make your own decision about the size and interval of the contribution (Figure 12-15). Treating savings as if it were a bill that must be paid regularly is the best approach for attaining real growth.

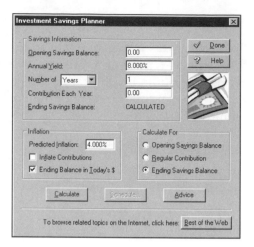

Figure 12-15 Investing for the sheer purpose of ending up with a bundle of cash is a worthwhile goal, and Quicken can help you calculate the results.

BONUS

Planning for the future and planning for large cash expenditures is the intelligent approach to handling your money. But life doesn't always work the way we plan it.

Dealing with emergencies

The best way to handle an emergency is to decide how much of your money can be applied against it. But if you don't have a great deal of money to spare, you have to take emergency measures:

* Plan for emergencies by budgeting for them. Have a budget that includes keeping a decent amount of cash in a liquid investment.

* Before borrowing, check the interest rate against the money you'd lose by liquidating one of your assets. Sometimes borrowing is smarter; sometimes liquidating is the better choice.

* See if you can borrow against your pension. If you can borrow against it, make sure that it doesn't cost you an enormous tax bite. If it does, it might be cheaper to take a bank loan.

* Borrow money from relatives.

Using financial advisors

Plenty of expert advisors are around that you can seek out for counseling. Do some homework first, however, by asking friends and relatives about their experiences. Advisors use several different payment methods.

Most advisors work on commission and make their money by selling you investment vehicles. If they're good, reliable, trustworthy advisors, you'll probably be able to choose from a wide variety of products.

Some advisors charge a fee based on a percentage of the money they handle for you. These advisors are really money managers, and they invest your funds. Some advisors charge an hourly fee for their professional services, which include going over your finances and making recommendations.

Quicken Financial Planner

Apart from all the nifty planning calculators discussed in this chapter, Quicken has a full-featured Financial Planner available for a very low price. The software is available on the Internet Intuit Marketplace.

Summary

All the Quicken financial planning calculators operate similarly. The information you have to enter and the specific calculations Quicken performs may differ from subject to subject, but the premise is the same.

But planning is more than just handling your money intelligently. It's even more than making your money grow. Good planning means you understand that emergencies arise and that carefully made plans for regular savings blow up occasionally.

CHAPTER THIRTEEN

PREPARING FOR TAXES

IN THIS CHAPTER YOU LEARN THESE KEY SKILLS:

SETTING UP YOUR SYSTEM FOR TAXES   PAGE 233

ENTERING SPECIAL TRANSACTIONS FOR TAX PURPOSES
    PAGE 236

CREATING TAX REPORTS   PAGE 237

TRANSFERRING TAX DATA TO TAX PREPARATION
    SOFTWARE   PAGE 240

FINDING MORE TAX DEDUCTIONS   PAGE 241

The Ides of April — tax day. It won't be the nerve-wracking experience it was before you began using Quicken. You can identify all the categories that have tax implications and get reports on them for your tax preparer (or yourself, if you do your own taxes). Even better, you can send all that information to a tax preparation software application and have the forms filled out automatically, using the information from your Quicken files.

It doesn't happen by magic, however, and you have to do a little bit of work. But it's not hard. The end result is that you won't spend all those nights at the dining room table with piles of paper, adding up long columns of numbers on an adding machine.

Setting Up Your System for Taxes

The secret to having a Quicken system ready for tax preparation is to use *categories* for tax links. You already know about categories, and you're probably assigning every expense to a category. But categories can fill two roles for you: They can point to tax-related information in addition to assigning your transactions to a category type.

Designating appropriate categories as tax-related is easy. In fact, some categories that Quicken provided for you are already linked to tax preparation. You can add the tax link to any categories you created yourself or to any that Quicken provided that fit your particular circumstances.

If you're using Quicken for business transactions, the tax-related information is extremely important, because you get tax deductions for many expenses that aren't deductible for individuals.

Linking categories to tax forms

Creating the link between a category and its tax form is quite simple:

1. Open the Category & Transfer List. Notice that categories that have a tax link are marked with the word *tax* in the Tax column (Figure 13-1).

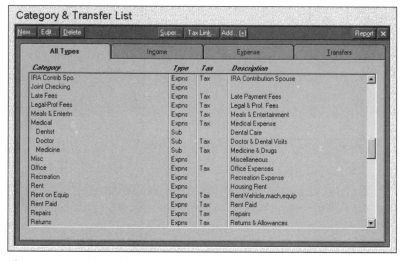

Figure 13-1 Identifying the categories that have tax links already is easy.

2. Select the category for which you want to create a tax link.

3. Click Edit from the button bar. The Edit Category dialog box appears (Figure 13-2).

4. Click the check box titled Tax-related. This tells Quicken that the category is tax-related.

5. Click the arrow to the right of the Form box to see a listing of tax forms and select the one that matches this category (Figure 13-3).

6. Click OK to finish the edit and link the category to your tax return.

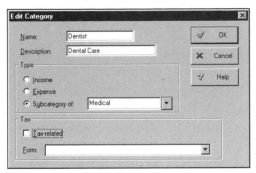

Figure 13-2 For an existing category, use Edit to add a tax link.

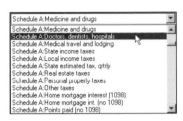

Figure 13-3 Select the appropriate IRS form for this tax category.

TIP Although you're not required to link a category to a specific tax form, doing so is certainly advantageous. If the correct form choice for the category is obvious (or if your accountant has provided that information), you should create the link, especially if you're planning to transfer your Quicken data to a tax preparation program.

Linking categories to tax form lines

Not only can you link a category to a specific tax form to make your tax preparation tasks faster, in most cases you can even designate the line number in the form. You'll be required to do this if you're going to use tax preparation software. The task is almost as necessary if you prepare your own taxes. Once you know the line number, you just take the total for any category and transfer it to the right line.

To create the link to a specific line on a tax form, follow these steps:

1. From the Category & Transfer List, click Tax Link from the button bar to launch the Tax Link Assistant dialog box (Figure 13-4).

2. Select a category that needs a line assignment from the Category column.

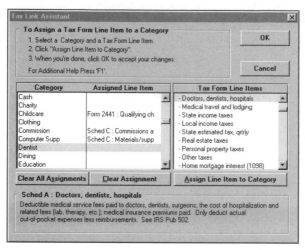

Figure 13-4 Use the Tax Link Assistant to assign a category to a specific line in a tax form.

3. Scroll through the Tax Form Line Items to find and select the appropriate form and line.

4. Click Assign Line Item to Category.

5. Repeat the process for every category that needs a line assignment.

6. Click OK when you're finished.

Entering Special Transactions for Tax Purposes

Some transactions are directly related to taxes that you'll want to track. These are mainly checks written to pay taxes over and above the taxes deducted from your paycheck.

Paying estimated taxes

If you have to send estimated tax payments to the federal or state government, create a new category for each of them:

* For federal taxes, mark the category as tax-related and assign it to Schedule 1040:Fed. Estimated Tax.

* For state taxes, mark the category as tax-related and assign it to Schedule A:State Estimated Tax.

Entering investment data

If you haven't been tracking your investment accounts in Quicken, you should enter all the tax-related information to get complete tax reports:

* Enter all dividend income in the category _DivInc.

* Enter investment interest income in the category _IntInc.

* Enter any long-term, capital gain distributions in the category _LT CapGnDst.

* Enter any short-term, capital gain distributions in the category _ST CapGnDst

You can get all the information you need for these entries from the mail you receive from your broker or the investment itself. Usually you won't have to go through every month's mail and put it together, because an end-of-year statement should summarize your tax liability.

Creating Tax Reports

Quicken provides reports that let you see all the data on tax-related transactions. The reports you run depend on what you're going to do with the information in the report. If you need information for your accountant, a report that summarizes tax-related transactions is probably sufficient. If you're going to prepare your own taxes (either manually or with tax preparation software), you need a more detailed report that helps you put totals on the right forms.

Tax Summary Report

The Quicken Tax Summary Report shows the totals for all your tax-related transactions. To produce this report, follow these steps:

1. From the menu bar, select Reports → Home → Tax Summary .

2. The Create Report dialog box appears with the Tax Summary Report selected (Figure 13-5).

3. Select Create to display the Tax Summary Report on your screen (Figure 13-6).

4. Scroll through the report to see all the lines. If anything appears that shouldn't be there, go to the account register and change the transaction so it isn't tax-related.

5. Click Print to get a hard copy of this report.

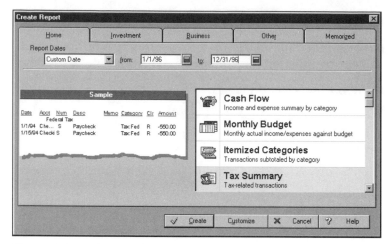

Figure 13-5 The Tax Summary Report is preconfigured to summarize all your tax-related transactions.

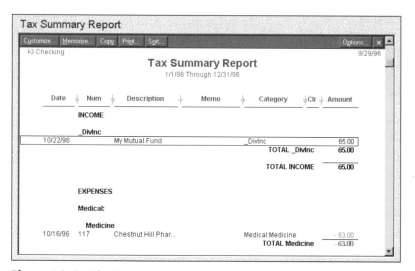

Figure 13-6 The Tax Summary Report displays all the pertinent transactions, with subtotals for each category.

The Tax Summary Report does not include tax-deferred account transactions such as your pension or IRA accounts.

Tax Schedule Report

The Quicken Tax Schedule Report lists all tax-related transactions for categories that have been assigned to tax-form line items. To produce this report, follow these steps:

1. From the Quicken menu, select [**Reports**] → [**Home**] → [**Tax Schedule**].

2. The Create Report dialog box displays with the Tax Schedule Report selected.

3. Select Create to display the report on your screen (Figure 13-7).

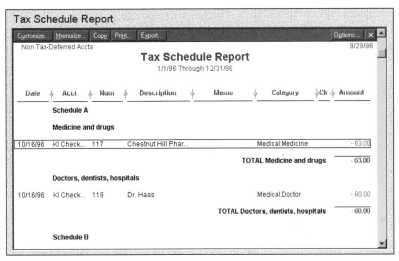

Figure 13-7 The Tax Schedule Report sorts transactions according to the tax form you need for the categories.

4. Scroll through the list to be sure that everything listed is appropriate. You can add or delete transactions in the account register and re-run this report if you need to make corrections.

5. Click Print to make a hard copy of this report.

The Tax Schedule Report is sorted by IRS form name, and it totals the transactions for each category within that form.

Capital Gains Report

The Quicken Capital Gains Report is another preconfigured report that is handy for tax time. The report, however, is only as good as the data you've entered into your Quicken system. To get an accurate report, you have to make sure that you enter all the data about your investment. You have to track the dates you bought shares and the cost of those shares. You also have to track the dates you sold those same shares and the price you received for them. Also, make sure that you've entered any fees. To produce the Capital Gains Report, follow these steps:

1. From the Quicken menu, select ⬛ Reports → ⬛ Investment → ⬛ Capital Gains .

2. The Create Report dialog box appears with the Capital Gains Report selected.

3. Select Create to see the report (Figure 13-8).

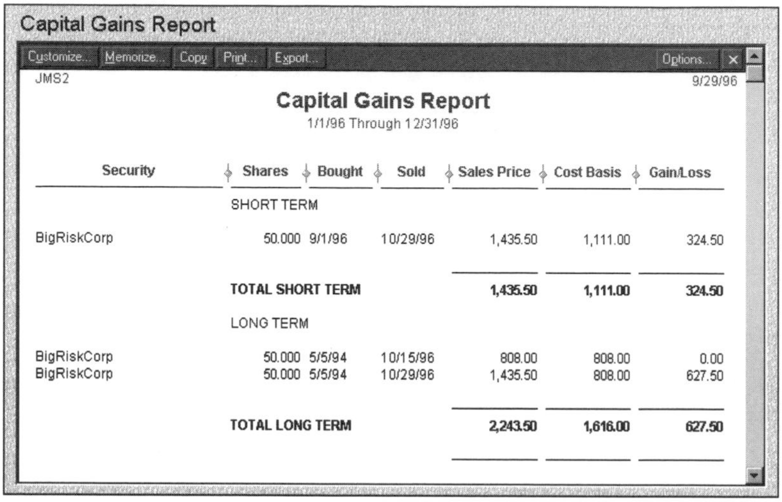

Security	Shares	Bought	Sold	Sales Price	Cost Basis	Gain/Loss
	SHORT TERM					
BigRiskCorp	50.000	9/1/96	10/29/96	1,435.50	1,111.00	324.50
	TOTAL SHORT TERM			1,435.50	1,111.00	324.50
	LONG TERM					
BigRiskCorp	50.000	5/5/94	10/15/96	808.00	808.00	0.00
BigRiskCorp	50.000	5/5/94	10/29/96	1,435.50	808.00	627.50
	TOTAL LONG TERM			2,243.50	1,616.00	627.50

Figure 13-8 The capital gains, both short-term and long-term, are summarized for you for all stocks sold this year.

4. Click Print to get a hard copy of the report.

The Capital Gains Report lists (and totals) short-term and long-term gains separately. When you sold stocks, if you didn't indicate the specific lot (if you'd purchased the stock at different times), the report assumes that you sold the oldest purchase first.

Transferring Tax Data to Tax Preparation Software

If you're using a tax preparation application to prepare your taxes, you can send data from your Quicken files directly to the tax software. The file format for the exported data is TXF (Tax Exchange Format), which is used by most popular tax preparation applications.

If you use Turbo Tax for Windows (from Intuit, the same people who bring you Quicken), you don't have to export your files. Turbo Tax for Windows will find and import the data for you.

The reports that can be exported and used in tax preparation are as follows:

* Tax Schedule Report
* Capital Gains Report

To export either report, follow these steps:

1. Create the report as described previously.

2. Select Export from the button bar to bring up the Create Tax Export File dialog box (Figure 13-9).

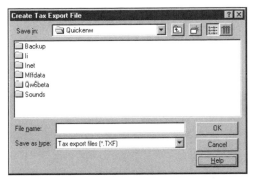

Figure 13-9   Choose a location and name for your tax data export file.

3. By default, the export file is saved in the Quickenw folder. You can change this if you want (you may want to save it to a floppy disk).

4. In the File name field, enter a name for this file (Quicken adds the extension .TXF automatically).

5. Click OK to export the file.

If you have both a Tax Schedule Report and a Capital Gains Report, you must export each of them separately, using distinct filenames.

Finding More Tax Deductions

Quicken has a feature that lets you know if you have something that may be a tax deduction that you hadn't realized was available to you. You answer questions (easy questions — don't worry, this isn't a test), and the answers help Quicken find these hidden deductions. This feature is called the Tax Deduction Finder.

Here's how to use it:

1. Put the pointer over the Planning icon in the Activity Bar to bring up the menu.

2. Select **Identify Possible Tax Deductions**.

3. Read the brief introduction (it tells you you're going to answer some simple questions) and click OK.

4. When the Deduction Finder window appears, the Deductions tab is in the foreground, and you can begin answering questions (Figure 13-10).

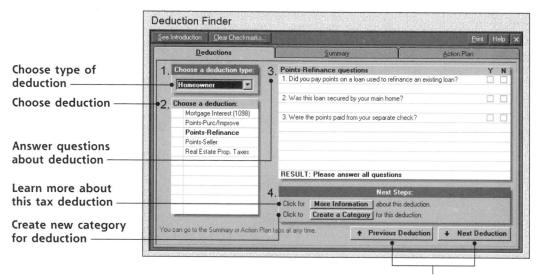

Choose type of deduction

Choose deduction

Answer questions about deduction

Learn more about this tax deduction

Create new category for deduction

Move to previous or next deduction for deduction type

Figure 13-10   A simple quiz can save you a lot of tax dollars.

5. Click the down arrow to the right of section 1 (the deduction box) to select a type of deduction with which to work.

6. In section 2, select a deduction on which you want to work.

7. In section 3, choose Yes or No for each question. Based on your answers, Quicken makes a decision.

8. If a green check mark appears next to the selected deduction, you probably have a tax deduction.

9. If a red X appears next to the selected deduction, sorry, there's no deduction.

10. If you're not sure about a deduction, click More Information to see some helpful hints about how this deduction works (Figure 13-11).

11. If you're eligible to take this deduction, you have to make sure all the transactions that apply are marked with the right category. If there isn't one, click Create a Category to take care of that task.

12. Continue to select deduction types and deductions, answer questions, and accumulate check marks.

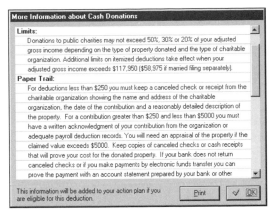

Figure 13-11 Everything you want to know about this deduction is displayed.

After you've gone through all the deduction types and the deductions you feel may yield some benefit, click the Summary tab to see your results.

If you want some help with your tax preparation as you use these deductions, click the Action Plan tab (Figure 13-12). A wealth of information is available about each deduction for which you qualify. You learn why you qualified, which tax form to use, and what the calculations are for using the deduction.

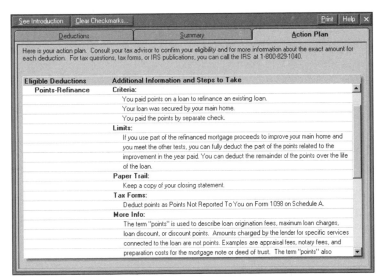

Figure 13-12 Want to know what actions to take to claim these deductions? Everything you need is in the Action Plan tab.

BONUS

Getting ready for taxes isn't the most fun you'll have with your computer, but Quicken certainly makes it easier than doing it manually. Here are some things to think about as you perform the tax tasks.

Some tax refunds are taxable, some aren't

If you receive a refund on your federal taxes, you need to create an income category for it (calling it Tax Refund is probably a good idea). Do not set up this category as tax-related. Although the refund is tax money, it has no impact on your next tax return. It's not taxable income and it's not a tax deduction.

If you took a deduction last year for all the state income taxes that you paid and then you received a refund from the state, however, that refund *is* taxable income (if you deducted it and then got some of it back, they're going to take taxes to wash out the deduction).

Get ready for business taxes

If you use a separate bank account for business, you can do some customization to get two separate tax reports, one for your personal tax return and another for your business returns:

1. When you create the Tax Summary Report or the Tax Schedule Report (or both), use the Customize button on the report window.

2. Eliminate any bank accounts that are for business use and save the results. Use a name for the report that indicates it's a personal tax report.

3. Then customize again to eliminate the personal accounts and include only business accounts. Save this report with a name that indicates it's a business tax report.

If you don't separate business and personal expenses by bank account and you're using categories or classes, follow these steps:

1. Use the Customize button to specify the categories or classes you need for gathering your personal tax information.

2. Save the resulting report as a personal tax report.

3. Reverse the procedure — eliminate the personal categories or classes and specify only those for business.

4. Save this report as a business tax report.

This is far easier than running reports and manually subtotaling before you visit your accountant (or, even worse, paying your accountant to pull apart the reports).

Special tax rules for wash sales

For Capital Gains Reports, Quicken does not report on wash sales (sales at a loss within 30 days of the purchase of a security) because special tax rules apply. Check your transactions in your investment accounts to locate any wash sales, then check with your accountant.

Summary

The capability to prepare reports that make tax preparation easier is a wonderful Quicken feature. However, the old computer adage "garbage in, garbage out" definitely applies here. You must be sure you set up your categories properly for tax links and you must be careful to enter all tax-related transactions accurately. This chapter covered what you need to know to take advantage of this Quicken capability.

MANAGING QUICKEN

THIS PART CONTAINS THE FOLLOWING CHAPTERS:

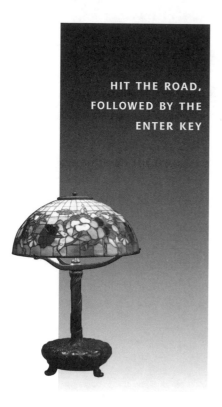

Planning a large trip is always difficult. Everyone stands around, crippled with anticipation, until the last minute, when they suddenly remember what they were supposed to do. Did someone tell the post office to hold the mail? Did I leave the iron plugged in? Did you defrag the hard drive? Um ... wait a minute. What was that last one?

Tagging the computer along might seem pretty frivolous to most vacationers, but not to Helaine Hepworth. Along with road flares and an atlas, Helaine's laptop is a necessary part of her trip. Helaine spends several months every year touring the country in her recreation vehicle — often for many weeks or even months at a time. With her laptop, modem, and cell phone, she no longer needs to worry about paying bills while on the road.

Without online banking, frequent travelers have a difficult time managing their home finances. Who pays the bills that come when you're on the road? One option is to have a spouse, partner, or close friend pay the bills. But what if the whole family is along for the ride? And to whom, outside the family, do you really want to give access to the checkbook?

Another option is to anticipate the bills and pay them ahead of time. This, however, requires too much extra money upfront, not to mention some amount of clairvoyance; who can tell how much the Visa bill will be in March? Of course, you could always hire an accountant to take care of things while you're away. Okay, okay, stop laughing. I was only kidding.

Thanks to Quicken and the online banking feature of her bank, First Interstate, Helaine doesn't have any of these problems. Quicken allows the user to do online banking, paying bills electronically. When Helaine is on the road, she uses her cell phone and modem to dial the bank's 800 number, and using Quicken, she pays her bills electronically. Says Helaine, "When I get a bill, I enter it in the computer checkbook account. Whenever I want, day or night, I just push a few buttons and the bills are paid. I know what day the checks will hit the creditor and can control the ebb and flow of the money in the account." Helaine has been online with Quicken about a year, and she pays every possible bill with it.

Before using Quicken, Helaine had used electronic transfer, but she was not pleased with the unpredictable time frame between giving the command to issue a check and the actual date the creditor received payment. With Quicken, bills get paid in two to four days. If she encounters a problem, she sends an e-mail message and gets a response the next day.

The best thing about online banking is that you don't have to be on a trip to use it. It works just as well if you're sitting at home.

IMPLEMENTING YEAR-END PROCEDURES

IN THIS CHAPTER YOU LEARN THESE KEY SKILLS:

The end of the year is an important accounting concept. A number of procedures take place then, although most of the complicated ones are designed for businesses (such as the determination of the profits for the year to get a basis for taxes). Year-end procedures for Quicken users involve running reports about tax-related transactions, cleaning up the file system, and, optionally, starting a new file for the new year.

None of this should take place at the end of the year. Year-end procedures should be deferred until you've taken care of all the bookkeeping details for the year. Lots of important tax information arrives in the mail well after January 1. Then tax reports have to be run and totals have to be compared to statements that arrive from investment accounts.

Waiting to implement all the suggestions in this chapter until after you've filed your income taxes is a good idea.

Running Year-End Reports

How much did you spend last year? On what? When did you spend it? What can you learn from this information? Running year-end reports can be an eye-opening experience. Did you really spend that much on restaurant dining? Why was so much of it spent in the summer? (That one's easy, at least for me. It's too hot to cook — who wants to stand near an oven or over a frying pan when it's 95 degrees? Someday I'm going to compare the dining out figure with the cost of air-conditioning the kitchen and see which is cheaper in the long run). This section discusses the types of year-end reports you can run.

Summary Reports

You can see all the money you received and spent in a Summary Report, and you can design the report to your own specifications. To begin, follow these steps:

1. From the Quicken menu bar, select **Reports** → **Other** → **Summary** .

2. The Create Report dialog box appears, and you can begin to design the report (Figure 14-1).

3. Because this is a year-end report, change the Report Dates to the entire year (from 1/1 to 12/31).

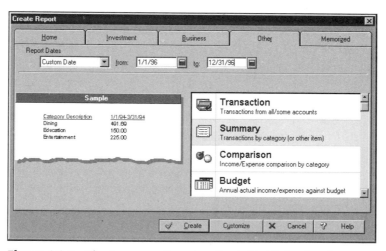

Figure 14-1   The Summary Report option is highlighted and a sample of its format is displayed.

Once the dates are in, you can choose among a number of different reports (although you will probably find you need all of them).

FULL-YEAR SUMMARY REPORT

The easiest report is a full-year report of activity, which requires no work to set up (except for making sure that the dates are correct on the dialog box). To see a Summary Report for the year (Figure 14-2), click Create.

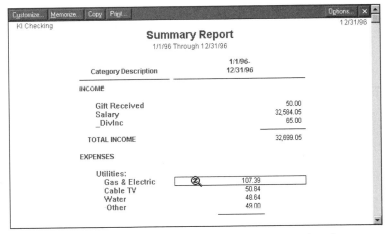

Figure 14-2 All your transactions for the year are sorted and subtotaled by category.

Scroll through the window to see all your category totals. To see where the subtotals come from, follow these steps:

1. Click a line item to put a box around it. The pointer changes to a Z (which means Zoom Down).

2. Double-click the line item to see the individual transactions that created the line item's subtotal.

3. Click the Summary Report QuickTab to return to the report.

CUSTOMIZED, YEAR-END SUMMARY REPORT

You can manipulate this report so that you can see anything you want to know. Customizing it to change the way information is presented is very easy.

Select Customize from the dialog box or click the Customize button from the Report window to begin. The Customize Summary Report dialog box appears with the Display tab in the foreground, and you can start to rebuild the report to your own taste (Figure 14-3).

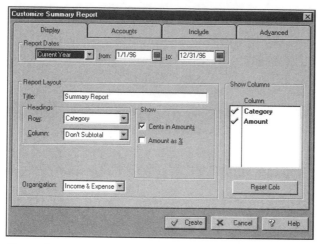

Figure 14-3 Customize the way the report displays with the Display tab.

To customize a report, follow these steps:

1. Enter a Title for this customized report.

2. Choose the Row Heading you want displayed. The default is to display Categories, but you can opt to display Class, Payee, or Account instead.

3. Specify the Column display, choosing separate columns for every time period (week, month, and so on) or for each category. If you leave the selection as Don't Subtotal, you'll see one column with a grand total.

4. In the Organization field, choose an option for the type of data you want to see in this report. The choices are as follows:

   ✳ Income & Expense, which gives you a total for all the income you received and a total of all the expenses you entered.

   ✳ Cash Flow, which looks at transfers in and out of asset accounts and treats them as income and expenses. If you spent money that you didn't count as an expense (such as a permanent improvement to your house, which is really an asset rather than an expense), it will report it.

   ✳ Supercategory, which groups transactions by any supercategories you've created instead of just totaling inflow and outflow by category.

5. Select Cents in Amounts to see cents; deselect it to see dollars only.

6. Select Amount as % to see summary amounts as percentages of the totals.

7. The Show Columns category is preset for this report, so you shouldn't have to change it.

Once you've entered all your configuration options, you can click Create to see the report. Because this is a year-end report and you need all the basic information, you shouldn't have to use the other tabs on the dialog box to select accounts and transaction types.

Tax reports

Part of your year-end plans must include getting tax-related information out of your Quicken file. Quicken saves data in a way that permits easy reporting, and a prebuilt report is even waiting for you. What could be easier?

To get the information, follow these steps:

1. From the Quicken menu, select Reports → Home → Tax Summary to see the Create Report dialog box with the Tax Summary Report already highlighted for you.

2. Check the Report Dates fields to make sure that the entire year is selected as the range.

3. Click Create to see the Tax Summary Report (Figure 14-4).

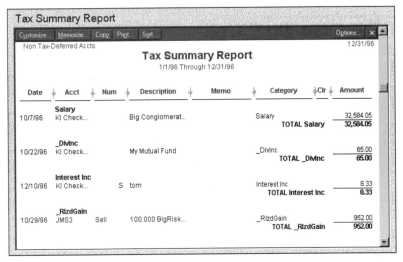

Figure 14-4 Every transaction that affects your income tax is reported, along with category subtotals, in the Tax Summary Report.

4. Click Print on the button bar to get a hard copy.

Just as with the year-end Summary report, you can choose Customize and change the categories, columns, or display of this report and create exactly what you need.

Archiving Files

Archiving a file means you store it separately from your working file. It's a safe-keeping device for information. It's normal for bookkeeping software to take all the transactions for a year and archive them. That doesn't have to mean that the information in those files disappears from your working file; it just provides a "year at a glance" file that is stored somewhere in case you need it later.

When you archive a data file, all the transactions that are dated before this current year are copied into their own, separate file (remember, you'd be performing the archiving process after the end of the year). Your working file isn't changed at all, and you won't notice any differences because all the transactions are still there.

TIP One advantage of archiving each year is that your current working file can continue to hold on to transactions so that you can actually create reports that span several years of information. This is a good way to check on the growth of assets or the decrementing balances of loans. And it's a great way to do year-to-year comparisons of account totals.

Performing a year-end archive

To perform a year-end archive, follow these steps:

1. From the Quicken menu bar, select File → File Operations → Year-End Copy to display the Year-End Copy dialog box (Figure 14-5).

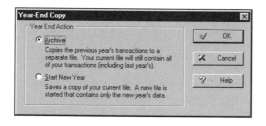

Figure 14-5 Start the year-end process off by archiving your file.

2. Choose Archive to bring up the Archive File dialog box (Figure 14-6).

3. In the Archive Old Data to File text box, you can change the name that Quicken picks for this file (although the name is awfully logical; I can't think of a better one).

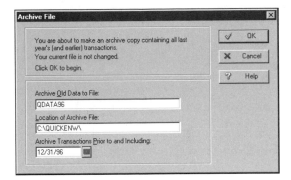

Figure 14-6 Tell Quicken what to name your archive file.

4. Click OK to create the archive file.

5. After the copy is made, Quicken notifies you of the successful operation and asks if you want to use the current file (your regular file, which is currently loaded) or the archive file (the copy you just made).

If you want to keep working in Quicken, select Current file. If you want to look at or manipulate the archive file, choose Archive file.

Making the archive file tamper-proof

If you can't think of any reason to load the archive file, I can, and I'll even tell you what it is. You want to make this file tamper-proof. There is no reason to change an archived file, or else you can't trust the historic numbers when you go back to look at them. So, bring up the archived file and password-protect the transactions so that nobody can change them (with the assumption that you know better and won't change them).

Here's how to protect the archive and then load the current file so that you can go back to work in Quicken:

1. Select Archive file as the file to work on when Quicken asks you which file you want to use and then click OK.

2. The archive file is loaded (you see its name at the top of the Quicken window), and a Quicken Tip appears just as if you were just starting Quicken.

3. Click Done to get rid of the tip (after you read it).

4. From the menu bar, select File → Passwords → File to see the Set Up Password dialog box (Figure 14-7).

5. Enter a password in the Password field. You can use up to 16 characters, including spaces. Then press Tab.

6. Re-enter the same password in the Confirm Password field.

Figure 14-7 Password-protect your archive file to keep it pristine.

7. Click OK to save the password and protect the file.

8. To go back to work on your current file, select **File** → **Open** to see the Open Quicken File dialog box (Figure 14-8).

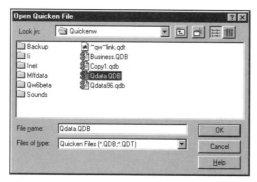

Figure 14-8 Choose your regular Qdata file to return to work in Quicken.

9. Select your regular Quicken file and click OK.

10. There's that Quicken Tip again; you're starting all over. Go back to work.

When you invent a password, be careful not to make it anything that has unusual characters and may be difficult to type. When you want to access your archived file, you have to enter the password blindly, because you won't see the characters you're typing on the screen. Every time you enter a character, you see an asterisk (*). If you make the password convoluted, it is very easy to enter a character incorrectly.

Creating New Files for the New Year

The other option for beginning a new year with Quicken is to start a new file in honor of the new year. Quicken calls this the Start New Year option. When you choose the Start New Year option, Quicken saves a copy of your current file, which becomes the "old year file." Then, returning to the current file, it gets rid of any transactions that aren't in the current year. Your working file now contains only the transactions from the new year (I'm assuming that you waited until some time after January 1 to do this). There are a couple of exceptions to these deletions — it doesn't delete any prior-year transactions that have not yet cleared the bank and it doesn't delete any prior-year transactions for asset or liability accounts. Only bank accounts are cleared of prior-year transactions. By and large, however, you will be missing the bulk of your previous transactions.

This method has some real disadvantages, because you won't be able to look at old transactions or use them in reports. More importantly, some real problems exist with deleting all the transactions from last year if you do your banking online. This method should only be used if you're getting worried about the size of your Quicken files, perhaps because you're afraid you might run out of hard drive space or because making backups now involves putting several floppy disks into your floppy drive.

If you aren't convinced to use archiving instead, and you want to start a new file for the new year, follow these steps:

1. From the Quicken menu bar, select File → File Operations → Year-End Copy to display the Year-End Copy dialog box.

2. Choose Start New Year from the Year-End Copy dialog box to bring up the Start New Year dialog box (Figure 14-9).

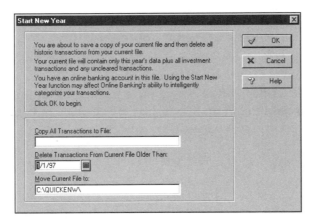

Figure 14-9   Create a file of all the transactions from last year to leave only this year's transactions in your working Quicken file.

3. The Copy All Transactions to File field is for naming the file that will hold last year's transactions. Choose a name that is meaningful (such as 1996).

4. Be sure the Delete Transactions From Current File Older Than field contains the accurate date.

5. If you want to change the location of your current working file, fill in the path and filename in the Move Current File to field (there is rarely any good reason to do this).

6. Click OK to copy the current file and then empty it of all transactions before the beginning of this year.

BONUS

Don't close your year too early; make sure that you wait until you've received all the documents about taxable income and expenses. And, if you're using tax software, be sure to transfer information to the tax software before you perform any year-end procedures.

Meanwhile, back at the shoebox, sort and label all those receipts you've been throwing into this container. If you ever have an audit, you can impress the IRS with your efficiency and honesty by showing the auditor how organized you are:

* Save cancelled checks and receipts for seven years.

* Save cancelled checks that were written for permanent improvements to your house until after you sell your house. Actually, save them for a couple of years after that in case there's some question about the taxes you paid (or didn't pay) on the profit from the sale of your house. Those checks increase the cost basis for your home.

Summary

After you've been backing up your Quicken data regularly (or should be), there is special treatment for the files that contain a full year's data. All your totals, all the information about the year that just ended, all the tax-related totals, are important to save as a one-year file.

You don't have to lose that information in the next year's file (unless you're dealing with files so large that it's impossible to work with them). You should just create a specific file for each year.

Quicken has all the tools you need to handle the end-of-year procedures built in. Just remember that before you use these tools you must make sure that all your transactions have been entered and all cleared transactions have been reconciled.

CUSTOMIZING QUICKEN

IN THIS CHAPTER YOU LEARN THESE KEY SKILLS:

T o fit the needs of a wide variety of users, computer software must be flexible and offer a broad range of customization choices. If the program is inflexible, it will satisfy only a small number of the potential users and relegate itself to a limited share of the market. Clearly, Quicken does not fall into this category. One reason for its tremendous popularity is the extensive assortment of options it offers.

The fundamentals of the record-keeping process remain the same for all users. However, the way in which you view, implement, and output those fundamentals is, to a large degree, your choice. Quicken offers a vast array of options for customizing the way things get done. Although several Quicken features have options available only while you're working directly with that feature, quite a few options with broader consequences are available that you can access from the main Quicken menu. You learn all about your options for customization in this chapter.

Changing the Quicken Desktop

The Quicken desktop refers to the arrangement of open windows and features that you normally maintain while working in Quicken. Because this is your private workspace, you should set it up so that you can work as comfortably and efficiently as possible. Making it your kind of environment is easy with Quicken's variety of options. To access a large number of the available options, select Edit → Options. The resulting options menu contains a variety of general options for many of Quicken's features.

Iconbar options

Although I find the Activity Bar and the QuickTabs handy, there is one Quicken tool that I find indispensable while I work — the *Iconbar*. The Iconbar is a toolbar that you can position at the top of the screen with buttons for each of your favorite features, thus allowing you easy access to those tools you use most frequently. Like the Activity Bar and QuickTabs, it provides you with instant access to many of the features you use regularly.

To activate the Iconbar as seen in Figure 15-1, follow these steps:

1. Move your mouse pointer to the QuickTabs column or to a blank area between the Activity Bar icons.

2. Click your right mouse button to activate the pop-up option menu.

3. Select Show Top Iconbar .

Figure 15-1 The default Iconbar offers quick access to the features you use most.

The icons function as follows:

 Move to the current account register

 Go to the Account List

 Balance your account

 Go to Reports

 Go to Online Banking

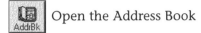 Display the Financial Calendar

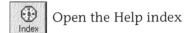 Open the Address Book

 Open the Help index

 Access Investor Insight

 TIP Investor Insight is a Quicken feature that lets you go online on the Internet to get information and stock prices for the investments you're tracking in your Quicken software.

 Start Home Inventory

 Go to the Mutual Fund Finder

Go to Quicken Help

CHANGING THE ICONBAR APPEARANCE

Perhaps you like the idea of the Iconbar but find the cute little icons unnecessary and a waste of valuable screen space. Or maybe you like the icons and don't need the text. No problem; just go the Customize Iconbar dialog and remove them, leaving the text label only.

To change the appearance of the Iconbar, follow these steps:

1. To reach the Customize Iconbar dialog box, select **Edit** → **Options** → **Iconbar** (Figure 15-2).

Figure 15-2   Change the Iconbar to suit your needs.

2. To include icons and their text labels in the Iconbar, select both Show Icons and Show Text.

3. If you want to show icons only (without text labels) in the Iconbar, select Show Icons and deselect Show Text.

4. To show text labels without the icons, select Show Text and deselect Show Icons.

ADDING AN ICON

Of course, there will be some features that you use more frequently than others, and some that you don't use at all. The solution? Simple; just add or remove features as often as you find it necessary.

To add a feature to the Iconbar, follow these steps:

1. Select **Edit** → **Options** → **Iconbar** to open the Customize Iconbar dialog box.

2. Select New to access the Add Action to Iconbar dialog box (Figure 15-3).

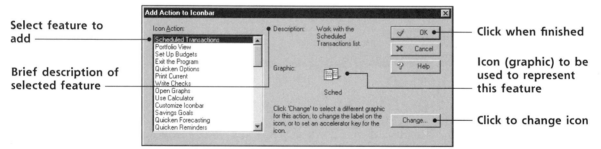

Figure 15-3   Add the features you most frequently use to the Iconbar.

3. Select the feature to add from the Icon Action window and click OK when finished (see Step 4 if you want to change the graphic previewed in the dialog box).

4. To substitute another icon for the default, select Change to access the Change Iconbar Item dialog box (Figure 15-4).

5. Scroll through the Graphic window to select an icon to your liking.

6. Enter a text label (not to exceed seven letters) in the Icon Label box.

7. If desired, enter a hot key combination in the Speed Key box.

8. Click OK when you're satisfied with your choices.

9. If you approve of the new graphic and label that now appear in the Add Action to Iconbar dialog box, click OK again to add the new icon to the Iconbar.

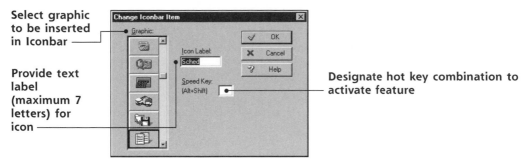

Select graphic to be inserted in Iconbar

Provide text label (maximum 7 letters) for icon

Designate hot key combination to activate feature

Figure 15-4 Quicken lets you choose the graphic, the label, and a hot key for each icon on the Iconbar.

TIP Although you can add as many icons as you want to the Iconbar, only a limited number appear at the top of the screen at any one time. The number of icons that appear depends on your screen resolution and the size of your monitor. If you decide to exceed that number, you have to scroll through the bar to find those not appearing on-screen.

EDITING AN ICON

If, after adding a new icon, you decide that the text label is confusing or the graphic is not appropriate, you merely return to the Customize Iconbar window and edit the icon. This applies not only to icons that you've added, but to existing icons as well. The steps for editing an icon are identical to those for adding an icon, except that you choose the Edit button rather than the New button from the Customize Iconbar dialog box.

DELETING AN ICON

When you begin using Quicken, there will no doubt be a number of features on the Iconbar that you use infrequently. You may decide to eliminate some icons and replace them with others.

To delete an icon from the Iconbar, follow these steps:

1. Select **Edit** → **Options** → **Iconbar** to open the Customize Iconbar dialog box.

2. Scroll through the icons in Current iconbar to locate the icon you want to delete. (Deleting an icon does not erase it permanently; it simply removes it from the Iconbar).

3. Select the icon to be removed by clicking it.

4. Click the Delete button and confirm by clicking OK when asked if you want to "Delete Icon from the Iconbar?"

5. Repeat for as many icons as you need to remove.

6. After you are finished deleting icons, click Done to return to your work.

RESETTING THE ICONBAR

If at any point you are dissatisfied with the additions and changes you have made to the Iconbar, you can restore the original (default) settings:

1. Select `Edit` → `Options` → `Iconbar` from the Quicken menu bar to access the Customize Iconbar dialog box.

2. Select Reset, which prompts Quicken to ask for confirmation, because it will result in the loss of any custom icons you have added.

3. If you're sure that this is what you want to do, click OK to confirm your choice.

4. Click Done to exit the Customize Iconbar dialog box.

Quicken Program options

Quicken affords different levels of customization, from simple keystrokes that affect a range of features to specific modes of operation that apply to a single feature only. To assure that the overall environment is suited to your needs, you should start with the broader options and then move to the more specific.

The Quicken Program option provides a General Options dialog box that enables you to customize some basic Quicken settings, including the way QuickTabs work. To access the Quicken Program option, select Edit → Options → Quicken Program. The General Options dialog box opens. Notice in Figure 15-5 that the dialog box contains three tabs: one for QuickTabs options, one for General options, and one for Settings.

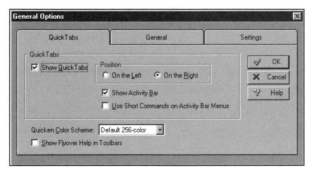

Figure 15-5 Start by setting some of Quicken's basic operating parameters.

QUICKTABS

QuickTabs give you a quick and easy means of navigating through open Quicken windows. QuickTabs options enable you to change the way QuickTabs and several other Quicken features behave:

* **Show QuickTabs.** Select this option to display QuickTabs. Deselect to hide QuickTabs.

* **On the Left.** Select this option to position the QuickTabs column on the left side of the screen.

* **On the Right.** Select this option to place the QuickTabs on the right side of the screen.

* **Show Activity Bar.** Check this box to have the Activity Bar appear at the bottom of your screen. Deselecting this box hides the Activity Bar.

* **Use Short Commands on Activity Bar Menus.** Shorten the Activity Bar menu items from descriptive phrases to one or two words by selecting this option.

* **Quicken Color Scheme.** Select this option to change the Quicken display color scheme.

* **Show Flyover Help in Toolbars.** Activate or deactivate Tool Tips (small, pop-up descriptors for each button) on the Iconbar by selecting or deselecting this option.

Once you are finished, click OK. To access more General options, click the General tab.

GENERAL TAB

The General tab has three options that can prove quite useful in the long run (Figure 15-6).

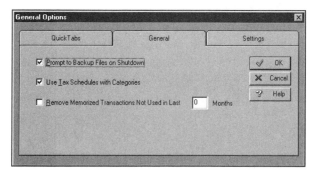

Figure 15-6 Quicken reminds you to make a backup copy of your records.

* **Prompt to Backup Files on Shutdown.** I highly recommend you select this option. Backing up is one of the most important things you can do with any computer data you value. This will become quite clear the first time you lose important data to an accidental erasure, a hard disk crash, or some other unexpected phenomenon. Having to rebuild information that you painstakingly entered over months, weeks, days, or even minutes is very frustrating, tedious, and sometimes impossible. Therefore, the question is not "Should I perform backups?" but rather "How often should I perform backups?" With this option selected, Quicken reminds you to back up every third time you exit the program.

* **Use Tax Schedules with Categories.** If you plan to use Quicken to generate tax reports, select this option. It enables you to assign categories to specific schedules or forms on your income tax return. Therefore, any check assigned to the particular category shows up on your tax reports as part of the information to be used in preparing the form with which you have associated it.

* **Remove Memorized Transactions Not Used in Last *x* Months.** If you have forgotten to remove memorized transactions you no longer use, this option can perform some housekeeping chores for you by eliminating transactions that have been inactive for the period of time you specify.

SETTINGS TAB

The third tab in the General Options window, Settings, gives you the two basic sets of options shown in Figure 15-7.

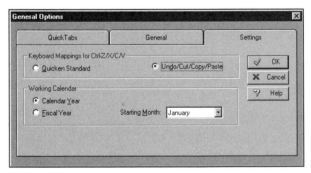

Figure 15-7 Keystrokes and calendars are the choices on the Settings tab.

* **Keyboard Mappings for Ctrl-Z/X/C/V.** You can choose to use the Quicken conventions for the hot keys Ctrl+Z, Ctrl+X, Ctrl+C, and Ctrl+V, or the Windows conventions. To select the Quicken conventions, choose Quicken Standard. To select the Windows conventions, choose Undo/Cut/Copy/Paste (see Table 15-1 for hot key conventions).

TIP If you plan to use the computer for more than keeping your checkbook, it is a good idea to familiarize yourself with the Windows keystrokes. You will use them extensively throughout most Windows programs. Trying to learn new uses of common keys from program to program can prove to be counterproductive. Therefore, unless you're going to use Quicken only and no other Windows software, I recommend that you select the standard Windows conventions Undo/Cut/Copy/Paste.

✳ **Working Calendar.** To make your financial year consistent with the calendar year, January through December, select Calendar Year. If, however, your financial year is different from the calendar year, select Fiscal Year and then select the month in which your year begins. Usually only businesses need this option.

TABLE 15-1 Hot Key Conventions for Quicken and Windows

Hot Key	Quicken	Windows
CTRL+Z	Quick Zoom (Report)	Undo
CTRL+X	Go to matching transfer	Cut
CTRL+C	Go to Category and Transfer List	Copy
CTRL+V	Void a transaction	Paste

Reminder options

Billminder, which Chapter 6 covered in detail, is a handy feature that taps you on the shoulder and lets you know it's time to pay a bill, print a check, or sell a stock. When and how Billminder works is up to you. To set the Billminder options, select Edit → Options → Reminders. The Reminder Options dialog box appears and offers you several ways to customize Billminder (Figure 15-8).

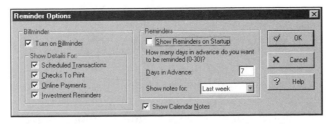

Figure 15-8 No need to tie a string around your finger unless you forget to set your Reminder options.

Your first choice is whether to turn on Billminder. Place a check mark in the box to left of the Turn on Billminder option to activate reminders about bill paying. The next set of options lets you choose which items you want Billminder to remind you about:

* **Scheduled Transactions.** Check this box if you want Quicken to let you know when it's time to process a scheduled transaction.

* **Checks to Print.** Don't forget to select this option if you want Quicken to remind you when a check needs to be printed.

* **Online Payments.** Do you have scheduled online payments to process? If so, check this box.

* **Investment Reminders.** In the investment register, you can write yourself notes about buying and selling. Checking this box includes the notes in the Reminders window on the appropriate dates.

In addition, you can choose to show reminders every time you start Quicken by selecting Show Reminders on Startup. To give yourself advance warning, you can set the number of days in advance of a scheduled event to be reminded. Finally, you can decide whether or not to include Financial Calendar notes and from what time period.

Desktop options

Once you have set up the desktop the way you want it, use the Desktop options to decide how the Quicken desktop should appear each time you start the program. To find the Desktop options, select Edit → Options → Desktop. The resulting Save Desktop dialog box offers only two options:

* **Save Desktop on Exit.** This option, which saves the desktop as it appears when you exit the program, is the default. Upon reopening Quicken, you return to the desktop as you last left it.

* **Save Current Desktop.** If you have a particular setup that you want to start with for each Quicken session, use this option. First make sure that the desktop is arranged the way you want it and then select Save Current Desktop.

Changing Quicken Components

Not only does Quicken allow you to modify the desktop to accommodate your work style, it also gives you the opportunity to change the features of many individual elements. Some changes are cosmetic, such as adjusting the color schemes, whereas others, like automating data entry, substantially change the way a feature works. From simple to complex, all the options give you more control over how Quicken responds.

Customizing the register

Because the account register is the heart of the Quicken program, customizing it is as fundamental as customizing the desktop. Regardless of what you're using Quicken for, every activity begins with entering transactions in an account. Therefore, you certainly want to have the register set up to suit your needs. The register options include changing its appearance and how it works, as well as automating some of its features. Select Edit → Options → Register to access the Register Options dialog box (Figure 15-9).

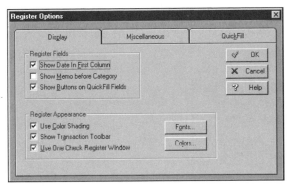

Figure 15-9 Quicken lets you modify how the register looks.

DISPLAY TAB

The Display tab options are primarily choices that control the physical appearance of the account register:

* **Show Date In First Column.** Selecting this option locates the Date field in the first column of the register. Deselecting it switches the positions of the Date field and the Num field.

* **Show Memo Before Category.** Like the previous option, this one lets you choose the location for one of the register fields. In this case, it is the Memo field. Selecting this option positions the Memo field to the left of the Category field. Deselecting it places the Category field to the right of the Memo field.

* **Show Buttons on QuickFill Fields.** As your drop-down lists increase in size, you may find it easier to begin typing the entry and then wait for Autofill to finish the job rather than to make a selection from the list. If you find that you do not use the drop-down lists, select this option to eliminate the buttons that activate them.

* **Use Color Shading.** Use this option in conjunction with Colors button to change the background color of the register.

* **Show Transaction Toolbar.** If you want to hide the Enter, Edit, and Split buttons that appear in the active transaction, deselect Show Transaction Toolbar.

* **Use One Check Register Window.** To create a new window for each register you use, leave this option unchecked. As a result, a QuickTab appears for each account that you open. When the option is selected, all registers utilize the same window, so only one QuickTab appears, named Register. To access different account registers, use the account tabs at the bottom of the register.

* **Fonts.** Clicking the Fonts button accesses the Choose Register Font dialog box, which enables you to select the font, its size, and whether to bold it (Figure 15-10).

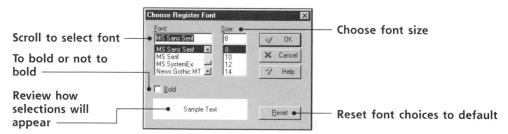

Figure 15-10 Make the register text as fancy or plain as you like.

* **Colors.** Used in concert with the Use Color Shading option, the Colors button enables you to choose different background colors for each of the different account registers (Figure 15-11).

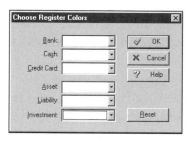

Figure 15-11 Don't want to clash? No problem; color coordinate with Quicken's color options.

MISCELLANEOUS TAB

The Miscellaneous tab contains Quicken's notification and alert options. Having the program warn you before you take a certain action can either be a blessing or a pain, depending on your viewpoint. Quicken realizes this and lets you decide when you want to be notified about certain actions. From the Register Options window, select the Miscellaneous tab, shown in Figure 15-12:

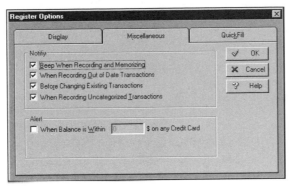

Figure 15-12 You can take or leave Quicken warnings. The choice is yours.

* **Beep When Recording and Memorizing.** With this option selected, Quicken beeps every time you finalize entering, deleting, or memorizing a transaction.

* **When Recording Out of Date Transactions.** This option comes in handy at the beginning of a new year. Choosing this option warns you when you attempt to record a transaction with a year different than the current one.

* **Before Changing Existing Transactions.** If you want Quicken to warn you that you're about to exit a transaction that you changed and failed to click Enter, select this option.

* **When Recording Uncategorized Transactions.** Provided that you have this option selected, if you attempt to record a transaction without assigning it to a category. Quicken reminds you that it is a good idea to use categories (Figure 15-13).

* **Alert When Balance is Within.** Can't remember what the limit is on your credit card? If you have a tendency to lose sight of your credit limit and get hit with charges for exceeding the limit, let Quicken help. Select this option, and Quicken lets you know when you're approaching your limit. Of course, this only works if you record all your credit card transactions as well.

TIP Don't forget to enter a buffer amount that more than covers the finance charges that accrue each month.

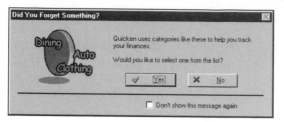

Figure 15-13 Quicken catches you when you try
to take the easy way.

QUICKFILL TAB

QuickFill, the last tab in the Register Options window, enables you to automate
a number of register procedures. If you repeat several of your entries, this can
save you a great deal of time and effort. To access these options, select the
QuickFill tab from the Register Options dialog box (Figure 15-14).

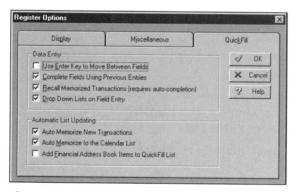

Figure 15-14 Set your data-entry options so that
Quicken does the work.

* **Use Enter Key to Move Between Fields.** If you're accustomed to using
  the Enter key to move between fields, check this option.
* **Complete Fields Using Previous Entries.** This option is a real time
  saver, so don't turn it off unless you're compelled to do things the hard
  way. Selecting this entry causes Quicken to automatically fill in the Date
  field with today's date and the Num field with the next sequential check
  number. It also auto-fills the Payee and Category fields once you begin
  typing and a match is found.

* **Recall Memorized Transactions (requires auto-completion).** Once a payee is entered, this feature fills in the remaining fields using information from the last transaction involving the payee. This feature does not work unless Complete Fields Using Previous Entries has also been selected.

* **Drop Down Lists on Field Entry.** Select this option if you want the drop-down list to appear every time you move to a field that has one. Turning this option off does not eliminate the drop-down list; it merely prevents it from popping up unless you click the drop-down button at the end of the field.

* **Auto Memorize New Transactions.** To add each transaction for a new payee to the Memorized Transactions List, check this option.

TIP **The Memorized Transactions List holds a maximum of 2,000 entries. When it reaches its limit, it automatically shuts off this option. To turn it back on, go to the Memorized Transactions List and delete some of the old and unused transactions. This does not affect the recorded transactions, simply the memorized data about the payee.**

* **Auto Memorize to the Calendar List.** Available only if the previous option is selected, this one records memorized transactions on the Financial Calendar's Transaction List automatically. It makes it a snap to create scheduled transactions. Simply drag the transaction from list onto the calendar date desired.

* **Add Financial Address Book Items to QuickFill List.** If you use the Financial Address Book, selecting this option is a good idea. When selected, it adds names and addresses from the Financial Address Book to the drop-down QuickFill list so that they are available in the register or when writing checks.

Customizing check writing

If you make use of Quicken's check-writing and printing features, the following options give you more control over both operations. Because many of the operations performed in writing checks are identical to those performed when entering transactions in the register, you will note that some options overlap with account register options. Select Edit → Options → Write Checks to access the Check Options window (Figure 15-15).

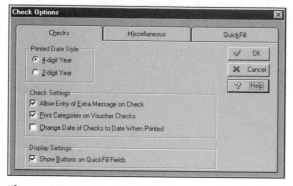

Figure 15-15 Use Check Options to print checks with the right information every time.

CHECKS TAB

The Checks tab offers you the opportunity to customize the way information appears on the checks that you print.

* **4-digit Year.** If you prefer the date printed on your checks to appear with a four-digit year (1997), select this option.

* **2-digit Year.** If you'd rather have a two-digit year (97) printed on your checks, select this option.

* **Allow Entry of Extra Message on Check.** Select this option to add an extra line for an account number or other information on the printed check. Information on this line does not appear in the transparent window of the envelope.

* **Print Categories on Voucher Checks.** If you use voucher (business) checks, this option enables you to include category from split transactions on the attached check stub.

* **Change Date of Checks to Date When Printed.** If you enter your checks on a different day than you print them, choosing this option changes the check date to the date of the printing.

* **Show Buttons on QuickFill Fields.** To hide the drop-down list buttons at the end of transaction fields, deselect this button. The drop-down list information remains intact; however, you can no longer access it by clicking a button.

MISCELLANEOUS TAB

With the exception of Warn if a Check Number is Re-used, all options on this tab are identical to those on the Miscellaneous tab of the register options (Figure 15-16).

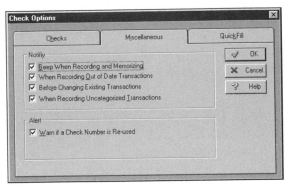

Figure 15-16 Check-writing Miscellaneous options are almost identical to register Miscellaneous options.

I highly recommend you select Warn if a Check Number is Re-used. It warns you if you attempt to use a check number that has already been recorded. Such a mistake is easy to make and tedious to correct.

QUICKFILL TAB

The QuickFill tab, which offers data-entry and automation options, is identical to the register QuickFill tab (Figure 15-17).

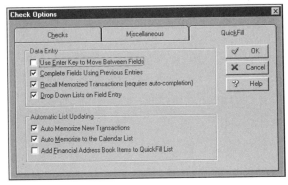

Figure 15-17 QuickFill options offer the same opportunities to automate the data-entry process as the account register options of the same name.

BONUS

I't's important to use Quicken for a while before you change the options, so you end up with the changes that really are significant for the way you work. If you do decide to make changes, start with only those configuration options that you've noticed while you work. Perhaps you found you were frustrated by the lack of extra space on a check for adding information. Change the check options to ease your aggravation.

Another good idea is to make one change at a time. It makes it easier to get used to the new configuration when you resume working in Quicken. Wholesale changes can be confusing.

Summary

As you can see, Quicken not only offers an abundance of features but a variety of options to customize those features so that they work exactly as you want them to work. From arranging the desktop to automating the entry of information, Quicken customization options give you control over how Quicken looks and operates.

MANAGING FILES

With the advent of truly "user friendly" software, it's easy to forget about the mechanics of an application. As much as the software may shield you from getting a little dirt under your fingernails, however, there are a few things that still require popping the hood and taking a look underneath.

That's what file management is — getting down to the basics and taking care of the internal engine. Quicken has made the file management tasks so easy that everyone can feel comfortable jumping in. In this chapter, you learn how to safeguard and manipulate your data by using Quicken's file operations features.

Using Backup and Restore

Although backing up data is one of the most important operations a software user can perform, it is also one of the tasks most likely to be ignored by most users. It's that "it can't happen to me" mentality that we all carry around inside our heads. Even though we know that disaster can strike at any time, we always convince ourselves that it will happen to someone else. Take it from one who knows: sooner or later, it will be your turn!

I'm talking about the disaster of losing your important data you have spent many hours toiling over. If you don't have a backup, you will be a very cranky individual when (note that I did not say if) your data disappears. Hard disks eventually fail, people make mistakes, and sometimes I think little sprites enter my computer at night and do strange things with my data. Whatever the reason, you should be prepared.

Backing up Quicken files

Backing up is a job that you should perform daily. What you're backing up is your Quicken file. It's important to note the way Quicken uses the word *file*, which is different from the way it is typically used in computer jargon. To Quicken, a file is a complete set of data. You can have multiple files in Quicken, which means you can run your personal financial life in one file and your business finances in another. Or you can have one file for your finances and another for another family member. The Quicken file is actually a group of files (using the word the way one normally refers to computer files).

Backing up is a rather simple procedure and can be accomplished by following these steps:

1. Insert a blank (if this is your first backup), formatted disk into the floppy disk drive of your choice.

2. Select File → Backup from the Quicken menu.

3. From the Select Backup Drive dialog box, select the letter of the disk drive in which you have placed the backup disk from the Backup Drive drop-down list. As you can see in Figure 16-1, the default is A.

Figure 16-1 Backing up is a breeze in Quicken.

4. Select the file to back up. If you want to back up the file in which you're currently working, choose Current File. If you want to back up a different file, choose Select From List to view a list of choices.

5. After you've made your selection, click OK to complete the backup process.

AUTOMATIC BACKUPS

One of the best ways to ensure that you don't fall victim to the "I'll back up later syndrome" is the Quicken reminder, which is set to nag you about backing up every third time you exit. This doesn't mean you can't back up any time you want. It simply guarantees that you won't forget.

TIP **You can change the setting for how often Quicken prompts you to back up if you're comfortable making changes to the Quicken.ini file located in your Windows directory. Be advised, however, that making changes in any .INI file has its associated risks. Changing the wrong parameter here can alter the way your program works or prevent it from working at all. If you choose to edit the Quicken.ini file, make a backup copy of it first. Then use the Notepad or some other word processor that saves files in text format to change the number in the line AutoBackup=3 to the number of times you exit the program before Quicken reminds you to back up. If you want to be reminded every time you close Quicken, change the 3 to 1; if you want to be reminded every fifth time, change it to 5.**

HARD DISK AUTOCOPIES

Every seven days, Quicken makes a backup copy (upon exiting) of its data files, placing these copies on your hard disk. They're placed in the Quickenw\Backup directory and named Qdata1. The default is to make two autocopies. When the second set is created, the first set is renamed Qdata2, and the new files are called Qdata1. This way, your most current information is always found in Qdata1. If you want to have more than two backups on your hard drive, you can change the number of copies by editing the Quicken.ini file found in your Windows directory. Change autocopy=2 to anything from 0–9, depending on how many copies you want to retain.

CAUTION **Don't be lulled into a sense of security by the fact that Quicken is automatically making backups on your hard drive. If your hard drive fails, you lose your backup along with your original files. In addition, it only makes a backup once a week. You can lose a great deal of information in seven days.**

A final word on backing up: Be sure to keep your backup copies in a safe place. It won't do you any good if a thief breaks into your house and steals your backup disks along with your computer because they're next to each other. Critical backup data is best kept in a safe deposit box or a fireproof container of some sort around the house or office. Even keeping a backup in a different location from the original (if the original is on your home computer keep a backup at the office) is safer than having the two sitting on your desk together.

Restoring Quicken files

Restoring is the other half of the backup equation. It's the part you hope you never have to do, but when the time comes, you're thankful that you've been backing up and have the capability to do the restore.

Restoring is quite simple as long as you have a recent backup:

1. Insert your most recent backup disk in drive A.

2. Select **File** → **Restore** from the Quicken menu.

3. Select drive A from the Look in drop-down list (Figure 16-2) in the Restore Quicken File dialog box.

Figure 16-2 It's only a few keystrokes from disaster to data recovery if you have a backup.

4. Select (highlight) the Qdata.qdb file that appears in the display window beneath Look in. This places the filename Qdata.qdb in the File name field.

5. Click OK to start the restore.

Restoring from a backup overwrites the existing file on your hard disk. Any changes made since the last backup will be lost. If you're restoring for any reason other than a damaged or deleted original file, you can rename the original file and later back up and restore from that if the need arises.

6. Unless the original data file has been deleted or renamed, Quicken asks if you want to overwrite the existing file. If you're sure this is what you want to do, click OK; otherwise, cancel and review the situation.

7. You receive a message that Quicken is restoring. Once you see the message telling you that the file has been restored successfully, click OK to complete the operation.

Managing Your Files

Although backup and restore may be the most critical file management tools available, they are by no means the only ones you will find useful. Copying, deleting, and renaming files are just a few other options under Quicken's file management operations.

Copy

Making copies of your Quicken files is a good idea for more than just safety reasons. If your file has more than one year's worth of data and is getting large and unwieldy, it may be a good time to make a copy that contains only transactions for the current year. You then can save the new file with current information under a new name and retain all your information in the original file. Or perhaps your backup is taking more than one disk and you really don't need all that information on hand at one time. Making a partial copy of the file reduces its size and therefore the size of the backup, while still retaining all your information in the original file.

Whatever the reason, you can make a full or partial copy of your Quicken files any time you want by following these steps:

1. Select File → File Operations → Copy from the Quicken menu.

2. Enter the name and location for the new file (Figure 16-3).

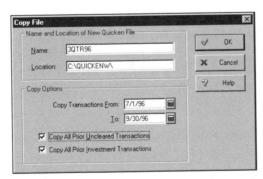

Figure 16-3 Making a full or partial copy of your file is as easy as filling in the blanks.

3. To set the date range, choose the beginning date in the Copy Transactions From field by typing it in or using the drop-down calendar.

4. Set the ending date in the To field.

5. If you want to include unreconciled transactions earlier than the Copy Transactions From date in the new file, check the Copy All Prior Uncleared Transactions box. Deselecting the Copy All Prior Uncleared Transactions option causes all prior, unreconciled transactions to be totaled and included in an opening balance for each account in the new file. The actual transactions do not appear in the new file.

TIP **If you have a transfer that falls in the date range, one side of which has cleared, only the cleared transaction appears in the new file. The uncleared part of the transfer is totaled and deleted. The amount is correct, but that side of the transfer is gone.**

6. If you use Quicken to track your investments and want to include all those transactions, select Copy All Prior Investment Transactions. This way, you do not lose the historical data for your investments.

7. When you're ready to make your copy, click OK.

8. Quicken makes the copy and gives you the option of continuing with the original file or opening the new copy. Make your selection and click OK.

Delete

When you decide that you no longer need regular access to an old file, you may decide to copy it to a floppy disk and erase the original from your hard drive. It's an easy task to remove a file from your hard disk using Quicken's Delete feature. However, don't be fooled by the simplicity of this procedure. It's easy to do but nearly impossible to undo without a backup or a third-party software utility. Deleting a file completely erases it from your hard disk, so be sure you truly want to take this action before clicking the final OK button that sends your file into digital oblivion.

Once you've made up your mind that the file has to go, use the following steps to delete it:

1. Select File → File Operations → Delete from the Quicken menu.

2. From the Look in drop-down list, select the location of the file (Figure 16-4).

3. From the display window, select the file to be deleted.

4. Once you're sure you have selected the correct file, click OK to proceed.

5. Before erasing the file, Quicken asks for confirmation.

6. Once you've double-checked that this file is the one you want to remove, type **yes** in the Type "yes" to confirm field.

7. Click OK to delete the file.

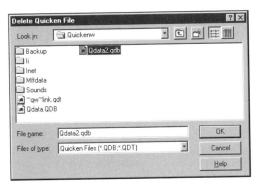

Figure 16-4 The results of this action are permanent, so look before you delete!

If you're using Windows 95, don't depend on the Recycle Bin to get your files back if you change your mind. Quicken does not use the Recycle Bin, and your files are gone.

Rename

When you first set up Quicken, it automatically names your file Qdata. Certainly not a name you'd choose for your firstborn, but heck, it's only a checkbook. Or is it? You may decide to create one file for your personal accounts and another for your business accounts. Or there may be more than one individual keeping track of her accounts on the same computer. In either case, it would help to have a filename that is more descriptive than Qdata or Qdata1. It's always a drag when you enter a half dozen transactions and then realize you opened the wrong file.

To avoid that potential problem, you can rename your data files by following these steps:

1. From the Quicken menu, select ⌷ File ⌷ → ⌷ File Operations ⌷ → ⌷ Rename ⌷.

2. Select the file you want to rename (Figure 16-5).

3. In New Name for Quicken File, enter the new name for the file.

4. Click OK to complete the procedure.

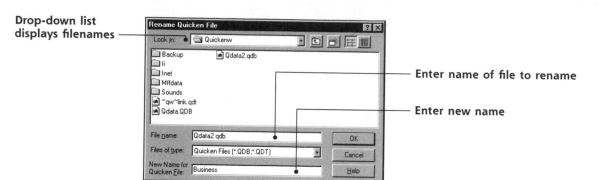

Drop-down list displays filenames

Enter name of file to rename

Enter new name

Figure 16-5 Changing the name makes it easier to identify your Quicken files.

TIP Quicken data files are composed of a number of different files, each containing various portions of your information. One file holds all your transactions, another your investment information, another your online banking information, and so on. It is not necessary for you to rename each of the individual files. When you use Quicken's Rename feature, it automatically renames all files associated with your main data file.

Validate

All files, including Quicken data files, can become damaged or corrupted from time to time. Quicken has a built-in utility that checks the integrity of your data file and, if possible, repairs any damage it finds.

If you're having trouble with a data file, you can run the Validate utility by doing the following:

1. Select `File` → `File Operations` → `Validate` from the Quicken menu.

2. Enter the name of the file you want to check.

3. Click OK.

4. If the file is undamaged, Quicken returns a message stating that no errors are found. Click OK to return to your work.

5. If errors are found, Quicken attempts to rebuild the file to fix it. Most of the time, this works.

6. If errors are found that cannot be corrected, Quicken returns a message indicating as much and recommends that you contact Intuit technical support. Click OK to return to your work.

TIP If the file contains important data and you don't have a current backup, a good idea is to contact the support department at Intuit. Very often the support staff can repair damaged files and recover the lost information.

Export

If you have a laptop and do a fair amount of traveling, you might keep track of your credit card expenditures on the road while your spouse is at home maintaining the checking accounts on the PC. Unless you merge the information you have input separately, neither of you will have complete records. The answer to this dilemma is Quicken's Import/Export feature. Like government and gridlock, you can't have one without the other. You won't have anything to import unless you first export it from somewhere else.

Follow these steps to export data from a Quicken file:

1. Open the file from which you want to export data.

2. Select File → File Operations → Export from the main menu to access the QIF (Quicken Interchange Format) Export dialog box (Figure 16-6).

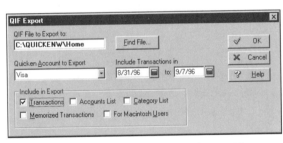

Figure 16-6 Taking your data on the road is a snap.

3. Enter the location and name of the file to export to or select Find File if you want to use a previously created file.

TIP If you decide to use an existing file, it must be a QIF file, and the new data will overwrite any data currently in the file. Before replacing the old file, however, Quicken prompts you for confirmation.

4. From the Quicken Account to Export drop-down list, select the account from which you want to export data.

5. Set the date range for transactions to include.

6. In the Include in Export section of the dialog box, check off the items you want to export to the new file. Your choices are all Transactions for the specified account, the complete Accounts List, the complete Category List, all Memorized Transactions, and an option for exporting For Macintosh Users.

Import

Quicken's Import feature enables you to bring information into Quicken from another Quicken file or from any other application that can create a QIF (Quicken Interchange Format) file.

Follow these steps to begin importing:

1. To secure your data in the event of a mishap while importing, make a backup of the file into which you are transferring the information.

2. Select `File` → `File Operations` → `Import` from the Quicken menu to bring up the QIF Import window (Figure 16-7).

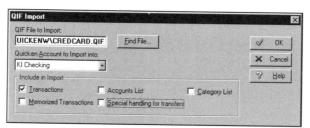

Figure 16-7   Import lets you merge data from other sources.

3. Enter the name of the QIF file to import or click Find File to select an existing file.

4. Select the account into which you want to import the new data.

5. Select the desired import options.

You use the Special handling for transfers option when you've been exporting data from multiple Quicken accounts into the same file. If you want to import that file in order to re-create those transactions, you now specify Special handling to warn Quicken to check transactions and prevent duplications (because you may have exported the same transaction more than once to various files).

BONUS

M anaging your system carefully is your insurance that your data will always be safe and available.

Don't back up on your backup

Having two or more sets of backup disks and rotating them is important. In other words, use backup disk 1 today, backup disk 2 tomorrow, backup disk 1 the following day, and so on. This setup is called an *A/B system*, and the easiest way to implement it is to think of Disk 1 as the "odd day disk" and disk 2 as the "even day disk." The purpose of this rotation is to avoid backing up onto your last good backup. The hard disk gremlins seem to know when you do this, and they manage to corrupt your data so that you're backing up bad data over the good data from yesterday.

Some people (like me) go so far as to use seven disks, one for each day. This way, you not only have additional backups, but you also have access to information that you may have deleted and then had second thoughts about. Of course, if you do restore the data from two or three days ago, you have to re-enter everything after that date.

Oops, no backup and I deleted my file

You may be able to recover a deleted file with the right software. The truth is, when you delete a file, you don't actually remove it. Instead, the space it occupies is marked as available for the operating system to use the next time it has information to write to the hard disk. It's kind of like rewinding a videotape and putting it in a pile to be reused. Until you put it into the VCR and record over it, the original information is still there. Once you tape over it, however, it is gone forever.

Third-party software such as Norton Utilities from Symantec can recover files that have been deleted as long as they have not been overwritten. Therefore, if you accidentally erase an important file by mistake and want to recover it by using disk utility software such as Norton, do not save anything to the hard drive. Doing so dramatically reduces the chances of your being able to undelete the lost file.

16

Summary

Although file management may not be the most glamorous of tasks, you can now see the important role it plays. Backing up is a must. Your data is only as secure as your last backup. Copying, deleting, and renaming certainly come in handy when your files become unmanageable or obsolete. Quicken's validation feature is like a spare tire — you generally don't give it much thought, but you're sure glad it's there when you get a flat. Last but not least, importing and exporting give you the flexibility to transfer your work between computers and applications.

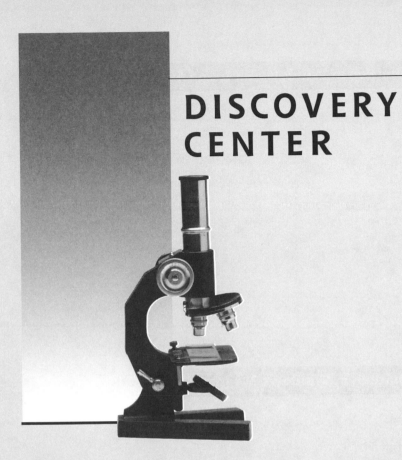

DISCOVERY CENTER

Shorten your learning time with this Discovery Center section. It high-lights, chapter by chapter, the Quicken features that can streamline and automate your finances. Try the procedures here as a quick preview of the book, or turn to this section for a handy reference or review.

CHAPTER 1

To Start Quicken in Windows 95 (page 10)

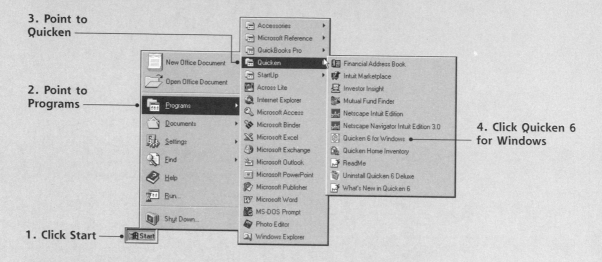

3. Point to Quicken

2. Point to Programs

4. Click Quicken 6 for Windows

1. Click Start

To Start Quicken in Windows 3.x (page 10)

1. Double-click the Quicken program group.

2. Double-click the Quicken icon.

To Set Up Your First Bank Account (page 11)

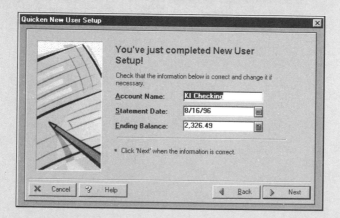

Follow the simple directions to enter an account name, a starting date for tracking the account, and the account balance.

To Find Your Way Around Quicken's Screen (page 18)

Advice   How Do I? help button

Menu bar

Register button bar

Account register holds transaction entries

Quick Tabs help you move through Quicken windows

To Do icon for Quicken Reminder feature

Speaker icon turns QCards on and off

Activity bar

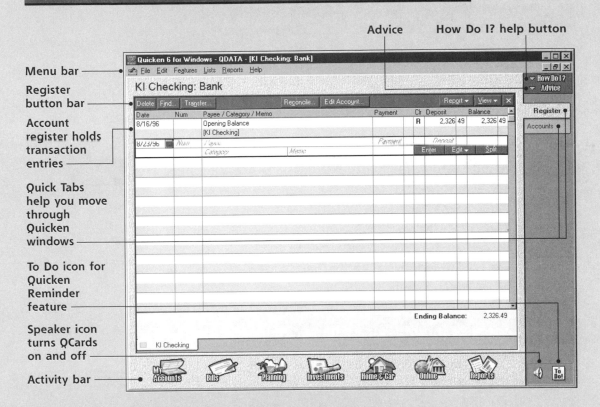

To Exit Quicken in Windows 95 (page 32)

Click the Close button (the X) on the right edge of the title bar.

To Exit Quicken in Windows 3.x (page 32)

Select File → Exit .

CHAPTER 2

To Enter a Check into the Register (page 38)

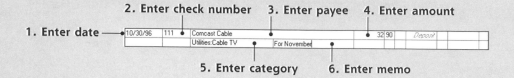

2. Enter check number   3. Enter payee   4. Enter amount

1. Enter date

| 10/30/96 | 111 | Comcast Cable | | 32 | 90 | *Deposit* | |
| | | Utilities:Cable TV | For November | | | | |

5. Enter category   6. Enter memo

To Change the Transaction Date Using the Calendar (page 38)

Today's date appears automatically in each new transaction. To enter a different transaction date, you can use the calendar as follows:

1. Click the Calendar icon next to the date field.

2. Click the arrows to move to the next or previous month.

3. Click a date to insert it as the transaction date.

To See a Graph of Your Expense Categories (page 46)

To view a pie graph that displays how much you've spent on each category, click the Report button on the register and select Expense Summary Graph.

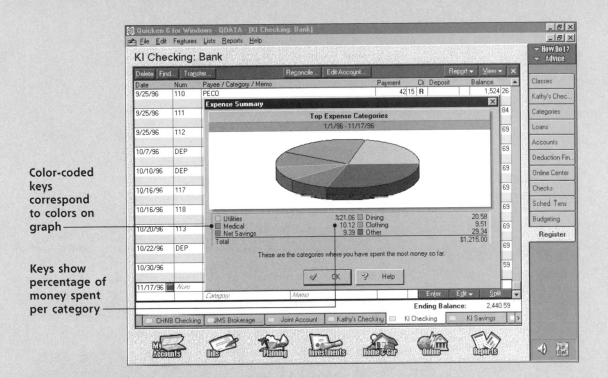

Color-coded keys correspond to colors on graph

Keys show percentage of money spent per category

To Delete a Transaction (page 49)

If you want to delete a transaction, do the following:

1. Click any field on that transaction's line in the register to highlight it.

2. Click Delete on the register.

3. Quicken asks if you are sure you want to remove this transaction from your file. Answer Yes if you are sure.

CHAPTER 3

To Start the Check-Writing Process (page 54)

1. Choose the account from which you want to write the checks.

2. Select Features → Paying Bills → Write Checks to open the Write Checks window.

To Write a Check (page 56)

Enter payee

Quicken automatically spells out amount in proper place

Enter date of check

Enter numerical amount

Click to finalize and save check

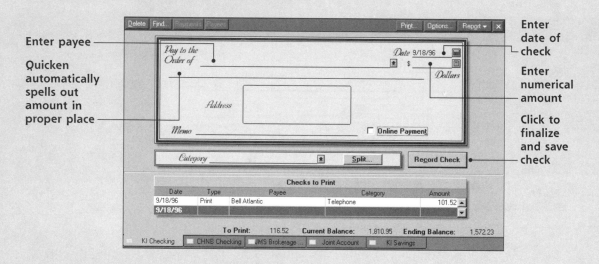

To Edit a Check (page 58)

1. From the Checks to Print register, select the check to edit.

2. Move to the fields you want to change and make the changes.

3. Select Record Check to save the changes.

To Delete a Check (page 58)

1. Select the check to delete from the Checks to Print register.

2. Click the Delete button.

3. Click OK to confirm the deletion.

To Void a Check (page 58)

1. In the Checks to Print register, click the check to void.
2. From the Quicken menu bar, select [Edit] → [Transaction] → [Void].
3. Click Record Check to complete the void.

To Set Up Your Printer (page 68)

Select printer

Select the type of check you're using

Click to insert partial pages of checks

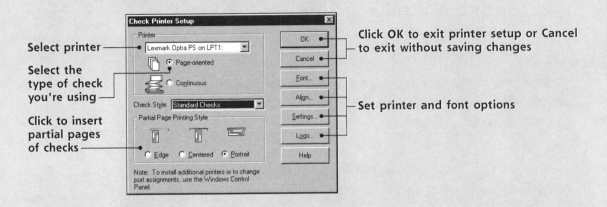

Click OK to exit printer setup or Cancel to exit without saving changes

Set printer and font options

To Print Checks (page 71)

Click to print all available checks

Click to print checks within a certain date range

Click to print individual selected checks

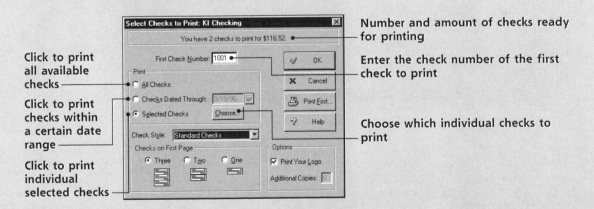

Number and amount of checks ready for printing

Enter the check number of the first check to print

Choose which individual checks to print

CHAPTER 4

To Void a Check (page 76)

To void a check (and put the amount for which it was written back into your checkbook balance):

1. Select (highlight) the transaction by clicking anywhere on the transaction's line.

2. Press Ctrl+V. The payment field of the transaction no longer shows an amount, and the word *VOID* is entered in the Payee field, in front of the payee's name.

3. Press Enter.

To Track Payroll Deductions (page 78)

To keep track of the deductions on your paycheck, go to the register for the bank account into which you deposit your pay and follow these steps:

1. Enter the transaction date.

2. Select Deposit in the Num field.

3. Enter the payee (use the company name as it appears on your W-2 form).

4. Click the Split button at the bottom of the register.

5. Enter the categories and amounts of the items on your paycheck stub. Use a positive number for your gross pay and negative numbers for the deductions. The resulting balance is the amount of your deposit. It looks like this:

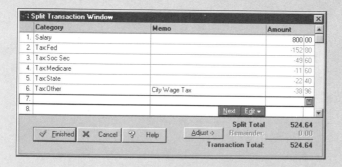

To Enter a Stock Purchase (page 81)

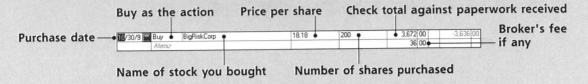

Enter the following information:

* Purchase date
* Buy as the action
* Name of stock you bought
* Price per share
* Number of shares purchased
* Broker's fee if any
* Check total against paperwork received

CHAPTER 5

To Begin the Account Balancing Process (page 85)

1. Switch to Register view by using the Ctrl+R shortcut.

2. From the account tabs, select the Quicken account to reconcile.

3. Click Reconcile from the register button bar. You see a dialog box to complete.

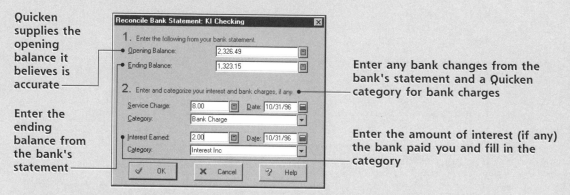

Quicken supplies the opening balance it believes is accurate

Enter the ending balance from the bank's statement

Enter any bank changes from the bank's statement and a Quicken category for bank charges

Enter the amount of interest (if any) the bank paid you and fill in the category

To Reconcile the Bank Statement with the Quicken Register (page 86)

1. Enter the necessary information from your bank statement in the Reconcile Bank Statement dialog box.

2. Click OK to proceed to the Reconcile window.

Checks sorted by check number instead of by date makes process easier

Clear Quicken items that match bank statement by clicking in Clr Column next to item

Bank charges and interest entered in previous dialog box are marked as cleared

Deposits listed in date order

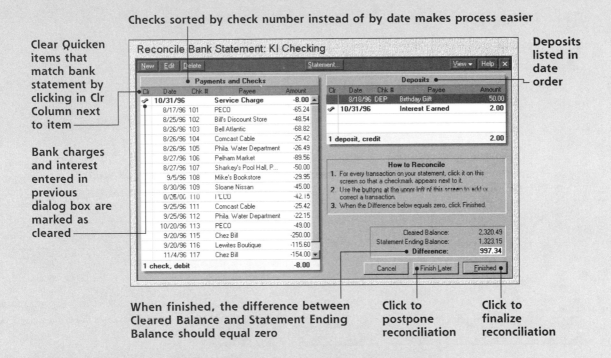

Reconcile Bank Statement: KI Checking

New | Edit | Delete | Statement... | View ▼ | Help | ×

Payments and Checks

Clr	Date	Chk #	Payee	Amount
✓	10/31/96		Service Charge	-8.00
	8/17/96	101	PECO	-65.24
	8/25/96	102	Bill's Discount Store	-48.54
	8/26/96	103	Bell Atlantic	-68.82
	8/26/96	104	Comcast Cable	-25.42
	8/26/96	105	Phila. Water Department	-26.49
	8/27/96	106	Pelham Market	-89.56
	8/27/96	107	Sharkey's Pool Hall, P...	-50.00
	9/5/96	108	Mike's Bookstore	-29.95
	8/30/96	109	Sloane Nissan	-45.00
	9/25/96	110	PECO	-42.15
	9/25/96	111	Comcast Cable	-25.42
	9/25/96	112	Phila. Water Department	-22.15
	10/20/96	113	PECO	-49.00
	9/20/96	115	Chez Bill	-250.00
	9/20/96	116	Lewites Boutique	-115.60
	11/4/96	117	Chez Bill	-154.00

1 check, debit   -8.00

Deposits

Clr	Date	Chk #	Payee	Amount
	8/18/96	DEP	Birthday Gift	50.00
✓	10/31/96		Interest Earned	2.00

1 deposit, credit   2.00

How to Reconcile

1. For every transaction on your statement, click it on this screen so that a checkmark appears next to it.
2. Use the buttons at the upper left of this screen to add or correct a transaction.
3. When the Difference below equals zero, click Finished.

Cleared Balance: 2,320.49
Statement Ending Balance: 1,323.15
● Difference: 997.34

Cancel | ● Finish Later | Finished ●

When finished, the difference between Cleared Balance and Statement Ending Balance should equal zero

Click to postpone reconciliation

Click to finalize reconciliation

To Resolve Unreconcilable Differences (page 92)

1. In the Reconcile Bank Statement window, click Finished.

2. The Adjust Balance dialog box appears because you need to make an adjustment to balance your account (Quicken figures the adjustment amount automatically and displays it).

3. Change the Adjustment Date to match the date of the bank statement.

4. Select Adjust to have Quicken make the adjustment transaction.

CHAPTER 6

To Create a Memorized Transaction (page 99)

1. Open the appropriate register or window and enter the new transaction.

2. When all the information is entered, press Enter to save the new record.

 T I P **If you have turned on the QuickFill option Use Enter Key to Move Between Fields, pressing Enter does not save the record. To save the transaction and move to a blank record, hold down Ctrl and press Enter.**

3. Right-click anywhere on the transaction you want to memorize.

4. Select Memorize Transaction from the pop-up menu.

5. Click OK to confirm your decision to memorize the transaction.

To Edit a Memorized Transaction (page 101)

1. Press Ctrl+T to open the Memorized Transactions List.

2. From the list, select the transaction to change.

3. Click Edit on the Memorized Transactions button bar to open the Edit Memorized Transaction dialog box. Enter or change information in the dialog box.

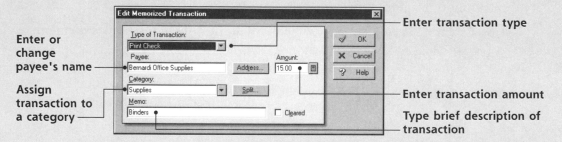

Click Address to edit the payee's address (only available for Print Check transactions). Click Split to assign the transaction to multiple categories. Check Cleared if the transaction has cleared the bank.

1. Press Ctrl+J to open the Scheduled Transaction List.

2. From the Scheduled Transaction List button bar, select New to access the Create Scheduled Transaction dialog box.

3. Indicate whether this is a regular transaction or an online transaction.

4. After you've selected the type of transaction, Quicken opens the Create Scheduled Transaction dialog box, where you do the following:

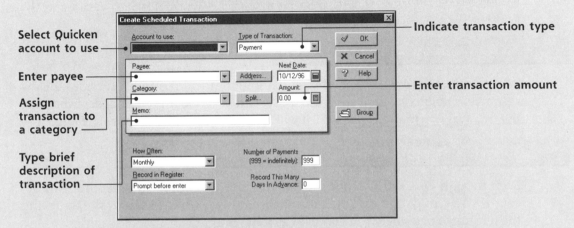

Select Quicken account to use

Enter payee

Assign transaction to a category

Type brief description of transaction

Indicate transaction type

Enter transaction amount

If this is a Check to Print, click Address to enter payee's address. Click Split to assign a transaction to two or more categories. In the How Often field, enter how often the payment is due. In the Record in Register field, indicate when the transaction should be recorded in the account register. Enter how many payments are left in the Number of Payments field. Enter how many days in advance Quicken should remind you under Record This Many Days in Advance. Click Group to create transaction groups for several transactions due at the same time.

CHAPTER 7

To Create a New Account (page 119)

1. Go to the Activity Bar and place your mouse pointer on My Accounts.

2. Choose `Create a New Account` from the pop-up menu.

3. Pick the type of account you want to create.

Now just answer the questions as the EasyStep program for creating new accounts walks you through the process. The questions are different for each type of account.

To Name an Account (page 120)

When you name an account, choose a name that will remind you about the account's contents when you see it listed. You can also add an optional description of the account when naming it, which will help you remember why you created it.

To Pick a Starting Date for a New Account (page 121)

Even though Quicken asks for the date of your last bank statement for this account, you can decide for yourself which date you want to use to start tracking the account's activities. You can use the following:

* Date of the last statement from the bank
* Date of an earlier bank statement that you reconciled to the penny
* Date of the last transaction in your manual checkbook
* First day of this year

If you want to see a list of all the accounts you've created, press Ctrl+A.

Use buttons on bar to make changes to selected account

Use tabs to view Account List sorted by type

Hand indicates hidden account

Lightning bolt means account set up for online banking

Select or deselect to view/hide hidden accounts

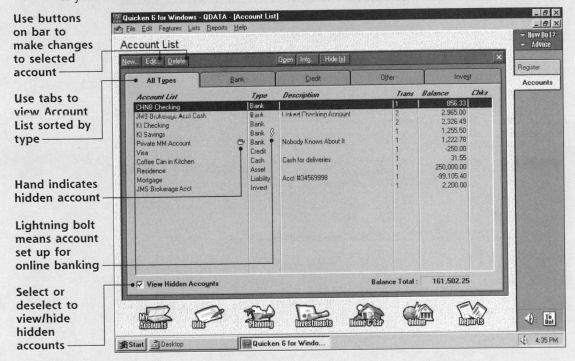

CHAPTER 8

To Enter Information for a New Category (page 147)

Enter category name

Enter optional description

Choose the type of categories you want to track

Indicate if this is related to a tax deduction, and if so, choose the appropriate tax form

To Modify Categories (page 150)

1. Open the Category & Transfer List.

2. Select the category you want to change.

3. Select Edit from the button bar.

4. Change the name, type (income or expense), or tax information.

5. Click OK.

To Add a Subcategory (page153)

1. From the Category & Transfer List window, choose New.

2. Enter a name and description for the subcategory in the Setup Category dialog box that appears.

3. Select Subcategory of in the Type section of the dialog box and scroll through the drop-down list to find the category you want as the parent.

4. If the subcategory is a tax deduction, select Tax-related and choose a tax form from the drop-down list in the Form field.

5. Click OK after you have finished filling in the information.

To Add a Supercategory (page 155)

1. Go to the Category & Transfer List window and select Super to bring up the Manage Supercategories dialog box.

2. Click New to open the Create New Supercategory dialog box.

3. Enter a name in the Supercategory Name field.

4. Click OK.

CHAPTER 9

To Use Your Existing Quicken File for Business (page 162)

The easiest (and safest) way to use your current Quicken file for business is to open a separate bank account for business use and then create that account in Quicken. Make sure that you use the business account for all business transactions (don't mix business and personal money). Make sure that you enter the transaction information in Quicken with plenty of details.

This detail gives all the information you need to analyze the state of your business and provides your accountant with the information needed for tax returns and business planning. It also should keep you safe from an IRS raid.

To Use Business Categories for Transactions (page 166)

1. Press Ctrl+C to bring up the Category & Transfer List.

2. Choose Add from the list's button bar to display the Add Categories dialog box.

3. Click the arrow to the right of the Available Categories field and select Business. The business categories are displayed in the box below the Available Categories field.

4. Choose Mark All to select all the business income and expense categories. Check marks appear next to each business category.

5. Select Add to add these categories to your system.

6. Click OK to complete the addition of these categories.

To Create a Class (page 163)

Use classes to sort your transactions by meaningful business criteria. You can use classes that represent customers, projects, or any other business element you want to track. Creating a class is simple:

1. Press Ctrl+L to open the Class List.

2. Choose New to create a new class.

3. Enter a name and optional description for the class.

To Use a Class in a Transaction (page 167)

During transaction entry, when you enter the category for a transaction, add a forward slash (/) and enter the class name. If the class doesn't exist, Quicken lets you add it right then and there.

To Use Subclasses (page 167)

You can narrow the way you track classes by using subclasses. Except there's really no such thing as a subclass. Instead, you can use any existing class as a subclass.

Therefore, if you have classes that are customers, projects, or services you provide, you can create a class for each. Perhaps you provide three or four different services, such as Sales of Goods, Minor Repairs, House Calls, and so on. When you provide one of those services for one of your customers, you can create a class for an entity of customer:service.

Once you've used classes and subclasses in transactions, you can build reports that use that differentiation.

To View a Quick Register Report on Your Business (page 169)

1. Click a transaction that contains either the Payee/Paid By entry or the category on which you want information.

2. Choose Report from the Register's button bar.

3. Select a report from either the Payee/Paid By field or the Category field.

If you choose a deposit transaction, the Payee report shows you all the income for that customer (assuming that the customer's name is in the Payee/Paid By field). If you choose a deposit transaction and the category is a form of business income, the category report shows you all the transactions for that type of income. If you choose an expense transaction, the category report shows you all those business expenses.

CHAPTER 10

To Create a Budget (page 182)

1. Place your mouse pointer over the Planning icon in the Activity Bar.

2. From the fly-over menu, select Budget My Spending.

3. In the Budget window, click New in the button bar. Complete the dialog box as shown here.

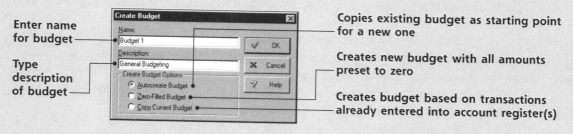

Enter name for budget ⟶

Type description of budget ⟶

Copies existing budget as starting point for a new one

Creates new budget with all amounts preset to zero

Creates budget based on transactions already entered into account register(s)

4. Then fill out the information to configure your budget.

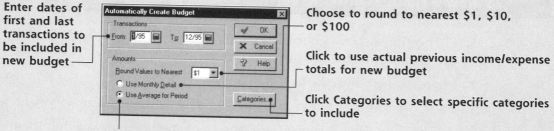

Enter dates of first and last transactions to be included in new budget ⟶

Choose to round to nearest $1, $10, or $100

Click to use actual previous income/expense totals for new budget

Click Categories to select specific categories to include

Click if you want Quicken to use monthly average of your total income/expenses

To Export a Budget (page 189)

1. Open the budget you want to export.

2. Click Edit and select Copy All.

3. Open the software application (spreadsheet, word processor, and so on) to which you want to export.

4. In the software window, select Edit → Paste .

To Create a Budget Report or Graph (page 190)

Use the steps outlined in the "Creating Budget Reports" section of Chapter 10, or follow these steps:

1. Place your mouse pointer over the Reports icon in the Activity Bar.

2. To bring up the EasyAnswer Reports and Graphs window, select Show Me a Graph or Report of My Finances. You see the dialog box shown here.

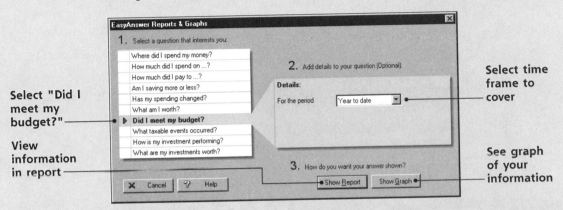

Select "Did I meet my budget?"

View information in report

Select time frame to cover

See graph of your information

To Create a Savings Goal (page 194)

1. Place your mouse pointer over the Planning icon in the Activity Bar.

2. From the fly-over menu, select Save for an Upcoming Expense.

3. In the Savings Goals window, click the New button to open the Create New Savings Goal dialog box and fill in the information indicated here.

Enter descriptive name for goal

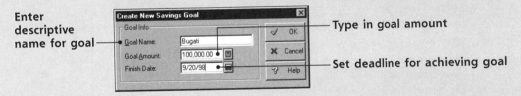

Type in goal amount

Set deadline for achieving goal

CHAPTER 11

To Create a Basic Forecast (page 202)

1. Select [Features] from the File menu and then choose [Planning] → [Forecasting].

2. Enter the date range for which you have transactions that Quicken needs to view to create a forecast for the future.

3. Select known items to forecast based on specific, existing transactions.

4. Choose estimated items to forecast based on the monthly averages for your existing transactions.

5. Select whether to use transactions from specific bank accounts or all bank accounts.

6. Choose whether to use transactions from specific categories or all categories.

7. Click OK.

To Examine and Change a Forecast Graph (page 210)

Color-coded legend indicates future and past balances

Use buttons to change, print, or save forecasts

Enter items to add to forecasting calculations

Change time period used for calculations

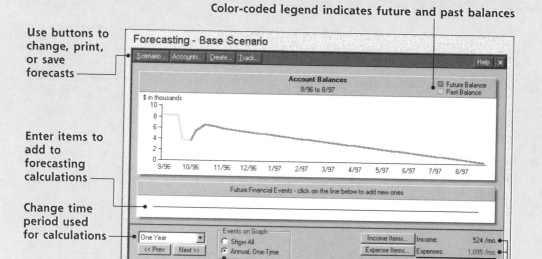

Specify what you want graph to display   Monthly averages for revenue and expense

To Compare Two Forecasts (page 212)

1. Select Features → Planning → Forecasting .

2. Click the Scenario button to bring up the Manage Forecast Scenarios dialog box and choose the first forecast.

3. Click the Scenario button again, and in the Display Options section, select Compare Current Scenario with.

4. Click the arrow to the right of the field and choose a scenario for this comparison.

5. Click Done to see a graph comparing the two scenarios.

To Create a New Income Item for a Forecast (page 207)

1. In the Forecasting window, select Income Items.

2. Click New.

3. Enter a description of the item.

4. Enter the amount.

5. Enter the frequency for this item. Click the arrow to see a drop-down list and then choose a frequency.

6. Select Average Amount to create an estimated item. This means the item will be considered an average amount that is spread out over the period of time you selected in the Frequency field.

7. Select Next Scheduled Date to create an item that is forecasted on the date you enter.

8. Choose More to open a category dialog box so that you can enter a category for the new item (this step is optional because it's a forecast, not a real transaction).

9. Click OK after you're finished. Quicken returns you to the Forecast Income Items dialog box.

If this new item is the only thing you want to add to the forecast, click Done.

CHAPTER 12

To Get Expert Advice on Planning (page 216)

1. Put the Quicken CD-ROM into your CD-ROM device.

2. Click Advice.

3. Select a topic.

Get information on related topics

See manual about using Quicken tools for this topic

See examples of how Quicken tools can help you carry out advice

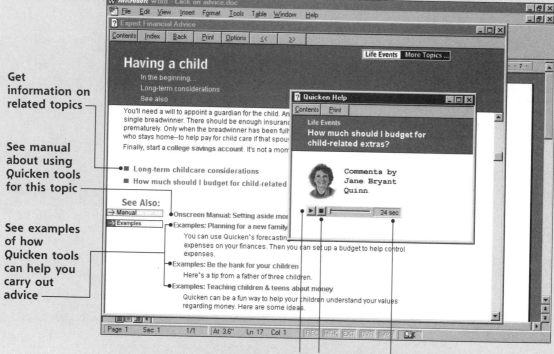

Hear audio again   Stop audio   Time remaining for audio

TIP If you're using Quicken in Windows 3.*x*, your advice screen looks a bit different, but the information is all there.

Click More Topics to jump to a new subject. Click the green text to see information on that topic. You have several other options in this window as well.

1. Place your pointer on the Planning icon in the Activity Bar to pop up the Planning menu.

2. Select Use Financial Planning Calculators to see the Financial Planners dialog box that features the five Quicken planners.

3. Select College and then click OK.

Tell the College Planner how you want it to calculate the figures:

* If you know how much you'll be able to contribute each year and have already begun saving for college, select Annual College Costs to have Quicken tell you the college expense you can afford (then you can pick a school that comes close).

* If you know the annual cost of the college and you know how much you can contribute from your income, select Current College Savings to have Quicken tell you how much you'll have to save to make up the difference.

* If you know the cost and have begun saving, select Annual Contribution to have Quicken tell you how much additional money you will have to find each year.

Fill in all the information on the College Planner dialog box and then choose Schedule to see what you have to do to accomplish your plans.

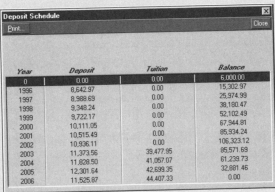

Year	Deposit	Tuition	Balance
0	0.00	0.00	6,000.00
1996	8,642.97	0.00	15,302.97
1997	8,988.69	0.00	25,974.99
1998	9,348.24	0.00	38,180.47
1999	9,722.17	0.00	52,102.49
2000	10,111.05	0.00	67,944.81
2001	10,515.49	0.00	85,934.24
2002	10,936.11	0.00	106,323.12
2003	11,373.56	39,477.95	85,571.69
2004	11,828.50	41,057.07	61,239.73
2005	12,301.64	42,699.35	32,881.46
2006	11,525.87	44,407.33	0.00

CHAPTER 13

To Link a Category with a Tax Form (page 234)

1. Open the Category & Transfer List by choosing `Lists` → `Category/Transfer`. Notice that categories that already have a tax link are marked with the word *tax* in the Tax column.

2. Select the category for which you want to create a tax link.

3. Select Edit from the button bar.

4. Click the box titled Tax-related. This announces to Quicken that the category is tax-related.

5. Click the arrow to the right of the Form box to see a listing of tax forms.

6. Select the tax form that matches this category.

7. Click OK to link the category to your tax return.

To Handle the Payment of Estimated Taxes (page 236)

If you have to pay estimated taxes, you should create specific categories and link them to the appropriate IRS forms. For federal taxes, create a category, mark it as tax-related, and assign it to Schedule 1040:Fed. Estimated Tax. For state taxes, create a category, mark it as tax-related, and assign it to Schedule A:State Estimated Tax.

To Create a Tax Summary Report (page 237)

1. From the menu bar, select `Reports` → `Home` → `Tax Summary`.

2. Choose Create to tell Quicken to look at all the transactions for tax-related categories and summarize them on your screen.

3. Scroll through the report to see all the lines. If anything appears that shouldn't be there, go to the account register and change the transaction so that it isn't tax-related.

4. Click Print to get a hard copy of this report.

Before you can produce an accurate report, you must go back through your transactions and make sure that you've entered all the data about your investment. For each purchase you made, enter the date, the number of shares, and the cost of those shares. Also enter any broker fees. For each sale you made, enter the date, the number of shares you sold, and the price you received for them. Also make sure that you've entered any fees.

Then you're ready to produce the Capital Gains Report by following these steps:

1. From the Quicken menu, select | Reports | → | Investment | → | Capital Gains |.

2. The Create Report dialog box appears with the Capital Gains Report selected.

3. Select Create to see the report.

4. Choose Print to have a hard copy of the report.

The Capital Gains Report lists (and totals) short-term and long-term gains separately. When you sold stocks, if you didn't indicate the specific lot (if you purchased the stock at different times), the report assumes you sold the oldest purchase first.

CHAPTER 14

To See a Summary of a Whole Year's Income and Expenditures (page 250)

1. From the Quicken menu bar, select [Reports] → [Other] → [Summary].

2. When the Create Report dialog box appears, the Summary Report is already selected.

3. Make sure the Report Dates are for all of last year.

4. Click Create.

Click for hard copy of report

Double-click for detailed report

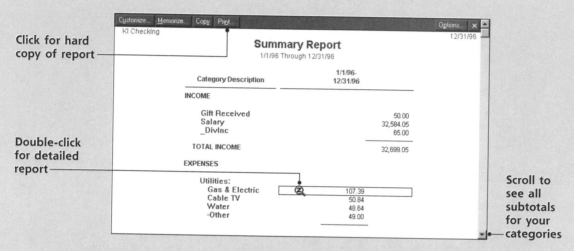

Scroll to see all subtotals for your categories

Click on a line item and, when the pointer changes its shape to resemble the letter Z (for zoom), double-click to see a detailed report on that item.

To Get a Report on the Tax-Related Data for the Year (page 253)

1. From the Quicken menu, select [Reports] → [Home] → [Tax Summary] to see the Create Report dialog box with the Tax Summary Report already highlighted for you.

2. Check the Report Dates fields to make sure that the entire year is selected as the range.

3. Click Create to see the Tax Summary Report.

Customize report to change way it displays

Memorize report to display it in future

Print hard copy

Change the way information is sorted

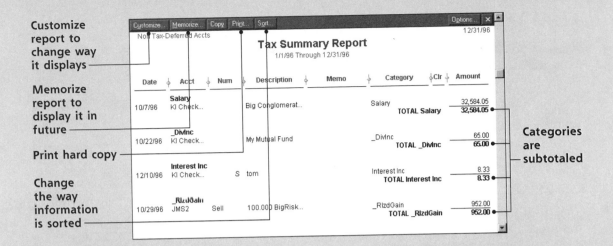

Categories are subtotaled

To Add an Iconbar to the Quicken Window (page 260)

Quicken Iconbar —

2. Click Show Top Iconbar —

1. Right-click anywhere in the QuickTabs column —

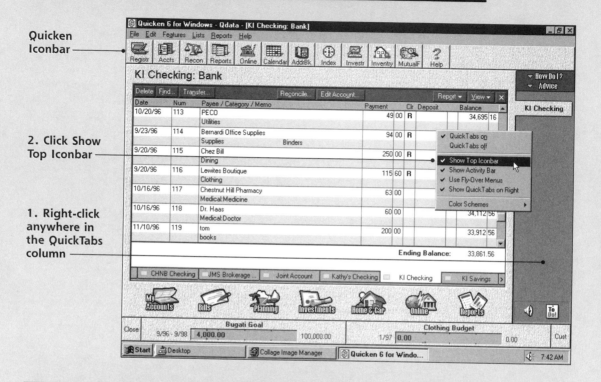

To Customize the Iconbar (page 261)

1. Open the Customize Iconbar dialog box by clicking Edit → Options → Iconbar .

Scroll to see icons in current Iconbar

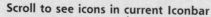

Check to show icons without text in Iconbar

Check to show text labels (without icons) in Iconbar

Check both boxes to show icons with text labels in Iconbar

2. Click the following buttons to affect icons:

* New to add a new icon to the Iconbar

* Edit to edit an existing icon on the Iconbar

* Delete to remove an icon from the Iconbar
* Reset to return the Iconbar to its original (default) form

To Customize Basic Quicken settings (page 264)

Activate the General Options window by clicking `Edit` → `Options` → `Quicken Program`. Then select the appropriate Options tab.

To Customize Billminder (page 267)

Click `Edit` → `Options` → `Reminders` to access the Reminder Options and tailor Billminder to accommodate your needs.

To Change the Desktop Settings (page 268)

To open the Save Desktop window, select `Edit` → `Options` → `Desktop`.

To Customize the Register (page 269)

Click `Edit` → `Options` → `Register` to activate the Register Options dialog box. Customize the register settings from the three available tabs.

To Customize Check Writing (page 273)

Access the Checks Options window by selecting `Edit` → `Options` → `Write Checks`. Then change the settings available on the three Check Options tabs.

CHAPTER 16

To Back Up Quicken Files (page 278)

1. Place a backup disk in the floppy drive and select File → Backup from the Quicken menu bar.

Choose drive containing backup disk —

Click to back up file you're working on —

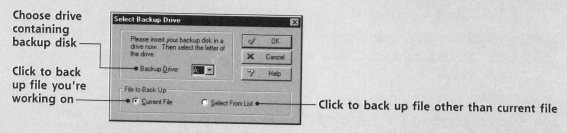

Click to back up file other than current file

2. Fill in the dialog box and click OK to begin the backup.

To Restore a File from a Backup Disk (page 280)

Insert your backup disk in the floppy drive and select File → Restore from the Quicken menu. Click the file you want to restore and click OK. If you're sure you want to replace the existing file, confirm your decision by clicking OK in the confirmation dialog box that appears.

To Make a Copy of Your Quicken File (page 281)

1. From the Quicken menu bar, select File → File Operations → Copy to access the Copy File window.

Type name of file to be created —

Type path (disk drive and directory) of new file —

Enter dates of first and last transactions to be included —

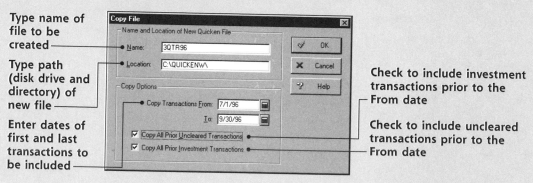

Check to include investment transactions prior to the From date

Check to include uncleared transactions prior to the From date

2. Fill in the dialog box and click OK to create the new file.

To Delete a Quicken File (page 282)

Activate the Delete Quicken File window by selecting `File` → `File Operations` → `Delete` from the Quicken menu bar. Click the file you want to delete and click OK. Because this is a permanent action, Quicken asks you to confirm your decision by typing in the word *yes*. If you're sure you want to delete the select file, type **yes** in the box and click OK to delete the file.

To Rename a Quicken File (page 283)

Click `File` → `File Operations` → `Rename` to access the Rename Quicken File dialog box. Click the file to rename and then type the new name for the file in the box provided. Click OK to complete the process and rename the file.

To Check the Integrity of a Quicken Data File (page 284)

Select `File` → `File Operations` → `Validate` from the Quicken menu. In the Validate Quicken File window, select the file to analyze. Click OK to start the validation process.

To Export Data from Quicken (page 285)

From the Quicken menu, select `File` → `File Operations` → `Export` to activate the QIF Export dialog box.

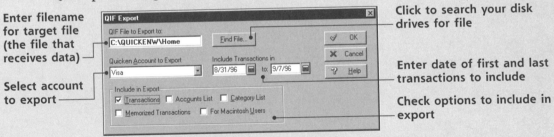

Enter filename for target file (the file that receives data)

Select account to export

Click to search your disk drives for file

Enter date of first and last transactions to include

Check options to include in export

Fill in the dialog box and click OK to export the data.

To Import Data into Quicken (page 286)

From the Quicken menu, select `File` → `File Operations` → `Import` to activate the QIF Import dialog box.

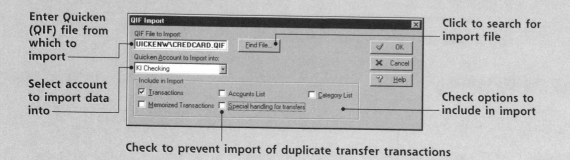

Enter Quicken (QIF) file from which to import

Select account to import data into

Click to search for import file

Check options to include in import

Check to prevent import of duplicate transfer transactions

Fill in the dialog box and click OK to begin the import process.

VISUAL INDEX

Setting Up an Account

When you set up an account, the more information you enter the better
Page 118

Enter tax information if account is tax-related
Page 137

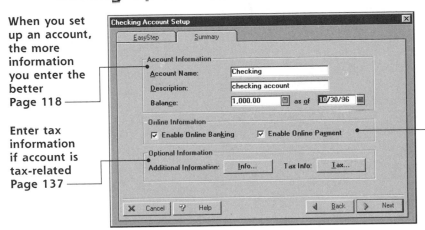

If you have an online agreement with your bank and/or pay bills online, mark account accordingly
Page 123

Writing Checks

Let Quicken print your checks
Page 54

Split expenses among multiple categories
Page 43

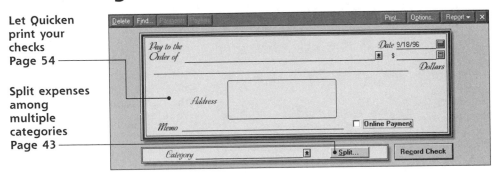

Balancing Your Checkbook

Enter information from your bank statement
Page 85

Bank charges and interest are attached to categories
Page 86

Icons for calculator and calendar
Page 86

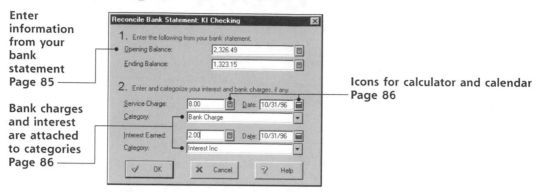

Creating a Budget

Create a budget to keep an eye on your expenses
Page 181

Select an option to tell Quicken how to put your budget together
Page 183

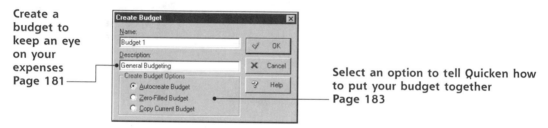

Using Categories

Set up categories to personalize the way you want to keep records
Page 145

If this category affects your taxes, tell Quicken and choose the right form
Page 147

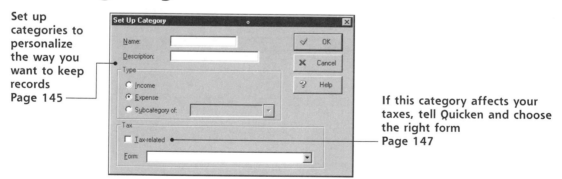

GOING ONLINE

The Internet is hot stuff, and buying a computer that doesn't come with a modem is almost impossible today. There's more to going online than exchanging e-mail, browsing the Net, and downloading nifty software and graphics; you can also make practical use of your modem and Quicken. However, this does complicate your bookkeeping a bit, because it makes it not so easy to correct errors, tear up checks, and so on. So, don't access that modem until you're really comfortable using Quicken.

Online banking is a way to use your computer, your modem, and Quicken to take care of business. Two features are available:

* **Online banking**, which is a way to keep an eye on your bank accounts, ensure that your Quicken registers have all the transactions (such as your ATM withdrawals), and even move money between accounts.

* **Online bill paying**, which lets you upload information about the bills you want to pay and, in a feat that seems like magic, gets your vendors their money without you having to write a check or lick an envelope flap.

Setting Up Online Services

If your bank participates in online services (the larger the bank, the better the odds are that it's part of the online movement), you can use Quicken and your modem to perform all sorts of banking chores. You can check your account, make sure that all the transactions in your account are transferred to your Quicken register (such as ATM withdrawals you forgot to enter), transfer money between accounts at the same bank, and generally keep an eye on your money.

The online banking service is also available at several investment companies, and you can go online to keep an eye on your portfolio.

To see if your bank is on the list of participating institutions, follow these steps:

1. Put your pointer on the Online icon of the Activity Bar.

2. Select Get Started with Online Banking & Investment.

3. Click Financial Institutions to see the list (Figure A-1).

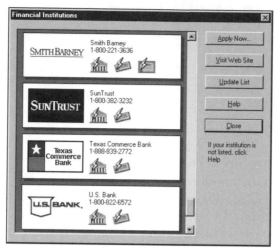

Figure A-1 The list of participating banks includes information about the services offered.

4. Use the scroll bar to move through the list to find your bank. Note the following:

* A lightning bolt on a bank building indicates online banking is available.

* A lightning bolt on a check indicates online bill paying is available.

* A lightning bolt on a stock certificate indicates online trading is available.

5. If a phone number is listed for your bank, give them a call. If no phone number is listed, call your bank and hunt down the online services department.

The bank will send you forms to fill out. You will have to keep track of secret passwords, codes, and all that CIA-type stuff. Once you have all the information, you have to set up Quicken for online services.

First, follow these steps to set up the bank account:

1. Open the bank account register and click Edit Account from the button bar to bring up the Edit Bank Account dialog box (Figure A-2).

2. Select Enable Online Banking or Enable Online Payment, or both.

3. Click Next to fill in the appropriate information for this account (Figure A-3).

4. After you have everything filled in, click Done.

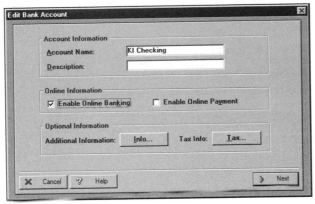

Figure A-2 Enable the online banking services you will
be using at this bank.

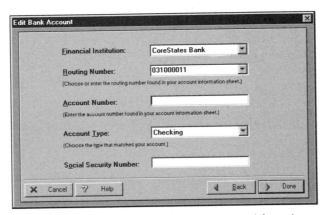

Figure A-3 Use the information you received from the
bank to make sure that all the data you enter
is correct.

Now that the bank account is set up properly, you can finish configuring
Quicken for online banking. Follow these steps:

1. Place your pointer on the Online icon of the Activity Bar.

2. Select Get Started with Online Banking & Investment.

3. Select Apply for Online Services to begin the EasyStep application
process (Figure A-4).

4. Indicate whether your account is an Individual or Business account and
then click Next. You will need to fill out a dialog box that asks for your
name and address. After you've completed it, click Next.

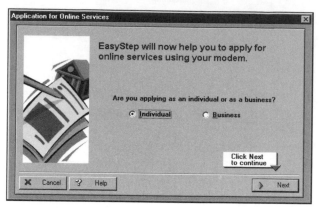

Figure A-4 Finish the setup phase for online services by letting Quicken walk you through each step.

5. Quicken asks you what made you decide to use online banking (software companies like to know these things) and presents a list of reasons. Pick the one that comes closest and click Next. You can also just click Next without answering the question.

6. Tell Quicken which financial institution you've made arrangements with and click Next.

7. Fill in the account information and the services you're applying for (Figure A-5) and then click Next.

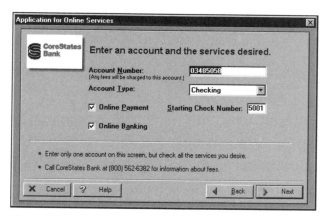

Figure A-5 The account information and the services you want are recorded.

8. Walk through the remaining EasyStep windows, filling out information as needed, including your Social Security Number, phone number, and some information the bank wants to protect the security of your online account information.

9. After all the data is entered, Quicken uses your modem to dial out to the bank's online site and finish the procedures for creating online access.

The information you enter differs from bank to bank, because some banks automatically make all your accounts available for online processing and other banks ask you to fill out information for each account.

If you're interested in online bill paying and your bank isn't a participating institution, check the Help files in Quicken to choose a way to use a third-party service for online check writing.

Using Online Services in Quicken

Once you have everything set up, you can easily go online to get your work done. It all starts with the Online icon in the Activity Bar, where you select Go to the Online Banking & Investment Center (Figure A-6).

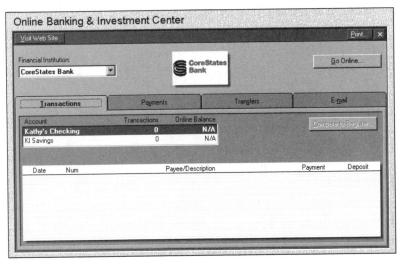

Figure A-6   The Online Banking & Investment Center window is the jumping-off place for your online work.

The online window has several tabs (which vary according to the online services you've selected).

Transactions tab

In the Transactions tab, you view data and perform tasks:

* Select the bank you want to work with in the Financial Institution box (for most people, there is only one bank).
* The Go Online button starts the process of connecting to the bank and retrieving transaction information.
* The Account List shows each account at the selected bank as well as the number of new transactions you've entered into that account since your last session online.
* The list of transactions is displayed for the selected account.
* Once you've downloaded transactions, the Compare to Register button is accessible so that you can reconcile the Quicken register with the bank's records.

The Financial Institution selection box and the Go Online button are available for every tab.

Payments tab

In the Payments tab, you can fill out information for online payment of bills:

* You can keep information about payees.
* You can fill out a payment form and assign a category.
* You can view a status report on payments you've entered.
* You can indicate a payment date for each transaction.

You can also view existing, repeating payments and cancel them to stop their online bill payments.

Transfers tab

Use the Transfers tab to move money between accounts at the same financial institution. To make it safe, Quicken displays the current balance for all the accounts.

E-mail tab

If your financial institution provides the service, you can send and receive messages. This is not a general e-mail system that you can use to send greetings to friends; it is a private mailbox system between you and the bank.

TROUBLESHOOTING GUIDE

The best troubleshooting advice I can give you is to try common sense before anything else. Start with the basics. If you can't print, make sure that the printer is plugged in, turned on, connected to your computer, and online. Even experienced computer users find themselves looking for complex solutions to problems that really have simple fixes. The next most important piece of advice is DON'T PANIC. Not only are you less apt to resolve the problem, chances are you'll make it even worse. This section helps you with common problems and is organized alphabetically by topic.

Accounts

Excuse me, I seem to have misplaced one of my accounts. This occurrence is not uncommon when you have more than one Quicken data file. You probably set up the account in the wrong file. To remedy this situation, you have to export the transactions from the account in the wrong file and import them to a new account in the right file (see Chapter 16 on managing files).

I'm trying to set up a new account and keep getting "Name already in use." What gives? Once an account or category name has been assigned, it cannot be reused. Occasionally when you delete an account and try to reuse the name, the problem persists. If this happens, check the Category & Transfer List. If the account name you deleted is still there, delete it again and try setting up the new account once more.

Budgets

Why can't I create a budget using AutoCreate? Try clearing the budget in the Budget window (Edit → Clear All), then save it and try AutoCreate again. If that doesn't do the trick, the problem may be that you don't have transactions in the register for the date range entered. Because AutoCreate uses information from your register, it cannot create a budget without existing transactions.

Why do I see an account that I already deleted? Occasionally Quicken is lax in doing its housekeeping and does not properly update your file. Go to the

Category List and delete the file there. Keep in mind, however, that you cannot actually delete an account from the Category List; this only works if it was previously deleted elsewhere.

Why aren't actual amounts and budgeted amounts the same when I use AutoCreate? You probably forgot to set the AutoCreate options to Use Monthly Detail and to Round Values to the nearest $1.00.

Categories

Why is one of my income categories displaying a negative amount in my report? Double-check your register entry for the transaction. You probably recorded a deposit in the Payment column or inadvertently assigned a payment to an income category.

Will transactions assigned to a category be deleted if I delete the category? Not to worry. The transactions will be safe, but they will not have a category. If you so desire, you can reassign them to a new or different category.

Why I don't see any categories on my Category List? Probably when you installed Quicken for the first time, you did not choose any categories to include in the file. This solution is easy. Simply go to the Category & Transfer List and select Add...[+]. From the Available Categories drop-down list, select the group of categories you want to add, mark the categories to add, click Add, and click OK to finalize the action.

Hold on. Now I have too many categories on my Category List. This is generally the result of duplicate transfers created when importing transactions from another Quicken file (see Chapter 16 on managing files).

Checks

Should I be concerned when I get the message, "Does not support full range of fonts"? As long as your checks are printing properly, you can ignore this message.

Why does Quicken tell me that there are "No checks to print" when I just entered them? You probably forgot to put Print in the Num field. This generally happens when entering a check in the register, because Quicken automatically does it for you when you enter checks in the Write Checks window.

How do I stop my printer from skipping and feeding blank checks? The first thing to do is make sure that you have selected the correct printer driver in Printer Setup. If you have, and the problem persists, try using the Generic/Text only printer driver.

Why isn't the address showing up in the window envelope.? I hate to ask, but did you enter an address for this payee? Okay, I'm sorry. No, you don't look that dumb, but it's my job to ask. Chances are the font you're using is too small. See Chapter 3 on printing checks for more information.

Why is only part of the date printing? This problem usually results from continuous feed checks that are not properly aligned. Use Quicken's printer adjustment features (see Chapter 3) to resolve this problem.

Data Files

I accidentally deleted my Quicken file. What do I do now? The first thing to do is nothing. Any action that causes one of your programs to write to the hard disk may make it impossible to recover your file. In reality, you have several options. If you have an unerase utility such as Norton's, run it and follow the instructions for recovering deleted files. You're looking for five files, not just one. They each have the name you gave them (Qdata if you didn't rename your file) with different extensions: .abd, .qel, qsd, .qmd, .qbd. If you don't have an unerase utility, you can restore from your last Quicken backup (you are making them regularly aren't you?). No? Shame on you. Fortunately, Quicken is prepared for such an event. Every seven days, it automatically makes a backup to your C:\Quickenw\backup directory. You lose any data input since it made the last backup, but at least you have most of your information.

Say, what was that password again? Okay, you memorized your password and ate the scrap of paper you wrote in on, and now you can't remember it. What do you? If you've recently added the password and have earlier backups without it, you can restore one of them and reenter the lost information. Your only other option is to contact Quicken Technical Support. You will have to send your file to them, and they will be able to remove the password.

Graphs

Why doesn't my color printer print color graphs? The first thing to check is the printer driver. Make sure that you're using the correct driver for your printer. If you have selected the correct printer driver, check the Graph options and be sure you have not checked off Use Patterns Instead of Colors.

Loans

Why is my current loan balance wrong? How do I fix it? Check to make sure that the loan was set up correctly. If it was, you may have incorrectly entered a loan payment. If the loan has been set up correctly and the payments are all accurate, you can adjust the balance from the View Loans window. Select Edit Loan, click Next, and change the Current Balance.

Why can't I reuse the name of a loan I've deleted? Because Quicken does not allow you to reuse an existing account or category name, you must delete not only the loan account but the liability account associated with it as well. If you want to maintain the liability account, you can simply rename it.

My loan schedule is wrong; how do I change it? This usually results from deleting a loan transaction without resetting the loan schedule. In the View Loans window, select Edit Loan, click Next, and change the due on date in the Payment section.

Quicken Options

Why did my Iconbar icons stop working? The most likely cause is damage to the icon settings file. Unfortunately, there is nothing you can do to fix it. You have to return the Iconbar to its original settings by using the Iconbar options (see Chapter 15 on customizing Quicken). However, be advised that you will lose any changes you made to the Iconbar. In addition, all scheduled transactions will be deleted. Be sure to make a note of them so you know which ones to reenter. Making a backup of your data file before resetting the Iconbar defaults is also a good idea. If this does not resolve the problem, contact Quicken Technical Support.

Reminders

Why am I still getting Reminders even though I turned Billminder off? Billminder and Reminders have separate on/off switches. You can possibly have one without the other. Go into Reminder Options and deselect Show Reminders on Startup.

Why aren't Billminder and Reminders notifying me of transactions that are due? First be sure that you have the Billminder and Reminders options set to on. The other possibility is that you have nothing to be reminded of. Double-check your Scheduled Transaction List.

Reports

Where do the columns go when I paste a Quicken report into my word processor? Because the formatting is different between the two programs, you must reset the tab settings in your word processor to regain the columns.

Why are my budget reports showing categories I haven't budgeted for? Unless instructed otherwise, Quicken shows budget items with zero amounts. To eliminate these items, select View in the Budget window and deselect Zero Budget Categories.

Why don't my printed reports appear as they do on screen? To get a truly accurate view of what your printed reports will look like, use the Print Preview option. In your report window, click the Print button and select Preview from the Print dialog box.

How do I get my printer to stop printing illegible characters? Check to be sure you have selected the correct printer driver. Be sure that your printer is in the same emulation mode as the printer you chose in the printer setup. Try a different type or size font.

How can I change the width of my report columns? You can adjust the width of only those columns that have column markers between the column headings (they look like little toy tops). Click on the marker and drag to the right to widen the column or to the left to narrow the column.

One of my report columns is missing. How do I get it back? Easy. In the report window, select Customize from the button bar, then click Reset Cols in the Customize Transaction Report dialog box.

Transactions

Where did that transaction go that I just entered? Because Quicken automatically sorts as soon as you enter a transaction, it puts the transaction where it belongs, according to the current sort order (by default it is date).

Hey, where did that blue line in my register come from? Pretty though it may be, it has a practical reason for being there. It separates current transactions from future transactions (anything dated later than today).

I really didn't mean to delete that transaction. Can I get it back? Unfortunately, the answer is no; you can't recover a deleted transaction. You just have to reenter the information.

Why can't I see the Category or Memo fields? You must have inadvertently switched from the two-line view to one-line view. Click View and deselect One-Line Display.

GLOSSARY

account — In Quicken, a group of entries that are related and kept together. You can create different types of accounts, such as bank accounts, assets, liabilities, investments, and so on.

accounts payable — The money you owe (your outstanding bills), usually a business term. Nobody says "accounts payable;" the jargon is "ay pee."

accounts receivable — Money that is owed to you (again, a business term) that is referred to as "ay are."

asset — Anything of value that's yours. This can include the money in your bank accounts, real estate, furniture, cars, investments, and so on.

backup — The process of making a safety copy of all the important files in your Quicken system.

balance — The cumulative total of an account.

balancing an account — The process of matching your transactions and totals to the statement the bank sends you each month.

billminder — A Quicken feature that keeps an eye on future transactions and reminds you to complete them.

budget — A plan for receiving and spending money. You can match the plan against what really happens and have Quicken point out where you missed the mark.

capital gain — The extra money you receive when you sell an investment or asset for more than you paid for it.

capital loss — The opposite of a capital gain; you sold something for less than you bought it.

category — A way to group transactions, such as utilities, insurance payments, wages received, and so on.

field — A blank spot in a dialog box or Quicken register where you enter information. Fields have titles that give you a hint about the type of information needed.

liability — Anything you have, or have the use of, that isn't yours. Examples are the mortgage money you used to make settlement on your house, the car loan money you used to turn over to the car dealer, and so on.

register — A list of transactions for an account. Each Quicken account has its own register.

restore — Using the backup files you made to put everything back together after some sort of disaster that made it impossible to work in Quicken.

split transaction — A transaction in which the total amount of money involved is split among multiple categories.

subcategory — A category under another category, for a way to break down information into even finer points.

supercategory — A selection of categories that you treat as a whole for special reporting.

tax deduction — An amount the IRS lets you deduct from your income to reduce your tax load.

tax-deferred account — An account that produces income on which the taxes are deferred until later. Retirement accounts defer the tax on their growth until you retire and start taking out the money.

transfer — The movement of an amount from one Quicken account to another.

INDEX

SIGNS AND SYMBOLS

$ (Amount) field, writing checks, 54, 56

* (asterisk), in password field, 256

: (colon), separating classes and subclasses, 164, 167

/ (forward slash), entering categories for business expenses, 167

% (percent sign), in split expenses, 100

_ (underscore character), in investment category names, 151

2-digit Year option, Checks tab of Register Options dialog box, 274

4-digit Year option, Checks tab of Register Options dialog box, 274

123 (.PRN) Disk File option, printing Reconciliation Reports, 90

401(k) accounts
described, 83–84
detailed information, 130
tracking, 79

A

Account List (Ctrl+A), 33, 139–141

Account Name box, 120

account tabs, Write Checks window, 54

accounts
See bank accounts; checking accounts; savings accounts

Accounts tab, Register Reports, 172

Accrued Interest investment category, 152

Action field, EasyStep dialog box, 82

Action Plan tab, Tax Deduction Finder, 243

Activity Bar
customizing with QuickTabs, 265
features, 19–20
voiding checks, 59

Actual column, Budget Report, 192

Add Action to Iconbar dialog box, 262

Add Categories dialog box, 149

Add Financial Address Book Items to QuickFill List option, 98, 273

S

savings accounts
  Quicken's planning features
    and, 216, 229
  Savings Planner and, 229
  setup considerations, 120
  transferring funds, 41–43
Savings Goal dialog box,
    194–196
Scheduled Transaction List
    (Ctrl+J), 33, 106, 109–110
scheduled transactions
  changing, 109–110
  described, 105–109
Scheduled Transactions
    option, Billminder, 268
scheduling future payments,
    114
securities, tracking, 133–135
  See also investment
    transactions
security
  See back-up files
  locking memorized
    transactions, 102
  password protection for
    transactions, 49–50
  Security Setup dialog box, 134
  tamper-proof archive files,
    255–256
  tracking nonmonetary items
    and, 81
  Windows 95 Recycle Bin, 283
Select Categories to Include
    dialog box, 185, 204
Select Checks to Print window,
    71

Sell/Remove Shares dialog
    box, 80
Set Up Category dialog box,
    147, 153
Set Up Class dialog box,
    163–164
Settings option, printing
    checks, 70
Settings tab, General Options
    dialog box, 266–267
Setup Category dialog box, 51,
    56–57
setup procedures
  automatic backups, 279
  categories, 147
  for checking account, 11–12
  investment accounts,
    130–136
  for online banking system,
    122–129
  for Quicken, 9, 10–16
  Quicken's basic operating
    parameters, 264
  for Reconciliation Reports,
    89–90
  tax information, 137
share prices
  Internet resources, 261
  investment transactions, 81,
    136
Shift key, selecting
    supercategories, 157
Short Term Capital Gain
    Distribution investment
    category, 152
shortcut keys
  See keyboard shortcuts

new annual files, 256–258
Summary Report, 250–253
Tax Summary Report, 253
time for, 249

Z

zero balance
  in Difference field, 88, 89, 92
  for new bank accounts,
    121–122
Zero Budget Categories option,
    185–187, 188
zoom option
  viewing Budget Report, 192
  viewing Summary Report,
    251

Have You Looked into Your Future?

Step into the future of computer books at **www.idgbooks.com** — IDG Books' newly revamped Web site featuring exclusive software, insider information, online books, and live events!

Visit us to:

- **Get freeware and shareware** handpicked by industry-leading authors found at our expanded *Free and Downloadable* area.

- **Pick up expert tips** from our online *Resource Centers* devoted to Java, Web Publishing, Windows, and Macs. Jazz up your Web pages with free applets, get practical pointers, use handy online code, and find out what the pros are doing.

- **Chat online** with in-the-know authorities, and find out when our authors are appearing in your area, on television, radio, and commercial online services.

- **Consult electronic books** from *Novell Press*. Keep on top of the newest networking technologies and trends presented by the industry's most respected source.

- **Explore Yahoo! Plaza**, the gathering place for our complete line of Yahoo! books. You'll find the latest hand-picked selection of hot-and-happening Web sites here.

- **Browse our books conveniently** using our comprehensive, searchable title catalog that features selective sneak-preview sample chapters, author biographies, and bonus online content. While you're at it, take advantage of our online book-buying—with free parking and overnight delivery!

Don't wait—visit us now. The future is here!

www.idgbooks.com

IDG
BOOKS
WORLDWIDE

IDG BOOKS WORLDWIDE REGISTRATION CARD

Visit our Web site at http://www.idgbooks.com

Title of this book: Discover Quicken® 6 for Windows®

My overall rating of this book: ❑ Very good [1] ❑ Good [2] ❑ Satisfactory [3] ❑ Fair [4] ❑ Poor [5]

How I first heard about this book:

❑ Found in bookstore; name: [6]

❑ Advertisement: [8]

❑ Word of mouth; heard about book from friend, co-worker, etc.: [10]

❑ Book review: [7]

❑ Catalog: [9]

❑ Other: [11]

What I liked most about this book:

What I would change, add, delete, etc., in future editions of this book:

Other comments:

Number of computer books I purchase in a year: ❑ 1 [12] ❑ 2-5 [13] ❑ 6-10 [14] ❑ More than 10 [15]

I would characterize my computer skills as: ❑ Beginner [16] ❑ Intermediate [17] ❑ Advanced [18] ❑ Professional [19]

I use ❑ DOS [20] ❑ Windows [21] ❑ OS/2 [22] ❑ Unix [23] ❑ Macintosh [24] ❑ Other: [25]_____

(please specify)

I would be interested in new books on the following subjects:

(please check all that apply, and use the spaces provided to identify specific software)

❑ Word processing: [26]

❑ Data bases: [28]

❑ File Utilities: [30]

❑ Networking: [32]

❑ Other: [34]

❑ Spreadsheets: [27]

❑ Desktop publishing: [29]

❑ Money management: [31]

❑ Programming languages: [33]

I use a PC at (please check all that apply): ❑ home [35] ❑ work [36] ❑ school [37] ❑ other: [38]_____

The disks I prefer to use are ❑ 5.25 [39] ❑ 3.5 [40] ❑ other: [41]_____

I have a CD ROM: ❑ yes [42] ❑ no [43]

I plan to buy or upgrade computer hardware this year: ❑ yes [44] ❑ no [45]

I plan to buy or upgrade computer software this year: ❑ yes [46] ❑ no [47]

Name: _____ Business title: [48] _____ Type of Business: [49] _____

Address (❑ home [50] ❑ work [51]/Company name: _____)

Street/Suite#

City [52]/State [53]/Zipcode [54]: _____ Country [55]

❑ **I liked this book!** You may quote me by name in future
IDG Books Worldwide promotional materials.

My daytime phone number is _____

IDG BOOKS WORLDWIDE™

THE WORLD OF COMPUTER KNOWLEDGE®

 **YES!**

Please keep me informed about IDG Books Worldwide's World of Computer Knowledge. Send me your latest catalog.